N TALES OF EHAMA

Impressions of the life and teachings of Nehama Leibowitz

LEAH ABRAMOWITZ

gefen
publishing house
JERUSALEM ◆ NEW YORK

Copyright © Gefen Publishing House Ltd
Jerusalem 2003/5763

Typesetting: Raphaël Freeman, Jerusalem Typesetting
Cover Design: Studio Paz, Jerusalem

1   3   5   7   9   8   6   4   2

Gefen Publishing House
POB 36004, Jerusalem 91360, Israel
972-2-538-0247
orders@gefenpublishing.com

Gefen Books
12 New Street Hewlett, NY 11557, USA
516-295-2805
gefenny@gefenpublishing.com

www.israelbooks.com

Printed in Israel   Send for our free catalogue

ISBN 965-229-295-8

Library of Congress Cataloging-in-Publication Data
Tales of Nehama: impressions of the life and teaching of
Nehama Leibowitz/Leah Abramowitz.
p. cm.
Includes index.

1. Leibowitz, Nehama. 2. Jewish teachers – Israel – Biography.
3. Women Jewish scholars – Israel – Biography. 4. Israel – Biography. I. Title.

BS1161.L45A27 2003 • 296.3'092 – dc21 [B] • CIP NO: 00-021076

Contents

Foreword

Professor Nehama Leibowitz was one of our century's outstanding personalities. A leading Bible scholar, an extraordinary teacher who established a new approach to learning Jewish sources, and a woman who single-handedly influenced a generation of *Tanach* educators, "Nehama," as she was fondly called by all, was actually even more talented in an additional field, human relations.

Despite the fact that she was widowed early in life and never had children, her wide circle of friends and admirers surrounded her, supported her, and were in turn enlightened and heartened by her. As her friend Professor Meir Weiss stated, "She was a genius not only in *parshanut* (commentary), but in *gemilut chassadim* (kindness)."

The love and affection that each person interviewed expressed, and the smiles that were exchanged when anecdotes were interchanged, indicate a special and close relationship with each and every one with whom she came in contact. "Everyone and His Own Nehama" is not only a chapter in this book, it is the way that people from all walks of life felt about this unique woman. She left her mark on so many, and inevitably was awarded the appelation: "There will never be anyone like her."

What was it about Nehama Leibowitz that made her so unusual, so beloved? She was, first and foremost, completely people oriented. She was truly interested in everyone and anyone who came her way, and got each to open up as only a therapist or a lover can. But she was also much admired for her chessed, her integrity, her commitment to principles, and paradoxically, her great modesty and humility. She had strong views on education, Zionism, religion, ostentation, technology, and a host of other subjects, but her complete self-deprecation and simplicity won over those who might otherwise have been her detractors and adversaries.

However, over and beyond everything else, Nehama was a teacher. She knew how to get even the most uninitiated involved in understanding text. She used a variety of pedagogical methods and initiated comprehension of the commentaries – both classical and unusual. She enlisted her talents in storytelling, drama, and brilliant rational insights to heighten the learning experience, and throughout it all she remained true to her mission – learning *Torah*.

In the words of one student, "It was a privilege to know her; it was a pleasure to know her."

Introduction

This book was really begun in 1954 when, as a student at the Machon L'madrichei Chutz LaAretz of the Jewish Agency, I first had Nehama as a teacher. Thereafter, at different stages of my life, I would attend her classes. Even though my background in Jewish studies was meager, she managed to ignite in me a lifelong love for learning Tanach, especially using her method, for which I am eternally grateful.

I was never one of Nehama's "inner circle" – those who visited her regularly, who helped her in the house, who held long discussions with her, or who cared for her. I did not know much about her history, and great sections of her background remain obscure at least to me. The few times I did drive her to a *shiur* or helped arrange sets of *gilyonot* (worksheets) in her house were outstanding and privileged quality time for me. As with so many, the impression that she left on me was unparalleled.

In 1993–94 I began attending her weekly Thursday night class, an extraordinary experience, actually an honor and a pleasure. The participants in that shiur, all mature professional people, some with outstanding intellectual achievements to their credit, were unified by the distinct atmosphere of the shiur, the physical spartan setting of Nehama's living room/library/office, and essentially by Nehama's orchestration of the evening. It was then that I first began scribbling the tales Nehama told, those used as vehicles to illustrate a point she was making, and eventually those she and others related about her life.

After Nehama died I began collecting stories from people outside the Thursday night shiur. I was amazed at the number of lives she had touched, the impact of that contact, and the love and affection that each person I interviewed expressed. Inevitably the fond memories that I elicited brought smiles and lit up faces as we exchanged anecdotes and impressions. Not one person of the sixty to seventy people I interviewed had a negative word to say about Nehama. Indeed the only person who ever spoke disparagingly about her was Nehama herself.

Collecting material on Nehama Leibowitz brought me into the musty library rooms of her contemporaries in huge, opulent Yekish houses in Rehavia or in university offices. I found her close friends in sparse utilitarian apartments in Talbiah and in kibbutz cultural centers; in comfortable, cultured homes of the academia; and in the "Israel modern" units of the working class. There were rabbis who received me in their book-lined *yeshiva* offices and others in the back seats of silent synagogues.

One complaint that I heard about this project was that I've made Nehama too hallowed, a virtual saint, and not the very real person that she actually was. However, the material collected speaks for itself, as her friends and associates experienced her. Similarly, the request she often made, "Write about my books and gilyonot, not about me," is not being fulfilled by this book. It remains for someone more knowledgeable and professional in the field of parshanut to do that. I assume there will be numerous scholarly works on her method, her biblical exegesis, her gilyonot, and the 'Studies,' in the coming years.

Some friends and associates who were interviewed found it difficult, even painful, to talk about their beloved teacher. Several turned down my request for an interview saying, "She wouldn't have wanted a book written about herself," and they refused to reveal anything of their special connection with Nehama. On the other hand, some found it therapeutic to both talk about their relationship or to hear how others had been affected by Professor Leibowitz. Most reactions were, "I'm so happy you've asked me to contribute," "It's imperative that her personality and her deeds are publicized," and "I wish I could write something about Nehama myself; maybe I still will."

With great reserve and timidity, I've undertaken to present some of the tales told or related about Nehama. As she wrote to Professor Bergman, "I may not be the proper *shofar* for this task," but until someone else comes along, I've written this book so that future generations can know about her outstanding personality and unique teaching skills. Just as I want my children and grandchildren to have an idea of the contribution she made as an educator and as a person, so too I venture to guess that there are thousands upon thousands of her students, who were taught either directly by her or indirectly by the generation of teachers that Nehama nurtured, and that they too want their offspring to know "who was Nehama Leibowitz."

1.

Everyone and
His Own 'Nehama':
כל אחד והנחמה שלו

Professor Nehama Leibowitz must have touched the lives of thousands of people in her lifetime. With a large number of them she had a very close relationship. Many of her students and friends felt that they had a special place in her heart, that she particularly wanted contact with them, and indeed Nehama was able to give everyone that feeling. Everyone had "his own Nehama."

Dr. Avigdor Bonchek is one of these disciples who had a special relationship with Professor Leibowitz. Although he only met her in 1975, he became very close to her, visited her often, and used her as a sounding board for his studies in Rashi. These conversations led to his books on the commentaries of Rashi. Nehama was very proud of his work, and his book often appeared on her table.

Here are his personal comments on "his Nehama": "When I was growing up, I never had any heroes – people I wanted to emulate, who I thought were the tops … Somehow Nehama elicited that in me … maybe because I both respected her and liked her at the same time.

"She developed a special personal relationship with each and every one of us. She knew that I was a behaviorist psychologist, so she confided in me her fears. They were real fears, not just gimmicks to keep my attention, or get me to talk about things that interested me, but they were revealed, to the best of my knowledge, only to me."

Rabbi Yochanan Freed, the director of the Torah Division of the Ministry of Education, was Nehama's "rabbi"; that is, she regularly attended services at his synagogue in Tikvateinu after she moved to Romema and consulted him for *halachic* decisions. "I think she's the most important teacher of Torah that has emerged in the last century," he proclaims with conviction. "The scope of her influence, the way she opened parshanut to the masses, and her special method of teaching are unparalleled. Like Rabbi Pinchas Kehati, who in this generation made the *Mishnah* available to the layman, she brought Torah learning within the sphere of thousands who would never have broached the study otherwise."

Nehama Ariel, wife of the Ramat Gan Chief Rabbi, and one of Nehama's disciples, relates a story she heard coming back from Nehama's funeral. At a ceremony at Bar Ilan, Nehama was asked to address the audience in the name of those being honored that day. Nehama began in her usual modest way, "I'm no public speaker; I'm only a teacher. *Melamdim* (teachers of little children), you know, are assured the World to Come. Do you know why? Because they've already experienced the opposite in this world!" After the laughter died out, Nehama added (almost to herself): "But I won't get to the World to Come." The audience stirred uncomfortably in their seats, until she continued. "And that's because I've enjoyed every minute of my teaching." And she meant it.

Frima Gurfinkle recalled how she first met Nehama as a student in the Foreign Students Program at the Hebrew University, a few months after she had made aliya from Russia. The first impression was of a powerful, somewhat fierce, and fearsome teacher, very demanding and harsh. "As I got to know her," Frima relates, "I learned she was actually a very warm, caring, and gentle person." She was very encouraging to the new immigrant and helped her advance in her studies with great personal input.

"I remember walking home with her along Rehov HaZvi one afternoon. Cars were shooting by in every direction, and it was really dangerous to stop and talk there. Yet she told me then, 'My contribution is not in the academic world, nor in the literary field, but only in that of teaching.'"

Indeed, she allowed only one word to be engraved on her tombstone: 'Teacher'. According to Frima, hundreds of students had a similar special relationship with her, and each one was convinced that he alone was her favorite. "She was an outstanding personality, a marvelous teacher, and I use her as a model daily."

For Dr. Ben Hollander, Nehama was also a model and really the reason why he changed his academic field. "I first met Nehama when I was a student at Machon Greenberg. I already had an M.A. in English literature and was sure I would continue and choose some specialty," says Ben. But learning Torah with Nehama was such an impressive experience that he began taking courses in Bible and Jewish Thought.

"She actually gave me my start as her teaching assistant at the Hebrew University," he continues. Today Dr. Hollander teaches at the Hebrew Union College and at the Beit Midrash of the Conservative Seminary as well. "My teaching is modeled on hers; I invariably quote from her *shiurim* and refer to her worksheets," he says. "Nehama taught me to activate students and get them to ask questions. She used to say, 'You can't teach anyone anything; you can only help them discover the meaning for themselves.' But she did have outstanding techniques to do that."

One of her earliest pupils, Tzila Adler Perle, was a student nurse at Shaare Zedek Hospital in the days of Dr. Wallach and Sweister (Chief Nurse) Selma. "We worked seventeen-hour days then," says Tzila. "Nehama knew that, and she offered us a lift in her taxi from her class at Terra Sancta. It made a big difference to us, because we didn't have money for the bus fare." Tzila remembers two features about Nehama. "She had a wonderful smile," she says, "and I've always been impressed with her ability to present complex material in an interesting way. She had this gift of relating theoretical or philosophical issues to everyday life."

Rachel Kosofsky used to take Nehama out for walks in the later years. "It was a real privilege, but when I'd say to her at the end of the walk, 'Nehama, that was a pleasure,' she would counter with a wry remark like, 'I wish you greater pleasures than taking an old woman out for a walk!'" Anyone who'd ever been close with Nehama, continues Rachel, could never, thereafter, engage in the little falsities of life that are acceptable.

"She was so extremely honest, and it rubbed off on us all. I can never go into a supermarket anymore and taste some of the samples, if I know I'm not going to buy that product. She taught us that it's considered a form of lying if you're standing waiting for a bus, and you're cold or it's raining, so you go into a shop and the clerk comes up to you and says, 'Can I help you?' So you ask the price of some item, or request information on some merchandise. And all along you know you're there only because you want to wait for the bus in a protected area. Well, after learning with Nehama, you just can't do that anymore."

Chaya Sara Benjamin first met Nehama as a student when she came to Israel to study Torah. She was in the process of becoming observant and wanted advice from Nehama about what she should study. Nehama agreed to meet her at the university cafeteria. The first thing Nehama did was say, "First get something to eat and we'll sit over there and talk. If you're going to study Torah you have to eat properly." Chaya Sara eventually took her course in Exodus for overseas students in English and got bitten for life.

A distant relative of Nehama's first met her as a student and later when she married into the family as a relative. "Nehama was always the same plain, simple person, a very good conversationalist, interested in everything, and very family minded."

Dr. Barry Samson saw pictures of Nehama before he met her. "They weren't very flattering, even when she was younger," he says. "But to me she was a beautiful woman. Beauty shone from her face." Barry continues, "When Nehama spoke words of Torah her mouth would inevitably turn up in a smile and her face would soften."

No one knows a person as well as his butler. Nehama never had a butler, but her housekeeper and companion for many years was Tzipporah Ophri, who now lives in a settlement in the Shomron. "I first met Nehama in 1954 when I was a nurse at Shaare Zedek Hospital and her father was hospitalized. She needed someone to care for him when he came home and it just suited my family situation at the time to accept the position." Tzipporah cared for the elderly Leibowitz until 1959 when he died, and then continued as Nehama's housekeeper until 1974.

"She treated me as a daughter. I learned a great deal from her – especially how to relate to people. She was always patient with everyone, even stupid or annoying people. She never showed any difference towards them…. Whenever one of her students called, no matter what time of the day or night it was, even if she was in the middle of eating her meal, she'd always answer them. She'd never say, 'Tell them to call later.' Nehama was always very generous, maybe overly so. In some ways she was too naive. She trusted everyone." Then after a moment's thought Tzipporah adds, "There is nobody, absolutely nobody like her."

Tzipporah's replacement, Yehudit Barashi, started working for Nehama twenty-four years ago. She was both a neighbor and a housekeeper. "Nehama loved to help people, but always secretly. Sometimes she helped people she didn't even know," says her former neighbor. "Whatever you asked her on any subject, she knew the answer. I used to get advice from Nehama about my personal life – if I had a problem with the children, or something, she always knew what should be done. She was like a mother to me – I miss her a lot."

"Sometimes in the middle of the night there'd be a ring at the door. It was Nehama, who often forgot her key and came to get her spare one from us." Eleven years ago Yehudit and her family moved to Har Nof. "Nehama was so upset. She tried to convince us to stay. She even offered to pay the fee for contract retraction. But I continued to work for her even after I moved. She really worried about us. If someone came late she'd start telephoning or if I went to the dentist she wanted to hear all about it. If it was raining she'd say, 'Never mind, don't come today. You'll get sick.'"

Dr. Zev Herzberg, another loyal student and colleague, gives an additional example of how Nehama was ever available to her public. Once when Zev and two other 'faithfuls' were sitting with Nehama preparing for a lesson, the doorbell rang. A couple came in. The man, who was obviously her student, told Nehama he wanted to introduce his fiancee. Nehama spoke very graciously with them, asked a number of questions, and wished them hearty congratulations. The

15

couple beamed. She merely cautioned, "Next time please call and let me know you're coming ahead of time." "She was very sensitive to people's feelings," Zev sums up.

Asher Hadad, a school principal in Lod, met Nehama while he was an advanced student at Yeshivat Hesder Maaleh Adumim. He and several colleagues had the unique opportunity of participating in her class for yeshiva students at the Lifshitz Teachers' Seminary. "I know she loved us and believed in us. She had a special rapport with our class," says Asher. "She invested everything she had in preparing us for our future, as teachers in Tanach.

"Later I studied at Touro College and we often had classes in her house," continues the principal. "Nehama always received us warmly. She was very strict about two things: using correct grammar and style, and being on time. She didn't want us to write down what she was saying in class; she wanted us to *think* and to understand. We actually got individual instruction in a class setting," Asher recalls.

Her publisher at the Jewish Agency, Shmuel Borstein, is the scion of a famous Hasidic family. "I once showed Nehama a section in a book of halachah that was written by my great grandfather, the Avnei Nezer, which validated something she had written in her *Studies*. Years later she still remembered it, and even wanted to know how a Hasidic *drasha* (lecture) is built. I could see she appreciated Hasidic thinking, even though she claimed she didn't know anything about it." Shmuel continues, "She herself was from a learned Lithuanian background, but, as in other matters, she was actually very well versed in Hasidism. Pity she didn't go into it more."

"When Nehama was about to retire from her teaching position at the Tel Aviv University," says Dr. Moshe Arend, "she suggested that I replace her. At first she continued to teach and I accompanied her. We traveled together by taxi and had many enlightening conversations." For almost ten years, Dr. Arend worked with Nehama on two textbooks for the Open University on teaching Tanach. "We would meet very often and discussed at length every chapter," he says. "I used to write a rough draft and she'd go over every word. Nehama was a tough taskmaster. Sometimes she would cross out everything that I had written. I didn't always agree with her. But those meetings were extremely enjoyable and enriching. Moreover, many classrooms of students have used the book we produced and Nehama even corresponded with some of these students years afterwards."

One of her oldest contacts, a colleague and good friend, was the late Professor Meir Weiss, who collaborated with her on some publications, especially their work, "Chapters of Comfort and Redemption" on the seven *haftarot* that are read between the Ninth of Av and *Rosh Chodesh* Ellul. "Nehama was the classic teacher, ever patient, encouraging, and enlightening. Her students saw her love for the subject she was teaching and her love for them, and they responded in kind." Professor Weiss, then in his nineties, spoke quietly and wistfully of his dear friend, "Personally I had a wonderful relationship with her for fifty years. We were very close. When she was working on the gilyonot and later on our essay she would show me what she'd written and I would write comments until we got to the final version. In the later years we used to visit each other. It was a relationship of platonic friendship of the purest kind. I cherish the books she gave me because of the fine dedication she wrote to me on the inside cover."

An even longer standing relationship was held with another colleague, Dov Rapell of Kibbutz Yavneh. "Sixty years ago Nehama was already a famous teacher," Dov declares. "At first I was a student at the Hebrew University and came to learn Torah from her. Later in 1941 I became principal of a Seminary for kibbutz women who studied at Beit Tzeirot Mizrachi and then I was her boss. For years, until the 1960s, wherever I was principal I always asked Nehama to teach there. She was much more experienced and older than I, so I was more a 'talent agent of a star' than her principal."

Dr. Joseph Walk knew Nehama from his earliest years in Israel. He believes that Nehama's 'secret' was her openness and willingness to share her feelings with others, and it was this that attracted people to her. "She always had some pet students," he recalls, "but she could also be very critical and demanding of her protegees." She used unconventional sources and commentaries in her teaching, even Christian theologists or Reform rabbis, although she was completely orthodox in her own religious practices, according to Walk. She often repeated, "Don't be afraid to ask *apikorsik* (heretic) questions – that's how you learn."

Walk, who became a supervisor for the Ministry of Education

17

and the principal of a teachers' seminary, once asked her to write a short introduction to a workbook he put out on one of the books of the Bible. She hesitated and delayed, and finally after some probing explained why she was reluctant to do what her good friend wanted. "Everyone knows how close we are. If I write an introduction to your book, people will think I'm praising it only because we're friends. You wouldn't want that, right?" And she refused to add her comments.

Dr. Techiya Greenwald, a chemistry lecturer, once had a free hour when her regular class was canceled, so she decided to attend a class in Tanach taught by Dr. Ben Hollander. He was replacing Nehama but Techiya didn't know that. She liked the class very much even though she'd never studied Tanach seriously, and decided to continue. One day her phone rang, "Hello, this is Nehama; I'd like to go over your last exam with you," she heard. "Nehama? Nehama who?" Techiya asked in amazement. It turned out that Ben was teaching the class, but Nehama still reviewed all the written work.

Techiya met with Nehama and from that day became her permanent disciple. "I got such personal attention from the first moment," says Techiya, still in wonder. "She encouraged me even though I'm not observant, and didn't have the background the other students had. She invited me to her advanced class and later to study with her personally. She wanted to know her students intimately – so she got to know my children and their activities; my history and my interests … I often wondered, she's so busy, how does she find time for someone like me who isn't even from her world?"

Shmuel Hershkovitz is also amazed at how much Nehama managed to do in one day, in one lifetime. He first met her when he was a young teacher in Shafir and later attended her classes while on a sabbatical at Mercaz HaRav. "She gave me such a lot; I learned from her the love of Torah, integrity, and many, many teaching tricks. She used both the carrot and the stick approach. In later years I'd come to study *Parshat Hashavuah* (the weekly Bible portion) with her on Friday afternoon. Where else could you find a *dati* woman sitting down to study on Friday afternoon!" On another plane, Shmuel mentions, "She always was appreciative of any small favor you'd do for her. Long afterwards, she'd still remember that I bought her a newspaper or set up the *Shabbat* clock."

Yeduel (Doli) Basok is another second-generation student and teacher who studied with Nehama. "At her funeral I was thinking she must have taught thousands of teachers who followed in her footsteps. And these teachers have by now taught hundreds of thousands of students, each adding something of his own background and his own personality, but using Nehama's method. For example, my mother studied with her, and then I did, and we're passing on to my children some of what she taught."

After the grave was filled up, Doli (and apparently several others there) did *kriya* (making a tear in one's clothes), the way family members do as a sign of mourning. "I just felt it was something I had to do," he says. "I feel indebted to her – the basis she gave me, the way to learn commentaries, no one else ever gave me that."

Dr. Bryna Levi also feels a need to express her special relationship with Nehama. "As a Bible student I used to work in the library a lot. All the books I needed were always on her desk. We got to know each other. Over the years I'd go to her with specific questions. I was careful not to take up too much of her time, because I knew how precious it was to her. But she always treated me graciously and even thanked *me* for coming."

Ariela Yedgeh, another veteran teacher who follows in Nehama's footsteps, and her whole family, felt very close with Nehama Leibowitz. "Nehama was very involved in her students' personal lives. Even though she was very exacting in her teaching, she was very big-hearted in her personal relationships. She had a lot of psychological insight in both her learning and her contacts … she demonstrated both concern and sensitivity."

Ariela recalls that Nehama never spoke gossip, but she did worry about those that weren't married. "She would hint that it might be a good idea to invite this one or that one over at the same time." On one occasion Ariela complimented Nehama on her life achievement in the field of Tanach: "What an accomplishment you've attained," she said with admiration. "Ah, but I never had children," Nehama answered with pain. Ariela understood then that Nehama felt she had missed something very basic in her life.

Shimon Ron of Givataim used to accompany Nehama on her rounds in Tel Aviv. "I'd take her from the University to the studio, where they taped her talks on the Bible for the blind. Then she'd give a shiur in a synagogue on Rehov Ben Yehuda. You couldn't get a pin into the place when she gave her class. Sometimes we'd just meet in a cafe and talk. I had the privilege of being her friend," he says with deep satisfaction.

Nehama once told Shimon something that surprised him. "You know I have a better rapport with you than with many people who pray three times a day daily, but who don't understand what they're saying. You aren't dati but at least you know how to think!" Shimon continues: "Her talent and her knowledge were just outstanding. She had an endless source of knowledge, yet she was able to give it all over and would include everyone and everything in her classes. They weren't really lectures; they were more like dialogues."

Dr. Yehudah Eloni, who had the distinction of being Nehama's student in Berlin when he was barely seven years old (and she was perhaps 19 or 20), renewed his contact with her when she gave two guest lectures at Seminar Lewinsky in Tel Aviv, a teachers' college where he taught history and served as a member of the board. "Her talks on Tanach were excellent. What impressed me and the students was her wide knowledge. Nehama had the rare combination of being erudite in three fields: Russian culture, German culture, and knowledge of Judaism (of which her knowledge was great). She merged these fields in an outstanding way." Dr. Eloni also notes that in her approach to people she demonstrated *chochmat chaim* (common sense) and tolerance – a scarce commodity in our generation.

The students she taught at Meretz in Mevasseret have spread out all over Israel and are working as rabbis, community leaders, and teachers by now. During the three and a half years that she taught them, Nehama made a great impression on them all. Avraham Davidson, who teaches at the *Midrasha* in Pardes Hana, recalls the pleasant atmosphere that accompanied her classes, even though she was very demanding and pedantic. "She'd give us homework, to answer certain questions, usually from her gilyonot," Avraham states. "She demanded that the answers be concise, no more than eight to ten words. Today I realize that short answers require deeper thinking. I use the same system with my students now."

"I knew about Nehama for many years. Many people used to

quote her or used her gilyonot for lessons," says Rivka Davidowitz, who became a member of her closest circle. "Shortly after I met her I had the opportunity to take her to Mevasseret by car. She was giving a class on Yonah to the students in Meretz. I thought to myself, what do I have to do with this famous woman? Here she is in front of me. What will I say to her?" Now Rivka laughs at the memory. "She made herself so available to me during that ride, she was so human. It was as if we had known each other all our lives."

"I went to a very good Jewish school in New York, and had the best Bible teachers," declares Esther Gross, another close friend and student of Nehama's. "Yet for me, until I met Nehama, Tanach was boring. She started me on a different way of learning Torah. She made it fascinating, exciting, a treat, an intellectual exercise.... I'm eternally grateful, because she opened up an entire new world for me."

Rabbi Nachum Amsel, who started a girls' school based on Nehama's method, wrote a memorial article that he titled "Reflections on my Rebbe, Nehama ZT"L." There he writes: "How can one describe such a complex yet simple human being? Of the many Rabbeim I have had the fortune to have, Nehama ... was the most dynamic and personable, even until her final shiur.... Although I became her student as an adult in the final 'era' [of her seventy-six-year teaching career] ... I feel privileged to have personally shared much with Nehama, which makes her loss more painful for me."

Nachum also mentions her qualities as a master teacher. "Of all her characteristics, her greatest, in my opinion, was her sense of humor. The jokes and stories all related to a particular point in the shiur, and made us laugh, even when we had heard them more than once. Nehama was an entertainer as well as a master teacher. She taught me that entertainment is an important component of successful teaching.... I will deeply miss Nehama, more than can be conveyed in print ... as my teacher, as my advisor, as my friend."

A member of her closest circle who prefers to remain anonymous has a similiar feeling of loss. This follower first met Nehama when he was in charge of courses for teachers from abroad at the Jewish Agency ten years ago. He quickly became not only a loyal disciple and follower, but a close associate and 'protector.' When Nehama was in

21

the hospital several years ago, one of the women in her room who had seen him visiting frequently and noted the relationship between them told Nehama, "While you were sleeping your son came to visit and left you some books." Nehama recounted that episode with *genuss* (deep satisfaction) – and the man involved loved it no less.

"The [parting] from Nehama is so painful," says this friend with distress in his voice. "I didn't realize how much it could hurt. It's not only missing her presence, the inability to ask her a question or get some advice ... She meant so much to me, to so many of us. She opened my eyes to Tanach." There's a picture of Nehama on the man's side table at which he glances as he talks.

The same picture is on the wall of a veteran teacher. Devorah Tashama recalls how she first heard a shiur from Nehama, and it changed her life. "A friend of mine told me, 'There's a lesson by Nehama Leibowitz tonight. Let's go.' I'd heard about her but I never had attended any of her lectures. The class was held at the old Horev School, in a prefab hut, in winter. I felt like Hillel; I didn't notice the cold or the rain coming in. Even though I was already an experienced teacher by then, I'd never heard anyone give a Tanach shiur like that. I was mesmerized. Ever since then I'd go wherever she gave a class."

Devorah remembers Nehama not only as an outstanding teacher, but also as a person of integrity and modesty – a role model to emulate. "She lived like the old *Yerushalmim*, very simply; but if she needed to get something done, she did it." Her niece twice removed, Miriam Shlossberg, expressed her own opinion of Nehama: "She was a living example of her principles."

Professor Shmuel Adler had a special relationship with Nehama as her physician and as her student. "From the time I first met her I was overwhelmed by Nehama, and my impression only strengthened along the years. She was not only an extraordinary scholar, with vast secular and Torah knowledge, but also a humane individual whose personal ethics were even superior to her great intellect."

Professor Adler referred to the synthesis that put harmony into her personality and explained her unique influence on so many. "To find a great mind like hers is a treasure in its own right, but to discover a full person on the human level is unprecedented. Her level of honesty, her deep concern for people, her incessant curiosity, her zest for life, made it a real privilege to know her." The physician was her student for only three and a half years, but he considers them very valuable years. "I grew because of my contact with her. It was an enriching experience."

Another person who spoke of Nehama as a role model is Dr. Moshe Shlomowitz, who treated her almost daily as a patient. "She was an important person for Yaffa, my wife, and me. She represented the ideals of religious Zionism – she embodied the complete person: very direct, very honest, but somehow also *tamim* (naive). Knowing her was an experience."

Moshe, who emigrated from Australia, was often asked by Nehama about the Jewish community in Australia. "She was very interested in that diaspora, their views on Israel, and how it continued to survive as a dynamic Jewish community," says Moshe. "She especially wanted to know why they don't come on *aliya*."

David Bar Yakov, a computer programmer from Neve Ilan, and his wife, Wendy, were other new immigrants who first met Nehama when she gave a class at the Absorption Center in Mevasseret. All her life Nehama had a special interest in *olim chadashim* (new immigrants). She went out of her way to make them feel comfortable and was genuinely concerned about their becoming acclimated, getting jobs, and integrating their children into the school system. She visited the Bar Yakovs in their home, first in the *Mercaz Klita* (Absorption Center) and then later at Neve Ilan. "Our children were duly impressed that we were her students," says Wendy. "Nehama could teach high-level thinking to people with *kita aleph* (first grade) level of Hebrew."

"She had a profound influence on our lives," says Wendy "She's the best teacher I ever had my whole life. I couldn't imagine that someone like her existed. I'd been studying Judaica and Hebrew for years [day schools, Boston Hebrew College] and had a B.A. in Jewish education. No one warned me what a special personality she was." David continues: "She challenged people, she made them rise above themselves. Even though she was herself so brilliant and so learned, she made it all available to everyone, no matter what their

23

level." Wendy takes up the theme: "I learned from her respect for students. She showed that everyone can learn from everyone. That's a tremendous lesson."

Bracha Ashual lived in a building behind Nehama for twenty-six years. "She was my neighbor, my friend, and my teacher," says Bracha with nostalgia. "I miss her very much." In the later years when Bracha and other 'faithfuls' would take Nehama for a walk, they'd walk around the corner and point in the direction of her house. "Can you tell which is your apartment?" Bracha would ask playfully. Nehama had very strong, three-phase electricity put in when her vision became dimmer, so the light from her house was always very prominent. Sometimes she'd be able to point out her apartment; sometimes not. "It's there," one of the women would say, "there where the great light's shining!" "That's what she was to me," says Bracha sadly. "She was a bright beam of light that shone out for all to see."

2.

Beginnings

Nehama loved to tell stories 'on' herself. "One day, when I was a young girl, I was late for school, and hurried out of the house without anything. Rushing across the street, I was knocked down by a streetcar. People carried me home, and luckily I was only slightly hurt. I told my parents, 'I know why I was run over today; it's because I didn't have time to recite my prayers this morning.' My father looked at me sternly and said, 'Do you really think that you're such a *tzaddekes* (holy person) that the Almighty sends you punishments immediately, special delivery?'"

Sometimes she would recall fondly how her father once told her, "I knew you were an idiot; but not such an idiot."

"She came from a family of geniuses," declares Yona Ben Sasson, who for years was her neighbor and friend. "Her parents were geniuses, her husband was a genius, her brother – everyone knows – was a genius, and so are her nieces and nephews." Already as a child she was the one who always knew all the answers in the family *verhorren* (when the patriarch of the family tested the children's knowledge of Parshat Hashavuah). Yet, years later, she claimed one of her cousins was the outstanding Bible student in those days. Many of the ideas that appeared years later in her gilyonot were already developed in her mind while she was a teenager.

Not everyone knows about her husband's contribution; she used him as a source of knowledge as well as a sounding board for many of her original ideas. Despite the fact that he was blind, he was extremely well versed in Jewish knowledge. She called him "Yonke" (Yom Tov), but his name was Lipman. He was her father's younger brother, her uncle, and they married in 1930 when he already knew that he was going blind. He had worked as a businessman but when he became blind he became a teacher of the blind. Already then they had a huge library. Her husband knew exactly where each book stood, and he could rattle off by heart the contents of most. He became very proficient in braille and translated several books into this 'language'. Lipman had a special hobby – he loved to compose riddles and used them on anyone, especially children.

Both Nehama and her husband loved children. They had very close relationships with their nephews and nieces and later with *their* children; they also were attached to the Ben Sassons' boys, who grew up in their very house. He was "Dod (Uncle) Lipman" to them all, but she remained "Nehama." Uncle Lipman, after he went blind, would take a daily walk once or twice around the house. When the first Sasson boy was born he would pass the baby's crib on his rounds. "Doesn't the baby's crying disturb you?" Dzunia (Junia) Sasson would ask. "No, not at all," said Lipman. "It gives me a good feeling." However, when subsequently twin boys were born, they were very weak at first and rarely could be heard crying. Uncle Lipman was extremely worried. He'd inquire as to why they never cried. After a while the twins grew, and had more strength. The old man was overjoyed to hear their wailing.

Dov Rapell recalls Lipman's riddles. During his university days Dov and a number of other religious students living in student quarters in the Old City often walked over to Kiryat Moshe on the long Shabbat afternoons to talk with the Leibowitzes about the Bible portion or any other subject. In addition to Lipman's riddles, impromptu Bible quizzes were also on the program. Later these *Chidonei Tanach* were transferred to Beit Tzeirot Mizrachi, where the school's outstanding Tanach teachers, Dov, Elyakim Ben Menachem, and Nehama, would answer questions from the 'audience'. Everyone tried to outdo themselves in stumping the experts. "That was our form of entertainment in those days," says Dov Rapell.

Yael Steifel, who worked for Nehama as a housekeeper, relates

26

that later when her husband was getting on in years, Nehama arranged to have different people read to him, especially when she was away from home. But to maintain her husband's dignity, she always explained that the reader came for his own benefit, to learn Hebrew or to understand some *sugiah* (issue) in Jewish learning from him. Yael also recalls, "For a number of years Nehama's widowed father lived first nearby and eventually with them. He always ate lunch with them and there was also an ancient rabbi from the neighborhood at the table. The three elderly scholars (all over eighty) would hold learned discussions, usually in Yiddish, around the dinner table." Her father died in his nineties, and her husband passed away at the age of ninety-six.

"We didn't go out much," Dzunia (Junia) Sasson relates, "but if we needed someone to look in on the boys, Nehama was always prepared to be the baby-sitter. She'd sit in our kitchen working on the gilyonot. Whenever we returned she'd have stories to tell us about the children; always some *nissim v'niflaot* (tales of wonder) regarding the boys. She could make great stories about the most banal incidents," recalls her former neighbor. "On the long summer evenings, we would sit with her on the porch, and she would often read aloud from world literature. She had such a beautiful voice, and a wonderful way of dramatizing."

"Even as a child she was a wonderful storyteller," relates Esther Reifenberg, her cousin, who knew Nehama all her life. "She used to tell stories to my younger sisters for hours, and they were entranced." Mira Libes, one of these younger sisters, recalls, "Nehama was very imaginative. We used to sit on the floor around her feet and she told us the most marvelous tales." These cousins and Nehama were born in Riga (although they were two and five years younger than she). They lived next door to Nehama until their father, Zvi, moved the family to Petrograd. Nehama's father, Mordechai, actually worked in his brother's (Zvi's) private bank, which specialized in lumber transactions.

Later both families moved to Berlin. Nehama studied at the Universities of Marlbourg, Heidelberg, and Berlin (not common for a Jewish girl in those days) and majored in German language and culture. Her doctorate was on "Biblical Translation Techniques in

Hebrew – German from the 15th and 16th Centuries, as Represented in the Book of Psalms." Other uncles moved to Warsaw or Vilna, but Lipman, the youngest and still a bachelor, went to Petrograd to work in business. When the Communist regime came to power he was sent to Siberia as a bourgeois and it's likely that the exile accelerated his eventual blindness. After his release in 1930 he came to Berlin, and married Nehama, but only after she finished her doctorate. He insisted that she needed the degree so that she could make a living in Israel. Shortly thereafter they made aliya.

Nehama told a lovely story about their arrival in Jerusalem. It was designed to show her own naivete and misconceptions. "When my husband and I arrived in Israel, we were ecstatic – everything impressed us. As we rode through the hills of Judea and observed the beautiful scenery we were overwhelmed with emotion. And then as we came nearer to Jerusalem, I saw a sign, "*lehamshich behiluch namuch*" ("Continue in Low Gear"). My husband could no longer see well, so in great excitement, I read it out to him. 'Isn't it wonderful,' I said, 'that they even have signs on the road telling people to approach the Holy City with the proper modesty.'"

Her cousin, Esther, remembers that Nehama was always a brilliant student, but modest and quiet. "She was in her brother's shadow. He was the one whom the mother spoiled and everyone fussed over." Even years later, Esther got a phone call from Nehama saying, "I was told that I'm getting the Bialik Prize. Surely they must be mistaken; they probably mean Shaya." Yeshayahu was home-tutored, and finished matriculations at the age of 16, whereas Nehama, after a few years of private learning, was sent to the regular school system. "She loved it," relates a distant relative. "The first encounter was overwhelming, as she told me several years ago. 'You don't only hear what the teacher says, but also what other students add.' It was exhilarating for her." Her cousin Mira says she was a very popular student, even though she was always the cleverest. "Her gift of the gab and her extraordinary imagination made all the girls like her."

However, in an article written by Rachel Salmon, Nehama had a different opinion of her education in the 'Gymnasia' in Berlin. "It was a terrible education. The teachers were boring; nevertheless, I had two good teachers [in my life]," writes Rachel from what Nehama told her. "One was a teacher in German literature who could draw things out of the students. He had a great influence on me. Here in Israel, there was an outstanding Mishnah teacher – I would go to his lessons, and see how he involved people, connected the Mishnah to the students' lives." Rachel adds that Nehama recalled these teachers from the beginning of the century to make a point: "The important thing in teaching is to activate the students, elicit thinking from them. In lectures people fall asleep."

Even as a girl Nehama rarely paid attention to her looks, her cousins remember. Esther's mother (who had three girls of her own) would suggest, "Come with us and I'll buy you a dress; or I'll get you a haircut," but those things didn't interest Nehama. Whereas they all received a very good German education, all the Leibowitz children also knew Hebrew from the age of three, from private tutors. They had to learn chapters and chapters of the Bible by heart. On the other hand, her cousins recall that Nehama's mother was very impressed by the German culture. The cousins used to call her "Potsdame" behind her back. She was quite Prussian in her attitude to children.

Nehama became a teacher in the afternoon school for Jewish instruction while still in her teens. Gershon Shalom was one of the students who attended classes there twice a week. Dr. Yehuda Eloni, a historian, recalls learning Bible from her at the age of seven. "She graduated from the Rabbinical Seminary in Berlin. Everyone said she was smart enough to be a rabbi. Only one other woman beside Nehama studied at the Seminary." Eloni remembers that Nehama took a trip to *Eretz Yisrael* in 1927. "When she returned she wore a white dress with Yemenite embroidery to class. With her dark black hair she was quite stunning in that Israeli dress," he recalls, now seventy-five years later.

"Nehama was one of the few teachers who knew Hebrew in the school," says Dr. Eloni. "She wasn't the typical 'Yekish' type of educators that we had there either." Eloni remembers Nehama Leibowitz well, even though he was so young. "She made an impression on me. Years later when I met her at Shimon Ron's house we spoke about the past and about that afternoon school which was headed by Rabbi Dr. Bleichrod. She thought the principal was a great personality."

Nehama once confided in Rivka Davidowitz that as a youngster she was, for a short time, a 'wanderer' (a hobo). At one point in her youth she put a knapsack on her back and wandered through the German countryside. She related how she used to sleep in youth hostels, pass through forests, meet very interesting people, and never dream of being afraid, even though as a young girl she hiked alone.

Few people know that Nehama's grandfather, Eli Leibowitz, lived for fifteen years in Jerusalem and is buried on the Mount of Olives. He came from a small Latvian town, Talsen (which is where Nehama's father Mordechai grew up), and was a Torah scholar. His wife ran a flour mill, as was common in those days, and she raised seven sons and two daughters. At some point, either in 1905 or 1911, the grandfather left Latvia and made aliya. Esther Reifenberg learned that their common grandfather worked with Dr. Wallach in Shaare Zedek Hospital as an assistant. He died in 1920, and her father, Zvi (Nehama's uncle), visited the grave when he came as a tourist in 1928.

All of the Leibowitz children excelled in something. Nehama's father went to study at the London University before his marriage; another sister, (Nehama's aunt) Rachel, studied medicine and became a psychoanalyst. She died young and her only son, Eli, was brought to Palestine before the War of Independence when he was barely 13. Lipman, who had no children of his own, adopted Eli, but in actual fact the boy grew up in his brother Zvi's household, where there were other young children. Esther thinks Nehama really wasn't very close to the boy because he wasn't observant. Eli grew up, attended the Haifa Technion, served in the army, and went to work at the Dead Sea Works. In 1954, in a terrorist attack on a bus on the Maaleh Akrabim Road, Eli was killed and subsequently buried in Jerusalem.

Besides Zvi's children, Nehama had another cousin in Israel, Professor Yeshayahu Leibowitz, the son of her father's brother, Zelig, who lived in Danzburg. This Professor Yeshayahu Leibowitz was Nehama's physician for many years, and she often visited him and his wife, Chana, socially. He taught at the Hebrew University Medical School and became the leading expert on Israel Medical History. For many years Chana attended Nehama's classes starting with the class she gave at the Tikvateinu Community Center and the cousins kept close contact. She too never had children.

Nehama's longtime housekeeper, Tzipporah Ophri, relates how this "gentle" Yeshayahu Leibowitz was once in Hadassah Hospital as a patient. "The nurse told me they'd never met a patient like him; even though he was half drugged with medicine he always smiled and always said thank you."

Nehama's father, Tzipporah recalls, was very sharp. He never spoke much but he was very bright and could size people up immediately. Tzipporah also thinks that Nehama's father and husband were her chief advisors in the years she was beginning the gilyonot.

Nehama Ariel, a very close student and disciple, recalls: "After her husband died, I came to make a condolence call. It was early afternoon, during siesta time, so I sat on the steps and waited until it was 4:00 p.m. I didn't want to disturb her. I'll never forget the sight of Nehama when I walked in, the first visitor that afternoon. There sat an old woman on a low stool, hunched over, all alone, reading the Book of Job. Gradually the room filled up with other visitors who had come to comfort her. As more and more entered the room, you could physically see the change in her. Her eyes lit up, she became animated as she talked, the mournful sight changed, and she was the old Nehama again. But that first view made me resolve to visit her as often as I could; and indeed at least once a week I would find an opportunity to come in [from Kfar Maimon in the Negev, and later from Ramat Gan]. She always thanked me profusely for my visits, and they were always enriching for me."

3.

Gilyonot (Worksheets)
and Publications

The worksheets that Nehama put out weekly for almost thirty years have been called "a one-woman correspondence course in Bible study." How did Nehama start putting out the gilyonot? In 1942 she taught a group of religious kibbutz women who were on a six-month sabbatical designed to replenish their spiritual strength and improve their learning skills. At the end of the course, which was held at Beit Tzeirot Mizrachi, some of them asked if she would continue to give them lessons via the mail. Nehama agreed and started sending each one of the twelve 'girls' weekly gilyonot; most of them answered and they were marked and returned to them at their kibbutz.

Word got around. The next year fifty people requested gilyonot; by the third year there were three hundred correspondents. Putting out the gilyonot in those early years was a joint project, in which both her father and her husband took part. Yael Steifel recalls how the elder Leibowitz even folded and addressed gilyonot from his hospital bed in Shaare Zedek. It was also his job (when he was well) to take the mail to the closest post office, which in those days was all the way to Macheneh Yehudah (at least thirty minutes from their neighborhood). "Every Tuesday the whole house was full of gilyonot," recalls Rabbi Aryeh Knoll, who as a child used to visit his aunt, Nehama's neighbor. "They were on all the tables, on the chairs, even on the beds."

Eventually Shmuel Ashkenazi became the distributor in Jerusalem. Producing the worksheets in the '40s and '50s was a tremendous undertaking – and at first no one gave official assistance. The Mizrachi Women of America Organization, eventually, paid for the mailing. The cost of typing and stenciling was either covered by the few *prutot* the recipients paid or by Nehama herself, and those were days of austerity and poverty. "Nehama never made a cent from the gilyonot," says Dov Rapell.

Aside from the tremendous effort of writing up the material, the research, and the care taken to get exact quotations, Nehama and her 'team' were meticulous in answering each and every respondent immediately. The sheets came out week after week, even during most of the difficult Siege of Jerusalem and the War of Independence. At one time a wall of their house in Kiryat Moshe was bombed out. Nehama didn't let this stop her. She got some students to help clear out the rubble and mess and continued producing the gilyonot. In all, some seventeen worksheets were not produced during the war years and a few others during the time Nehama sat *shivah* for her father and her husband.

Few people realize the amount of office work that was involved. The sheets had to be typed and run off by hand on a mechanical stencil machine, by an office work company. Dov Rapell recalls a Mr. Dagani, the head of *Misrad HaMedeiyek*, who was bitten by the 'Nehama fever.' "He would get the pages typed and stenciled even if she brought her handwritten notes to his shop after hours. Nehama would wait, sometimes until after midnight, to proofread the gilyonot and only then would they be stencilled and taken home for addressing. This too was Nehama's concern."

Paper was expensive and therefore of the plainest kind. The stencils were difficult to read. Only in the last ten years was there an improvement in the quality of the print. Yet generations of students used these old, browning sheets to study Nehama's method. Only weeks before she died, some of her steady students were still 'drafted' to organize sets of gilyonot from years back for a kibbutznik from the north, for a library in a settlement, and for educators all over the world. Nehama continued putting out the worksheets until 1971, at which time she claimed she had nothing new to offer. Nevertheless for years she continued to mark and return any answers to gilyonot that people sent her. Only when she became sick did she relinquish her "Parsha Pen Pals," as Dr. Bonchik calls them, "thus summing up fifty years of marking papers for a vast, unseen audience of students all over the world." A close associate has a letter that she sent to one of her "regular" correspondents five years before her death. In it she writes, "It is with great sorrow that I have to inform you that I will no longer be able to mark and return your gilyonot. Of course those that are still in my possession I will get back to you at my earliest opportunity. Unfortunately I no longer have the strength to return submissions." However, she assures him that he's already on a level where he can learn on his own and that he doesn't need her replies. "There are still a few beginners who need my assistance, and with them I can't break off yet. I want to thank you," she writes at the end of her letter, "for the gift you gave me all these years through our mutual learning." In 1957 Nehama was awarded the prestigious Israel Prize for her lifework on the gilyonot (thirty-seven years before her brother was awarded that prize). Over the years she received many additional honors: the Lieberman Prize for Dissemination of Torah Knowledge in 1980, the Bialik Prize in Judaica in 1982, and the Saul Rothberg Prize in Jewish Education in 1986, among others.

Hadassah Zalkin remembers working on the gilyonot while she was a young teacher in Rosh Pina. In those days (1943) Nehama did not yet receive answers and send them back with comments. "Whenever I came into Jerusalem, I would go to Mr. Ashkenazi, sign up for some more gilyonot, and pay a modest fee," she recalls. "The gilyonot were an important link for me in my isolated outpost."

Even as a girl, Nehama Ariel recalls, she used to work on the weekly gilyonot with her father, but she never sent in the answers. Later, in Bnei Akiva, her *shevet* (age group) would also plow through the sheets. "Our teachers, who were among the best in the National Religious School System, used the gilyonot in their classrooms," she recalls. "After I was married I finally began sending in my answers, and always got personal attention. And as a young teacher, whenever I began teaching a new book of the Bible, I would go to her house and stock up on all the relevant worksheets."

Dr. Yosef Walk was a regular subscriber to the gilyonot. Like

34

hundreds of others, he and his family would work on the sheets over Shabbat. Then after *Havdalah* he would send in their answers. "We always got the sheets back within a few days, marked and often with her commentaries. Thus I had weekly contact with Nehama, over and beyond our professional meetings, over all the years."

Similarly, Dr. Rafael Posen recalls how he started corresponding with Nehama when he was still a yeshiva student. "The first time I sent in replies to a sheet, I was confident that I knew all the answers. However, when after a few days it was returned to me, the sheet was riddled with corrections in red ink in Nehama's distinct handwriting. I was devastated. However, at the bottom there was a special message that she had written, that was so typical of Nehama," recalls Dr. Posen. "Don't be put off by the '*adom, adom hazeh*' (these red, red [the reference is from Esau's and Jacob's discussion about lentils] marks)," wrote Nehama. "You have potential and with a little practice, I'm sure you'll do better next time." But Nehama didn't leave it at that. She also took the trouble to call the young Posen and encourage him to keep trying, and ever since then they have been friends.

Gerti Urman of Lavi remembers the envy with which she regarded her learned friends at *hachshara* (training camp) in England who were able to work on Nehama's worksheets. Years later after they'd all come on aliya, "*I* also learned Hebrew (somehow) ... and a group of us began doing the gilyonot together every Shabbat under the guidance of David Reiss. What a pleasure it was! I began to understand the magic and the intellectual enjoyment that these worksheets gave week after week to thousands of people all over the world. It was pure logic, crystal clear, and easy to understand, without an unnecessary word, like a fine laser that cuts right to the point."

David Reiss's widow recalls that Nehama heard about her husband's *chug*. On her regular visit to Lavi, Nehama came to their house and asked if he had the whole set of her gilyonot. David made a list of those that were missing. Sure enough, within a week of her return to Jerusalem, she sent him a package with the missing worksheets. "That was Nehama!" says Esther Reiss, "practical and to the point all her life." Nehama Ariel once attended a Yom Yerushalayim dinner in Kibbutz Berot Yitzhak. There she talked to one of Nehama's regular 'correspondents.' He told her that after writing one week's answers he

35

got a curious reply from Nehama. "Please let me know what country you're from. That answer is suitable to a *Galizianer* [someone from Galicia]." "Believe it or not, I'm from Galicia." On one of the sheets on *Shemot* that dealt with Pharaoh's decree to stop giving the Jewish slaves straw with which to make bricks, Nehama asked her correspondents: "Do you think Pharaoh acted out of malice or economic considerations?" Most of the replies were that he wanted to save money, but one veteran 'regular' answered: "If someone is forced to undertake a task in which he's inexperienced, it's generally wasteful. Pharaoh knew his workers would expend a lot of time and energy with this new undertaking; therefore I don't think he was being cost conscious. He was just being mean." Nehama was duly impressed by this original approach. She wrote back asking him, "What is your profession?" Sure enough, the reply came: "Efficiency expert."

When Nehama stopped producing the gilyonot, Rabbi Yochanan Freed mentioned the fact in his Shabbat sermon (much to her dislike). He included two stories she told of her wide-ranging correspondents and how the paper on which answers were received often told a tale. In the early years two of her respondents sent letters covered with grease marks and dirt. It turned out they were from two Jewish soldiers serving on the front in El Aleimin, deep in the Sahara Desert.

One of her weekly correspondents was a woman from Tel Aviv who inevitably got the answers all wrong. She also made terrible spelling mistakes and had very poor grammar. Nehama decided she wanted to meet this correspondent and maybe tell her (gently) that she was wasting her time. They met in a cafe near the sea. Nehama was surprised to see that she was a young woman, in her twenties, and worked as a waitress in the same cafe. Nehama asked her, "Why do you have such difficulty writing the answers?" "I never had any formal education," replied the young woman. "That's why I make my living as a waitress. But this is the only Torah I ever learned." Needless to say Nehama said nothing about stopping the correspondence; quite the opposite, she even offered to help the girl learn writing skills.

Nehama had other such stories to relate, and was especially proud of the 'amcha', the simple people who worked on her worksheets. Zvi Perle was her student in Meretz. He recalls one such tale: Nehama got a letter from a Yemenite street cleaner. He wrote, "I'm sending my regular *gilayon*, but I apologize if the handwriting isn't clear. I worked very hard after the first rain. There was a lot of mud in the streets. When I got home tonight I was worn out and thought I wouldn't work on the gilayon, just this once. But I overcame my *yetzer harah* (bad inclination) and just finished writing the answers; but please excuse the scribbles."

Nehama once admitted to Zvi that she often worked on the gilyonot until 3:00 a.m., marking and sending off the answers. But she had great satisfaction from the progress she noticed in certain correspondents. "Some of my correspondents didn't know anything when they started doing the gilyonot," she told a Meretz class. "There were new immigrants or uneducated people, who nevertheless had native intelligence." At the end, Nehama realized, many of them could read commentaries without difficulty and reply even to the most advanced questions. That was her reward.

At a memorial service for Nehama at *Machanaim*, a Russian new immigrant center in Jerusalem, one of the leaders of the refuseniks recalled that they were already putting out translated copies of her gilyonot in the 1970s. The printing was very cramped so as to get maximum use of every page. These underground sheets would be put out in batches of 100–150 copies and circulated among those who had learned a little Torah. "Anyone who had ever gone through the Five Books of Moses with Rashi was already sent out to teach," said Pinchas Polvovski, one of the directors of *Machanaim*.

He explained why *dafka* (specifically) Nehama's teachings were among the first works they bothered to distribute. "The questions she raised were suited to our generation, and elicited interest even among people who had never learned Torah in depth," he said. "Furthermore, Nehama always cited a wide range of commentaries, many that didn't appear in the *Mikraot Gedolot* that we had at our disposal. She explained everything in everyday language, which plain people could understand." Polvovski was proud that now her works are available for Russian readers in book form and even on the Internet.

Some of her works also appeared in French, Spanish, and Dutch. Her complete set of *Studies* in book form appeared in English long before they came out in Hebrew. Nehama was very meticulous and insisted on going over every line and every commentary several times, to be sure there were no mistakes. That's why, according to Shmuel Borstein, it took so long to put out the last two books. Shmuel was in charge of publications for the Division of Torah Culture at the Jewish Agency. He first encouraged Nehama to put out study pages for teachers and community rabbis in English and in Hebrew to accompany the gilyonot. "The *Studies* were very warmly received," says Shmuel, "and many sermons in synagogues throughout the world are based on them."

Of course the main 'clients' have always been teachers. Many of them wrote to Nehama to ask for more information, or to comment on how the lesson went. Some of these teachers remained in close touch with her until her last days. The *Studies* were published and distributed by the Division of Torah Culture for seven years. They formed the basis of her five books: *Studies in Bereshit, Shemot, Vayikra, Bamidbar,* and *Devarim.*

In addition, Nehama put out a collection of didactic articles; a fascinating pamphlet on how to teach history (translated into English); lessons on the Book of Jeremiah; the book of Psalms in English for Hadassah's Education Department; chapters on the Seven Haftarot (Additional Readings from the Prophets) of Comfort and Redemption, written with her lifelong friend, Professor Meir Weiss; two correspondence-course textbooks on Rashi's method for the Open University; and innumerable articles – even for nonacademic publications, for example, WIZO women or *Kibbutz HaDati.* No one has yet put out the Teachers Guides that accompanied the gilyonot for fifteen years, which were meant to help teachers use them in the classroom, explaining what points to stress, in what sequence to ask the questions, and how to elicit discussions.

Her *Studies* on the five books of the Torah were published over a period of twenty-seven years. Professor Moshe Arent, who replaced her as lecturer at the Tel Aviv University, and also worked with her on the Open University textbooks, explains why it took so long. "Many Torah scholars never put their lessons into print, and Nehama looked at publications as a sideline. Her main task in life, after all, was teaching, lecturing, and putting out the gilyonot. But probably the main reason for the long delay was that Nehama took a long time with her writings, especially as she grew older. She was very critical and exacting, with others and, of course, even more so with herself."

Shmuel Borstein says that her admirers in Kfar Blum (a non-religious kibbutz) invited her to stay at their Guest House for six months to finish her last two books (*Devarim* and *Bamidbar*) – but she couldn't keep away from teaching that long. Once at 1:00 a.m. a man called up from America and demanded to talk to her. "Do you know what time it is here?" said Nehama sleepily. "I don't care what time it is," said the person. "I just want to know one thing. When are you going to put out your last book already? I'm an old man and I want to see that book before I die."

Yael Stiefel knew Nehama very well. When people asked her about that last book, which took a long time in coming out, Nehama would often complain that she couldn't write. Her listeners thought that she meant she was getting old, or it was difficult to collect her thoughts. But Yael accompanied her to a doctor's, where it turned out her difficulty was orthopedic – her gnarled hands wouldn't allow her to hold a pencil and complete the act of writing 'mechanically'. The doctor suggested an apparatus to connect to her fingers, which Nehama quickly acquired, and then the work on the book proceeded again.

Another source of Nehama's lessons, which Shmuel Borstein mentions, was the radio. She often broadcasted lectures and Bible classes on Kol Yisrael, some even before the State was established. Unfortunately there do not seem to be any tapes of these broadcasts.

Today students all over the world still use her books, learn her *Studies*, and work on her sheets; individuals in Melbourne, San Paulo, or Dallas, or groups in youth movements, army camps, and kibbutzim study Parshat Hashavuah with her gilyonot. Nehama's books continue to sell well and are used for reference by lecturers, teachers, rabbis, and laymen alike. Her group of faithfuls, Amitei Zion, hold a monthly class where the marked gilyonot of former students are often used for reference, especially if the participants are stuck and asking, "What would Nehama say if…"

At the Van Leer Institute there were regular lessons in her memory, organized by Michael Bahat of Kfar Blum. Some gilyonot have been translated into English and put on the internet while Rabbi Stan Peerless for several years continued a series begun by the Torah Department of the JNF in 1999 and which appeared weekly via e-mail and on a website through the auspices of the World Council for Torah Education.

These reissued gilyonot appeared with answers (something Nehama never allowed) and relevant excerpts from her *Studies*. They were edited by Yitzhak Reiner and associates who also produced them for CD-Rom in English and Hebrew. According to Reiner, they represent "thirty years of feedback from students throughout the world."

4.
Teacher

There were many stories of Nehama's skills as a teacher: how she made difficult points simple, how she was able to learn moral lessons from grammatical commentaries, how she could teach people of all levels with equal success, and how she compared the approach of different commentators, which made students understand their system. But being a paramount educator meant that she could also be a strict disciplinarian. If a student entered her class without a Tanach or came late, she was capable of throwing him out no matter what the plea.

A group of Machon Gold students from abroad returned from a *tiyul* (trip) and went directly to her shiur. Their teacher had convinced them to enter the classroom even though they were very tired and wanted to shower. He assured them that they were in for a treat. Instead Nehama yelled at them for not having brought *Tanachim*: "Did you come to look at my beautiful face?" she shouted and left the room in protest. The teacher was distressed. Not only were his students terribly insulted, but Nehama had walked out of the class. Outside Nehama beckoned him over and said in her normal tone of voice, "Don't worry. I'll wait here in the next room until they all bring their Bibles, and then I'll come back to teach."

Yeduel (Doli) Basok, an excellent teacher himself, has many stories to tell about Nehama's didactic methods. "Nehama always used to say that the teacher must activate the student; frontal lectures were not worth anything. In the Teachers' Training Program she once talked to us for fifty minutes on this point. I felt close enough to her to raise my hand in class and tell her, 'Nehama, we're sitting here for almost an hour listening to you give a fascinating lecture. So why are frontal lectures out?' She gave me a dirty look, but didn't say anything."

Doli remembers that he first met Nehama as a Yeshiva student doing a teachers' course in the Lifshitz Seminary. "Here we were, a group of young rabbis who had learned Torah for years. We attended her class reluctantly, only because we needed the points for the teachers' certificate." What they expected to be a burden turned out to be sheer pleasure. "She held us enthralled," he recalls nostalgically. "The shiur flowed. She was outstanding, but also very strict."

It was forbidden, for example, to miss even one class. She informed them from the beginning that if someone didn't attend even one of her classes he would have to take her course over again the next year. "When I had several children already," Doli relates, "We moved to the Moslem Quarter in the Old City. I was so busy that I nearly forgot it was Thursday, the day of Nehama's class. I called her by phone, thinking that for a reason like this she would certainly let me off. 'Hello, Nehama,' I said. 'This is Doli Basok. I want to inform you that we're just moving into the Moslem Quarter today, into a house where my father's grandfather once lived – the Diskin Orphanage.' She was most impressed. 'I have so much unpacking to do, and my wife's pregnant. I don't want to leave all the work to her, so I don't think I can make it to the shiur today.' Nehama was very sympathetic. She said, 'O.K. Never mind, I'll see you next year.' She wished me a *yishuv tov* (Good luck in your new home) and that was it – no arguments, no reprieve, no special treatment, even though she had taught my mother … What shall I tell you? I didn't want to lose the whole year. I beat it down there quick. I even took a taxi to get there on time."

Nehama had the ability to mesmerize whole classrooms of students, of all ages and backgrounds. Nehama Ariel often took the first class of each Tanach course she taught at the Open University to Nehama's house for an introductory lesson. "There were people from every walk of life; academicians; plain workmen, retired people, and youngsters, secular and religious of all persuasions. She held them all in the palm of her hand, as she taught a commentary from Rashi, or a chapter from Jeremiah. No one looked at his watch; no one yawned. It was positively magic to watch her get her message across and teach."

She was always open to teach groups, and until her later years was prepared to travel all over the country to give a shiur. Once, Idit Izkovitz relates, she was invited to give a shiur in Ofira. "Do you think people will come to hear me?" she asked the organizers. They assured her there would be a sizable audience, and that she would be flown down there. In the end practically the whole population of Ofira turned out to hear her. They were not disappointed. Nehama returned to the southernmost point of Israel several more times before it was relinquished to the Egyptians.

Rabbi Aryeh Knoll, the Rav of Kfar Etzion, relates that after the Six Day War, Nehama was invited to give a shiur when their settlement was reestablished. "She was very happy that we invited her and for a long time she returned every *Motzei Shabbat* to give additional classes. In fact Nehama would usually go to teach wherever she was asked. It didn't matter who was in the class and even how many people were attending. She once told me, 'A good teacher is one who is prepared to instruct even one pupil.' The truth of the matter is that she could relate to every individual in a *big* class as if he were the only one." Rabbi Knoll also thinks that Nehama actually liked being invited to places all over the country.

For example, she often gave lectures in Eilat. Machon Meir would send her there by plane and she'd stay over at a hotel. Azariya Ravivi, who would pick her up from the airport and take her to the lecture hall, remembers fondly the long and intimate discussions they would have deep into the night after her official shiur. "She was the most popular speaker we ever brought down to Eilat," he says emphatically. She was also influential in bringing about an 'awakening' of interest in Judaism among some of the old-timers there, like Azariya.

"Nehama was actually an ugly woman," he says bluntly, "but when she began to talk she became very attractive and almost enchanting. Her curiosity and her range of learning were outstanding." Her friend, Shimon Ron, once pointed out to her, "Nehama, why don't you get down to finishing your *Studies?* Traveling around the way you do, to Eilat and all, doesn't leave you time to finish your books. In Eilat maybe 100 people will hear your lecture. But if you get your last book out (*Bamidbar*) you'll reach thousands!" Nehama heard him out and even said, "You're right. I promise to work on the book." But she continued to lecture in Eilat and other far-flung places until she was well into her late eighties, and *Bamidbar* came out only in 1996.

She was very supportive of housewives who took the time to learn Torah. Chana Tuval recalls that twenty years ago she gave shiurim in Mevasseret Zion to Yeshiva students who were studying in a program called "Meretz" to be teachers in development towns and border settlements. She allowed some of their wives to attend the classes. "Nehama was very strict with the yeshiva men and kicked out any of them who appeared without a Tanach or who came late. But with us [the women] she was much more lenient. She would say, 'Any of you housewives/mothers of small children who attend the Friday morning shiur can come in whenever you like.'"

One rabbi suggested that if there were women in the class they should sit behind the *mehitzah* (the partition). The organizers asked Nehama her opinion on this. "After all," said the rabbi, "It is a yeshiva." Nehama agreed. She said, "No problem, but I'll also stand behind the mehitzah." The matter was dropped, pronto. Someone else raised the question of whether a woman could teach at all in a yeshiva. The Haredi rabbi who was consulted asked: "If there's a man who can do the job as well as the woman speaker, then no." However, states Rabbi Uri Cohen, the *Rosh Kollel* (Dean), "Since there was no alternative to Nehama, ever, we had our *heter* (religious licence or permission)."

Zvi Perle was a yeshiva student at Meretz. His mother had studied with Nehama forty years earlier. During class one Friday morning, Nehama, as usual, gave out a question or two to solve in writing. While everyone was hunched over his notebook, she came up to Zvi and asked to see his answer. Zvi said, "I'm sorry, I don't know it yet." Nehama shook her head. "Your mother solved it in half the time it takes her son." Then looking beyond the yeshiva students to where the women participants sat, she noticed that some of them had already finished writing and were waiting for the shiur to continue.

She quoted the verse from *Bereshit*, "*V'yevan HaShem Elokim et hazelah shelakach*" ("And God built the rib He had taken..."), and the explanation of the word, "*V'yevan*" in the *Midrash Raba*: "*binah yeterah nitan laisha*" ("He endowed women with more understanding"), and added, "Here we have proof of that explanation!"

All kinds of groups would come to Nehama's house to study. She was prepared to teach anyone who wanted to learn. Chana Tuval brought a group of non-orthodox women from Mevasseret to her home for a class. "They were very impressed with her, but even more so with her simple living conditions," says Chana. Dr. Ben Hollander often brought classes from the Hebrew Union College at the end of the school year to hear a shiur from her. "I don't think we should use Torah to separate us; Torah should link all of us," she would say if someone asked her how she felt about teaching future Reform rabbis.

Similarly, Nehama Ariel had no trouble getting her to receive a group of women from Netiv HaAsarah shortly after the evacuation from Yamit. These women were at the time terribly demoralized by the loss of their homes, and the negative views on settlement by certain politicians and even by Nehama's own brother. Nehama Ariel recalls that Nehama received them very cordially and to raise their spirits taught them the chapter on Navot's vineyard. "She had gone to the trouble of preparing handwritten charts to make the lesson clearer; she herself made carbon copies for each participant. She also told them how she was often invited to lecture abroad, but wouldn't dream of leaving the country. 'I ask those who invited me, "Have you already been to Hanita? Have you seen everything there is to see in Israel?"' She made the women laugh and forget their sorrow for a while; they felt uplifted when they left her home."

Naomi Ragen belongs to a group of five professional women who have been 'doing' Nehama's gilyonot for the past five years. "I've learned to respect Nehama very much through these worksheets," says Naomi, a popular novelist. "She's changed the way we learn Tanach. We're now called upon to use our intellect, which is what we use in the other aspects of our lives [the group consists of a teacher, a lawyer, a doctor, a psychologist, and a novelist]. That's not what we were taught in day school. It's liberating!" Naomi also thinks that knowing there were groups that were continuing to learn according to her method gave Nehama great satisfaction.

Dr. Tamar Ross, who was also her student, says: "It's hard to second-guess what Nehama would say today, but I imagine she would be very gratified by the burgeoning of women learning [all over the country] in the last few years.... I'm familiar with Nehama's attitude to family and motherhood; she most definitely regarded these as the most worthwhile activities a woman could engage in. On the other hand, she was totally outspoken amongst men.

"She felt that a lot of the modesty bit in segregating the sexes was a bunch of stuff and nonsense, as well as the limitations upon women teaching men, etc., and many other attitudes that go with the chugim (circles) that promote the above. Although she was very respectful in her manner when addressing rabbanim [speaking to them in the third person singular, as a sign of deference], she often expressed her impatience ... with yeshiva-ish values, such as the ideology that would have all men learning full time, wholesale submission to formal authority, and uncritical, blind *emunah* (faith)...."

Nehama had very down-to-earth methods of teaching Torah principles. To illustrate the difference between *p'shat* (literal explanation) and *drash* (non-literal) she'd bring an example that everyone could understand. "A husband comes home from work and says, 'I'm dead' to his wife. She doesn't call the emergency ward, she doesn't get a mortician; she simply replies, 'Why don't you lie down a few minutes until dinner is ready.'" Then she would show how the literal meaning is not the real meaning in a Bible verse. Once while traveling in a taxi, she heard the popular song on the radio, "*S'heat omeret Lo, I'ma at mitkavenet*" [about a girl who says no to her boyfriend, but means something else]. "Oh, that's exactly what I'm trying to explain," she told her class on the subject of p'shat and drash."

Dr. Bonchik wrote an article (in English) on Nehama's unique pedagogical achievements. Nehama never acknowledged any special talents. "I only teach what the commentators say. I have nothing of my own in a lesson," she would say in characteristic modesty. It's true that she generally did not teach anything original, but she definitely developed an original way of getting people to think, to learn the commentaries, and to understand the underlying meaning in every phrase.

She taught her students to question why an expression was there or elsewhere, why a precise word is used, and what approach is hidden behind each *peirush* (commentary). For example, Rashi and the Malbim had different interpretations for the word "*L'hozi*", which appears in *Shemot* 8:14, "*Vayahasu hahartumin b'loteiham l'hozi hakinim, v'lo yochlu*" ("and the magicians did so with their enchantments *to bring forth* lice, but they could not..."). Rashi explains the word as in "*l'hozi lechem min haaretz*" ("to bring forth bread from the earth"); whereas the Malbim stresses the meaning to take out, to remove, as in "*l'hozi B'nei Yisrael miMitzraim*".

Nehama wouldn't accept a rewording of Rashi and the Malbim's words; she insisted that the essence of their difference be exposed. Thus Malbim relates to the specific plague, the lice, and explains why Pharaoh's magicians were unable to get rid of them, "*l'hozi otam*," and even suffered from them themselves. Rashi sees the sentence in the contents of all the plagues, which, like this one of lice, were brought forth – "*L'hozi*".

Despite the literal meaning that was important to her, Nehama inevitably managed to find moral and spiritual lessons in the most obscure phrases, thus turning her Bible lessons into ethical seminars as well as intellectual experiences. In fact the subjects she chose to teach were generally also moral issues. Many of her female students were delighted with her lesson on *Bereshit* 30:1. When Rachel pleads with her husband Yaakov, "*Hava li banim v'im ain meta anochi*" ("Give me children, or else I die"), she had the students read three different explanations to Jacob's seemingly callous reply, "*Hatachat Elokim anochi*" ("Am I instead of God?").

The clincher was a little-known commentary from Akedat Yitzhak. He explains that Yaakov wanted to remind Rachel that women have more than one function in life. The name 'Chava' refers to her function as a mother, to bear children, "the secondary purpose," according to Akedat Yitzhak; but the name 'Isha' refers to the aim of every woman, just like every man, to advance intellectually and morally in the service of God. Thus the childless woman has every reason in the world to live. Then Nehama (who never had a child of her own), using only Akedat Yitzhak's words, never her own, seems to reprimand Yaakov – and maybe the male commentator as well, by subtle use of exclamation points and quotation marks. "She (Rachel) in her yearning for a child saw her whole world circumscribed solely by this second purpose of woman's existence (which the Akedah calls 'the secondary purpose'!?!)."

Dr. Gaby Cohen, a veteran educator and scholar, claims, "In Nehama's classes the Torah commentaries from all generations 'sat' around the table with us, arguing and debating among themselves in talmudic fashion, their understanding of the text. Nehama didn't just teach what Rashi said – rather she highlighted what initiated his commentary; what's the basis of his views in the text; and what's the central point of his explanation." Dr. Cohen points out that Nehama encouraged students to compare the various commentaries and verify where they differ, where they are similar, and which, in their opinion, is closest to the Written Word. He admits that "there might be those who take issue with her for allowing fifteen to sixteen-year-olds (and even scholarly adults), to *choose* their 'preferred commentary' or give their opinion about the virtue of the revered and time-honored interpretations."

To this criticism Nehama would reply, "If the comparisons and appraisals are conducted in the right spirit, in an attempt to get the students into the habit of understanding the commentaries in depth, and if the purpose is to deter superficiality or rash conclusion, I don't think there's a danger of any lack of respect or frivolousness. Quite the opposite, reverence for the spiritual leaders and diligent study of their words should result."

What characterized the subject matter and commentaries that Nehama chose to emphasize, according to Dr. Rachel Salmon, a lecturer in Bar Ilan University, is their moral application and relevance to everyday life. "Nehama does not recognize intellectual activity as separate from the conduct of life. To study Torah for its own sake means, for her, to realize its teachings in our lives.... [She maintained] an allegiance to the view that reading should have a pragmatic effect on conduct – that the study of Torah should lead to practice."

To this Dr. Gaby Cohen would add, "Despite her rational intellectual approach, one always felt Nehama's deep commitment to Judaism. Like Rabbi Soloveitchik, one could feel the _Shechinah_ (the Divine Presence) looking over her shoulder at every step." "She was a very religious woman," says her close friend, Shimon Ron, himself a non-observant Jew.

On another plane, Dr. Cohen credits Nehama Leibowitz with bringing about a renaissance in the use of _midrash_ (legend) for understanding the Bible. "When Nehama started her career sixty to seventy years ago there were few books on midrash and, even more difficult, the approach and way of thinking used by allegory was foreign to most teachers." By opening up this additional route to understanding Tanach, Gaby Cohen believes Nehama achieved three things. She forced her students to be textually exacting. She focused on value issues, thus making the contents even more of a "Living Torah" (_"Torat Chaim"_), and she added an additional approach to understanding the material.

For example, Dr. Cohen shows how legend fills in the gap of what happened during the three days when Abraham and his son, Yitzhak, went on their way to the _Akedah_ (the sacrifice). "The fact that nothing is written allows the Midrash to raise all kinds of options," he explains. One legend has Satan continually appearing to Abraham in an attempt to change the patriarch's mind. Satan uses arguments like "God promised you that Yitzhak will be your successor" or "You're supposed to be an example to others regarding moral behavior. What can be more immoral than murder?" It's as if the Midrash is expressing Abraham's subconscious.

In the discussion between the brothers, Cain and Abel, Dr. Cohen pointed out, "The Midrash is not dealing with these two forefathers only. Rather the explanation of the phrase "_V'yehi bihiyotam basadeh v'yakom Kayin al Hevel achiv v'yehargeihu_" ("and when they were in the field, Cain arose and killed his brother Hevel"), deals with the three basic reasons why people fight. The word 'sadeh' (field), which seems superfluous, is explained in one legend as being actual land [economic source]. In another one, it is a symbol of the Temple, and in a third midrash, _sadeh_ is analogous to woman. Indeed, most human strife, Nehama would point out, stems either from arguments over land, religion or woman. Then she would add with a twinkle: 'Is it an issue that concerns Marx, the Pope, or Freud?'" All in all, Dr. Cohen counted seven hundred uses of *Midrashim* in Nehama's works (and only three hundred sources from the Talmud).

Most teachers teach knowledge; Nehama taught understanding. The audible "Ah" that one often heard in class when 'the coin fell,' so to speak, when the whole group caught on to a beautiful explanation, was a common and uplifting sound. A longtime student, Idit Itzkovitz thinks the percentage of material remembered in her class was probably higher than in other classes simply because of her flair for using dramatics and stories to make her point. For example, in teaching the expression '*noval b'reshut haTorah*' (fraudulent within the letter of the Law), she'd use the colorful simile "like a woman who wears a long skirt but flaunts a low-cut bodice."

Nehama gave such theatrical feedback to answers written or verbal (feigned horror at mistakes, heavy praise for correct answers) that instantly the participants were compelled to try even harder. Her dramatic flair was one of her great attractions as a teacher, and on many occasions she quite hammed it up, to get across a point. "A man carrying two heavy baskets got on a crowded bus and pushed his way to the back. On the way he stepped on a lady's foot. 'Oh, I beg your pardon,' he said, 'I didn't mean to…' 'I should *hope* you didn't mean to,' came back the irate reply." Nehama gave this striking rendition, in her raspy voice and tone of righteous indignation, as she illustrated the difference between inadvertent sin and premeditated sin.

Using mock shock, pathos, or feigned anger, Nehama was most effective in bringing across a point. Once she read out Moshe Rabbeinu's plea to be allowed to enter the Land of Israel. It was so moving and realistic that the class was completely caught up in her narration. "I really wanted to get a professional actor to read this midrash," she said, little realizing how beautifully she had put the story across herself.

Indeed, Professor Moshe Arend, in an article in *S'deh Hemed* (1968), lists "entertaining" or "actualization" as the prime characteristics of "Nehama's method" in making Bible study not only relevant, but also intriguing. The other two characteristics are "rigorous adherence to the text" and parshanut (use of commentaries). Professor Yairah Amit, of the Bible Department at Tel Aviv University, shows the danger in this first tendency. "… Nehama's tendency to seek out what is relevant has led to a selective coverage of texts. She is more likely to focus on passages which are interesting by virtue of their subject matter or the exegetical response they aroused … She often shows a preference for passages with a moral message…."

On the other hand, Professor Yairah Amit wisely points out that Nehama's popularization of the traditional commentaries has forced adherents of biblical criticism to reexamine their approach. "Such problems as duplications or even (seeming) contradictions, which served as the starting points for historical criticism, are nothing new. Jewish exegesis had already taken note of these problems and had dealt with them…. Now any scholar who is really after the truth must take serious note of the solutions proposed by traditional Jewish commentators."

Professor Amit concludes an erudite article she wrote on Nehama's method of teaching Tanach, in honor of her eightieth birthday, with a quote by Nehama: "A scholar can have no honor greater than the knowledge that his students cherish the words of the Torah, thanks to him." Amit writes, "She was, of course, referring to the exegetes drawn upon in her commentaries – but these words, certainly, apply to Nehama Leibowitz herself, for her students cherish the words of the Torah and the words of its interpreters, as well, thanks to her."

For her students, the selectivity of her subject matter, and her eclectic, non-traditional choice of commentaries were of small concern. "She was a different type of teacher," claims Shmuel Borstein, who first studied with Nehama fifty-two years ago. "She didn't lecture; she activated the students. She got them to use their heads, to independently crack open the commentaries – classic and nonconventional alike; to understand the text through midrashim, philosophy, and grammar. Bible criticism didn't interest her – although she understood it; she opened the gates to knowledge and understanding."

When one of her doctorate students asked her if she shouldn't take some classes in Bible criticism, Nehama answered tersely, "That's not at all necessary." However, she herself was well versed in their school of thought and knew how to refute each one's contentions. For example, many 'modern' Bible critics claim that the two incidents where David refuses to harm Saul, when he twice has the opportunity to do so, is really a repeat. Nehama scorns this "uneducated" and "unpsychological" view. She points out that letting off a sleeping adversary once is a matter of chance. David may have had a moment of weakness or pity for Saul, and undoubtedly his colleagues berated him for the lost chance. By giving the future king a second opportunity, and having him forego an act of revenge despite the pressure no doubt applied on him, demonstrate David's character traits and suitability to lead Israel as one incident never could.

Nehama sprinkled her classes with outside sources from the world of literature and modern sciences, especially psychology, to explain a point. She was wont to do this when addressing 'beginners' in the field of Bible study, so that they could relate to the familiar 'commentators,' and only afterward she would introduce the classical *peirushim* to them.

Moshe Bodek, an educator from Haifa, describes the way Nehama managed to get everyone in the classroom involved. "When a teacher asks a question in class, some raise their hands to answer but more are passive or involved in something else. Nehama had a different method. In her class every student had to answer the question – in writing. That way there's a break, both for the teacher and the students, from the frontal approach. Moreover, everyone has to think; the teacher passes through the room and comments on what she sees they've written ... It's my experience that this is the preferred way to teach – it gives every student the opportunity to participate and answer the question. Those teachers who adopted her method were rewarded immediately with a good response."

A similiar description of Nehama's didactic method was given by Rabbi Uriel Kessing, another veteran teacher and longtime student of hers. "Nehama never gave a dry shiur. We all had to write, and she'd pass among the students and comment on what we'd noted. '*Yafeh kotavta*' (You've written nicely); '*Zeh lo nachon*' (that's not correct); '*Tichtov od pa'am*' (write it again) – these remarks prodded us on to do better. Her method had three purposes: (1) to provide a break in the frontal teaching, and allow teacher and students a respite period; (2) to assure a personalized approach; and (3) to provide feedback and reinforcement. I use this approach in my teaching at the Jerusalem

College, and I tell the girls who will one day be teachers to use this system when *they* educate as well."

Moshe Bodek also points out how Nehama advised teaching aspects of nature that appear in the Bible. "Because we sinned and were exiled from our Land," she quoted, "we were dislocated from our natural habitat; and unlike our forefathers we no longer understand the plant and animal metaphors that appear in the sources." By way of example, Bodek mentions the verse in Isaiah 7:2, "And the House of David was told, Aram has descended on Ephraim, and his heart is moved … as the trees in the forest are moved by the wind." According to Nehama, trees in the forest do not all bend to the wind at the same time. Rather, row follows row, or individual trees bend after other trees have bent. That is what happens among people, when one gets frightened or a group becomes terrorized, the effect passes through the crowd like fire – and the result is mass panic. This is the picture that the prophet transfers to the people of his generation when he uses the tree and wind metaphor. And the farmers of his generation understand the phenomenon, from their contact with nature.

Another close disciple, Dr. Bryna Levi, once approached Nehama for personal advice. She was teaching in many places and was equally taken up with her small children at home. She couldn't decide where to put her emphasis and which positions to give up. Nehama answered her sympathetically but emphatically. "You have to continue teaching at all the seminars and all the courses," she said to Bryna. "You never know the influence of a Torah class. Even if one student decides, after he goes back to his country of origin, to donate money to a hospital in Israel and not in Argentina, you've made a dent."

Bryna found that Nehama was extremely supportive of women teachers just because they had families to bring up. "I don't know how you young mothers do it," she would say. "The Catholic nuns are the best teachers, because they're not married, and they can devote their whole lives to their mission." Bryna gasped, but Nehama quickly added, "But you manage to teach, to prepare lessons, to mark them, and to bring up your families too.…" And she would shake her head in wonderment.

Rachel Burg was a student of Nehama's in the 1930s. "When

we were studying for our final exams in the Teacher's Seminary we had to know the entire Bible, not like today, when the matriculations concentrate on only certain chapters of several books of Tanach," she relates. "We complained to Nehama that we would never be able to remember all that material, so what was the use of learning so intensely. She answered us, 'At least you'll know where to look up material.' And she was so right!" Mrs. Burg thinks Nehama was probably her most significant teacher, and taught her an extraordinary amount, above and beyond the understanding of text.

Esther Gross was once present at a curious incident in Nehama's house. It was Shabbat and a group of her regulars were gathered for a spontaneous shiur. One woman came in with her eight-year-old daughter. It was obvious that Nehama was not comfortable with the child there. "She'll get bored," she told the mother. "No, no, it's O.K. She's a quiet child, she won't disturb us," said the woman. Nehama began the shiur, but she continually mentioned that the child didn't belong there, that she'd find it tedious. Finally, she simply told the mother, "You can go now." After they left, Nehama continued the lesson. Later Esther asked Nehama, "Why did you send them away; the child wasn't disturbing anyone."

Nehama hemmed and hawed. She repeated something she often claimed: that it's a sin to bore a child, so that they won't be put off of learning Tanach in the future. But she had another reason. "The child will show off in front of her friends," said Nehama, with great reluctance. "She'll say, 'I attended a class at Nehama Leibowitz's house.'" Esther was amazed. "She was right on the mark!"

Yaakov Rubin knows of another incident where Nehama asked a student who came to a class with one of her children to leave. In that case, when afterward Yaakov asked for an explanation, Nehama said something else. "I'll ask everyone to write an answer. Assuming her mother's answer will be incorrect, or I yell at her mother, what kind of an impression will that have on the child? No, better she shouldn't sit in on the class with us."

Similarly, Shifra Aviner reports, Nehama didn't approve of certain assignments teachers often gave to elementary students. "Writing about 'A Good Deed I Performed' may lead a youngster to use his imagination and lie," she claimed. "Better not to give such an essay subject." She once told Rivka Davidowitz that she overheard a kindergarten teacher explaining the opening prayer, *Yigdal*, to her class. "Do you think they can understand the concepts in that prayer?" she asked the *gannenet* (teacher). "Do these tots understand a Being that has no body, or One who is inconceivable and incomparable?" The kindergarten teacher thought for a moment and then shot back, "Do you understand those concepts?"

Nehama never considered herself original. Her strength, she admitted, was in her ability to explain and analyze text. She opened the door to many *parshanim* (commentators) that most laymen would never approach were it not for her special integrated method. "I would never have had an acquaintance with Yitzhak Arama, Ibn Ezra, Abarbanel, Ramban, and others were it not for her special screening of sources," says Professor Shmuel Adler. Learning with Nehama was not only an intellectual experience, however; it was a spiritual one as well.

Her intellectual integrity led her to use unconventional sources. Professor Adler thinks she helped rescue Benno Jacob from obscurity. Even though he was a Reform rabbi and anti-Zionist, this never bothered her. Her references included Martin Buber, Yehezkel Kaufmann, and even Christian sources, even though her faith was irrefutable and she was extremely halachic-minded. She pointed out that the Abarbanel suffered greatly at the hands of the Church and the Spanish government. He fought for the survival of the Jewish community in the Iberian Peninsula and failed. Yet when he came to interpret the prophet Samuel's reaction to the Israelites' request for a king, he presented the interpretation of a Spanish bishop, the best source he could find – which to Nehama showed the openness required in the pursuit of knowledge.

Wendy Bar Yaakov searches for a way to describe Nehama's special teaching charm. "She made learning Torah *kef* (fun). I'd come back from a shiur on a high – especially if she approved of something I'd said. She'd say, 'Interesting, the Ramban says something very similiar,' or 'Oh, I never thought of that angle,' or simple, '*Yaffe*' (nice), '*Nachon*' (right). That challenged people and made them rise above themselves."

Dr. Moshe Shlomowitz, who also attended her Thursday night

shiur regularly, says, "She was a great teacher; she made people love Torah. It meant something to them because she turned the Tanach into a living thing, not just the realm of Torah scholars; not something that is relegated to the dusty back rooms of the synagogue. I suppose that's what they mean by 'living text.'"

"When I first attended her classes, I would get upset that people argued with her and took up class time. She had so much to say, and I thought that they were stealing valuable minutes from the shiur," says Chana Tubal, who first heard Nehama in the Meretz classes in Mevasseret. "Only later I understood that it was her *shitah* (method) to get the participants involved, by igniting controversy and discussion."

David Bir, one of her older students, thinks one of Nehama's talents was her jokes – her dry humor, the Englishman stresses. "She always made us laugh; she told us about her own experiences," and indirectly the material she was getting across was absorbed much more smoothly. Nehama could also be critical, Bir points out, but it was an "encouraging" type of criticism – a "you can do better" approach.

Nehama had a special relationship with the yeshiva students she taught at Meretz. They were all post Army Hesder service, studying to become teachers and spiritual leaders in outlying areas, and they applied themselves to their learning with extra fervor. Zvi Perle relates, "Shortly after the war in Lebanon, Nehama gave a class in *Tehillim*. It was the first class after they had all come back from their army service. She wrote a verse on the blackboard and asked us to punctuate it. One after the other the students came to the board, but no one could do it to her satisfaction."

"Did she yell at us!" continues Zvi. "She berated us, 'It's a shame and a scandal! If in the university they don't know something as simple as punctuation, I can understand it. But Yeshiva students, *B'nei Torah*, can't write a plain verse from the Bible....' She really let us have it. Everyone was in shock. No one wanted to say a word," he goes on. "Nehama stopped in front of my table. 'Zvi, what's going on here?' she asked. I told her, 'Nehama, everyone's afraid to open his mouth. They're all intimidated.' She looked at us all with her slight smile and a look of wonder came over her. 'Men who fought like lions on the front in Lebanon; who weren't afraid of anything in battle – they're afraid of an old woman well into her eighties, who only wants "*doresh elbono shel Torah*" ("protect the Torah's reputation")! From her they're afraid!' Everyone broke out into cheers and spontaneous clapping, and the ice was broken." When Zvi's class at Meretz was graduating, Nehama gave them a closing talk, which turned out to be a type of ethical will. "I love you all; you're all dear to me. Remember never to be ashamed of being a teacher. But don't use the title of 'rav' – it's *Bizayon LaTorah* (an insult to the Torah). Today anybody who knows a little Rambam and a few chapters of *Shulchan Aruch* calls himself a rabbi." The students were dumbfounded. Here they were being educated to serve as rabbis and teachers in outlying settlements, and Nehama was negating the whole concept.

One student asked her, "Who is entitled to call himself a rav, Nehama?" Without a second thought she said, "Rav Herzog (Chief Rabbi of Israel in her time); he was a rav, no one less." "Why him?" the student asked. Nehama put her finger to her forehead, as the rabbis do and said, "Every question I ever asked him, he knew how to answer. He'd move his finger from this side of his forehead, saying 'It's not in the *Yerushalmi Talmud*' and he'd move his finger to the other side of his forehead, saying, 'And it's not in the *Bavli Talmud*' – he really knew," Nehama said. "He was erudite in 'the fifth book of the *Shulchan Aruch*' [there are only four] – in experience and common sense."

Another student asked, "If Rav Herzog is the maximum rabbi in your opinion, then who fits the minimum requirements?" Again Nehama answered quickly, "Rav Min-Hahar" [a noted educator and neighborhood rabbi with years of experience]. "Why him?" the student asked. "It never happened that I'd ask him a question and he didn't know the answer," Nehama replied once again. "He'd already been asked my question many times before." The boys could only sigh and wonder what she would say next.

Nehama continued with her closing talk, "I don't want to hear from your principals, when I come to visit, that you're late for class. I think I've taught you enough that being late is a form of stealing." She quoted a number of verses from the Talmud to back up her claim, and went on: "This business of 'honor examinations' [unsupervised tests, based on trust], I don't believe in them. You can't let children endanger themselves. It's a form of *"Lifneh iver lo titen michshol"* ("Do not put a stumbling block in front of the blind"). I don't put a wallet on the table when there's a new cleaning woman in the house to test her honesty. I think these honor exams are an English invention. That's all well and good for the English; but for *Am Yisrael*, where we're not crooks and swindlers, we have other standards to go by."

"Another thing," Nehama continued. "Don't express an opinion on things you don't know anything about. It will only show up your ignorance." She then brought an example of a young rabbi who disqualified a new Bible edition that contained certain abbreviations. He thought the abbreviations were first written by missionaries, when indeed they appeared in Jewish sources from the Middle Ages. The graduates were all very impressed by her forthrightness and practical advice. "It's served me well, on more than one occasion," admits Zvi.

Nehama stressed the same points to many classrooms of teachers. Asher Hadad, a school principal in Lod, was her student at the Lifshitz Teachers' Seminary program for Yeshiva students. "Nehama always emphasized the need to be on time, to keep the students interested in the material, and to be careful of our Hebrew grammar and style." Dr. Tamar Ross first met Nehama when she taught a class on Hebrew style at the Beit V'gan Seminary. "Nehama would walk into the room, mimicking some type of Israeli, and we would have to describe in great detail what we'd observed. She was a terrific actress, and that was a wonderful way to teach us nuances of language."

In the 1980s Nehama conducted a special class on didactic methods twice a week. The shiurim were held in her house, and many teachers, some of them from abroad, participated. "It was a very intensive, closed group, not very large, but with a great deal of interaction," says Frima Gurfinkle, who became a close disciple of hers. "Amitei Zion" grew out of this nucleus. In addition to teaching new material, Nehama taught tricks of the trade: making associations, arousing interest, using stories.

"She never purposely collected the anecdotes from taxi drivers, storekeepers, or elementary school children with which she sprinkled her lessons," says Frima Gurfinkle. "She just had an uncanny talent for making the mundane interesting and illustrative." It didn't even matter if the events she related actually happened or were embellished for the sake of explaining a point. Nehama's examples were classic and became a model for all her students.

Frima relates that once, only once, the students of the didactic class came to her door and it was locked. She wasn't in. "I was very worried; we all were. There wasn't a note on the door, and no one knew where she could be." Finally Nehama arrived and we all went in. I remember we were studying Ibn Ezra or Malbim's view on liturgical poetry. After the lesson I asked her why she'd been late." "I was in the library, preparing for our shiur, and I forgot myself," Nehama told her somewhat sheepishly. "How long were you there preparing the shiur?" Frima asked her. "Three, four hours," said Nehama.

Frima continues in wonder, "I suddenly realized, here was a woman who had taught this material for sixty years, and still she sat for three or four hours preparing for a forty-five-minute shiur!" Frima says this example remained a lesson for her – and for many other teachers besides her. Nehama admitted to another close associate that even after all these years of teaching she never went into a class without preparing. "The results speak for themselves," he added.

Rabbi Uri Cohen, director of the Meretz program, had a similiar experience. He once asked Nehama to substitute for a teacher who was ill. "When do you want me to come?" asked Nehama, always accommodating. "Tomorrow morning at 8:00 a.m.," he replied. Nehama was shocked. "No, I could never prepare by then." "But Nehama," Reb Uri said, "you know the material by heart." "No, no," Nehama assured him, "I prepare every lesson I give for several hours." "I must admit," Rabbi Cohen says in appreciation, "all her classes were tip-top."

She was not just a teacher – she was an educator. Most of her students agree that her high standards and expectations were generally met – eventually. She combined high intellectual qualities with strict moral standards and a humane attitude toward all. "She was extremely bright," says Frima Gurfinkle, her student since she came on aliya in 1975. "But she was a model on the personal level, the complete person – even though she never considered herself more than a teacher. Her shiurim were like a revelation to us.

5.
Qualities and Convictions

SIMPLICITY

Nehama was a no-frills person in every respect of the word. Her house was decorated down to the essentials; she always dressed very plainly in the inevitable brown or blue dress, matching beret, sensible shoes, and that's it. Rabbi Yochanan Freed believes there may be a connection between her way of life and her *derech* (approach) in learning. She always sought out the simple explanation, p'shat; her approach to commentary was plain, unembellished, just as her appearance. There was a certain negation of self in this approach, an "I don't really exist."

Nehama rarely said, "This is my idea"; instead she would say, "I saw this somewhere...." Miriam Falk remembers when she was a student teacher and Nehama often took her and her friends back to Shaare Zedek Hospital in her cab, Nehama would say, waving aside their thanks: "You're performing *avodat kodesh* (holy work); I only teach."

Even certain *chidushim* (original ideas) that she claimed were Rashi's or some other commentary's thought were probably culled from their writings, but were really her 'find'. Professor Shmuel Adler gave a shiur in her memory in which he used some famous explanation she assigned to Rashi. "I searched through all the Rashi commentaries again and again, but couldn't find where he said that. It's obviously one of her ideas, which she developed and claimed it was Rashi's."

Aesthetics and luxuries were foreign to her. Gerti Urman of Kibbutz Lavi, where Nehama stayed every *Chol Hamoed*, was holiday director of the Guest House. "Nehama always stayed in the same simple room, No. 51. Once when it was raining – and you had to go out of the main building to get to 51 – she finally agreed to stay overnight in one of the more luxurious rooms. What shall I tell you: She was *umlala* (distressed) and never again took a newer room." Gerti also says that Nehama ate very little on these visits. "I don't know why she had to pay!"

However, whenever there were visiting professors or a judge in the hotel, Gerti would sit her next to them for stimulating conversations that went on for hours, "while they ate and she picked at her food pretending to be a diner." When Nehama had to curtail her visits to Lavi due to ill health, the 'regular' guest house visitors got together the first year and wrote her a letter, telling her how much she was missed.

One of her closest associates once tried to get Nehama to improve the aesthetics of her apartment. "You see, there's a black spot there over the electric outlet," he told her. "Listen," asked Nehama, "did you ever notice it before?" He had to admit that he'd not seen the black mark before. "So," said Nehama triumphantly, "I don't have to paint."

Dr. Tamar Ross commented on these qualities when Nehama died. "I feel that she represents the end of an epoch," wrote the Jewish philosophy scholar. "The old die-hard Torah v'Avodah values, *Histapkut B'meat* – forthrightness, no frills, a certain vitality.... It's a different world now, more urbane and distracted, and we are much the poorer." Dr. Ross feels that, in addition to her spartan ways, Nehama stood for the ideals of Kibbutz HaDati (the religious kibbutz movement) and therefore felt so at home in that environment.

Nehama couldn't understand why people devoted time and money to external matters. Showy *s'machot* (celebrations) and expensive weddings always raised her eyebrows (and often her ire). She couldn't understand, for example, why people needed a professional photographer at weddings – some friend could gladly take a few pictures, she would contend. If someone sent her an invitation to a *simcha* she'd get angry. "Why doesn't he just invite me verbally?"

she'd ask. She also couldn't understand why people invited so many guests and fed them when everyone had enough to eat at home.

She didn't attend the s'machot of even those with whom she was very close. She once explained to Ariela and Shaul Yedgeh, her good friends and long-term students, "You understand that I can't attend your bar mitzvah. I can't go to one person's party and not to the other." But Ariela thinks it's mostly because she was against the 'tra-la-la' of the functions, not only because she didn't want to hurt people's feelings. Dr. Zev Herzberg points out that she did attend funerals and visited mourners.

When she was invited to give a seminar or series of lectures in a hotel or kibbutz, she refused to take money, and even asked if she didn't have to pay for her stay. Dov Rapell of Kibbutz Yavneh who knew Nehama first as a student, then as a colleague, and finally as her boss, relates a characteristic tale. "Sixty years ago I was a student at the Hebrew University. Nehama was already a famous teacher. Several of us religious students would walk over to her house on Shabbat afternoon for very stimulating discussions. She became a kind of cultural center for the *chevra* (the gang).

"One day in 1936 I saw her walk into the Hapoel Hamizrachi office. 'I want to pay my dues for July,' she told the clerk and gave him money." After she got her receipt and left, the clerk asked Rapell, "Do you know who that was? That was the famous Nehama Leibowitz. She's crazy." "Why crazy?" asked Dov Rapell in shock. "She's the only one in Jerusalem who pays her dues on time, and without being reminded ten times."

Years ago, before the invention of small tape recorders, Nehama would often turn up at a shiur with a huge, old-fashioned tape recorder that had large reels. She would play dramatized readings of psalms on tapes, or other sections she was teaching. But she stopped doing this so that she wouldn't trouble people who ran to help her carry the huge, unwieldly contraption on her travels.

SELF-DEPRECATION

Frima Gurfinkle recalls that Nehama liked to mention her mistakes and her weaknesses. She would tell how she insulted a student, or ignored someone. For example, Bracha Ashual, her neighbor, relates a story she heard from Nehama. "Once two students came out of a matriculation examination, looking very tense. Nehama asked one of them, 'How was it? Did you find it very difficult?' She didn't know the other student as well and didn't ask her anything. Years later Nehama got a letter from this second student. 'You won't remember me, but many years ago when I finished my matric examination in math, you asked my friend how it was, but me you treated like air – you ignored me completely.' Nehama admitted sadly, 'That's something I'll never be able to fix.'" She used the story to warn teachers how important it was to show no favoritism.

Frima isn't sure Nehama told these tales to instigate discussion or to show she made mistakes and so was like everyone else and not entitled to more admiration than the next person. She once told a class that she had asked her brother, the late Yeshayahu Leibowitz, to explain the Theory of Relativity to her. "No problem," Professor Leibowitz (whom she called Shaya) told her. "Just read this and this volume on physics; and these chapters on mathematics ... and after that I'll explain it to you."

There was once a debate in her house over whether the government erred in canceling the Lavi Project. Nehama finally asked the participants in the debate, "Do we actually have enough information to discuss this matter?" Even as she made fun of her own foibles she'd laugh with (not at) the common character weaknesses displayed by 'everyman.'

Here's one story she liked to tell, to illustrate what we call human nature. It's written in the form she relished, direct dialogue. In the era when most people still used iceboxes, she overheard two women talking:

"My son just bought me a refrigerator," said one lady. "How does it work?" asked her friend. "Do you put ice in it?"

"No, no more ice for me; it's wonderful."

"So how does it cool?"

"It works on electricity."

"Oh. (Pause.) Electricity!" (As if to say, now I understand fully.)

Nehama had a healthy suspicion of academic pursuits – research for no practical reason or assurance of validity. She'd often make fun of certain professors who took themselves too seriously. For example, she once mentioned that someone was getting his doctorate on the fascinating (!) subject: Did people in Shakespeare's time believe in ghosts? After many months of investigation the conclusion was "some did; some didn't." Nehama's reaction to such academic undertakings was "So what?"

Everyone knew Nehama had very strong convictions. For the most part she couldn't be budged on her preconceptions. However, she admitted that once she had thought anyone who paid too much attention to her personal grooming, who wore makeup and jewelry, couldn't be a serious person. "She admitted to me," says Frima, "that she'd learned to change her mind on this point."

On another occasion she argued vehemently that there was no lasting value in making bar mitzvah ceremonies for non-religious boys. However, a young rabbi in the Negev who was her student described how important such affairs were both for the boys, at that impressionable age, and for their families. She not only changed her mind on mass bar mitzvah celebrations, but she became an ardent supporter of such projects.

Dr. Barry Samson remembers his first impression of Nehama. He came to visit her with his fiancee and they got to talking about Rav Kook. "I don't understand what Rav Kook wrote. I thought I understood him," said Nehama, "but I don't." Then she related how she had read an article about some subject Rav Kook had developed. She disagreed with the author and, as was often the case, called him up to tell him where he had gone wrong. But instead the author convinced her *he* was right. "So you see," she told the new couple, "I don't understand Rav Kook."

RELATIONS WITH BROTHER

Then as a final thrust, she added, "And you know what, Shaya (Professor Leibowitz, her brother) doesn't understand Rav Kook either." Dr. Samson adds in passing, "I think that's the only time I ever heard any slight (almost offhanded) criticism of her brother from her. Usually she was extremely talented in getting out of expressing any opinion of him, even when he made outrageous remarks and students would try to get her reaction."

Nehama was very close to her brother and his family. Yet even though she loved him strongly, she differed from him in two main ways, according to her student, Dr. Rabbi Rafael Posen. "She wouldn't let herself be interviewed, and she refrained from making bombastic public statements – as the plague."

Rabbi Uriel Kessing, one of her steady students, remembers once attending a shiur when Professor Yeshayahu Leibowitz entered the house. It was obviously an unexpected visit. Nehama excused herself and went into the kitchen with her brother. There was a lot of loud talking, and Uriel heard Nehama say emphatically at one point, "That's not what we learned from our sacred father." "We all wanted to know about what they'd been shouting," says Uriel, "but Nehama just returned to the room and continued teaching where she'd left off."

GIFTS

On one subject she remained adamant: she refused point-blank to receive gifts. Every Adar she would announce: "I'm going away for *Purim* (even if she'd stay at home), so no one is to bring me *Mishloah Manot* (food presents exchanged on Purim)." Uriel Kessing once visited Nehama with his 22-year-old daughter. He wanted the girl to meet his mentor. They considered buying something for Nehama, but in the end there wasn't time. "What luck!" says Rabbi Kessing. "She hated gifts." We began to discuss *mitzvot bein adam l'chavero* (social mitzvot). "In that context, she said something very interesting to us that day. 'Do you know there are some young couples who get invited for Shabbat, but can't go, because it's expected that they bring a gift – and they can't always afford it.' I looked at my daughter and she looked at me and we sighed in relief."

Esther Gross recalls overhearing the following conversation. A woman came to visit her and said, "Nehama, I wanted to buy you something, but I didn't know what to get. So I've brought you this small blackboard which you can use in your classes, and some chalk."

65

Nehama was very uncomfortable. "No, no, I have no room to keep it. Look how every space is taken up with books." "But it's collapsible, see," said the woman, demonstrating how little room the board took up. Still, Nehama tried in every way to get rid of the woman and her present. She kept muttering to herself (and to the guest, who began feeling very uncomfortable herself), "Why do people insist on giving me things that I don't need; that I have no room for?" Esther doesn't know how the incident ended, but there was no blackboard in her house later.

Similarly, if someone brought a plant or even a book, Nehama always gave them away, unless the presenter found a way to put it somewhere in the apartment without being observed. "She lived by the maxim '*Soneh matanot yichye*' ('He who hates gifts will live')."

INTERVIEWS AND PERSONALITY CULT

She never liked to be interviewed or have her picture taken. Dr. Moshe Shlomowitz believes that this may have been a reaction to the cult of hero worship, to building up personalities, to which she objected so strenuously. "Write about my books, not about me," she told a potential interviewer. Naomi Ragen, a writer, who tried, unsuccessfully, to interview Nehama, wrote, "Nehama's example provides me with a role model on how one should deal with all the peripheral nonsense that one is bombarded with [when you're famous] … Nehama was ready to meet with those who wanted to meet her only if she could teach them something of value. She didn't want to be a 'museum' that people visited."

Once against her better judgment she allowed a classroom of girls to write about her after a class interview. Sure enough most of the essays that the children wrote afterward, entitled "Professor Leibowitz's Visit to Our Class" described her dress, her hat, her bag, and so on, and very little about what she had taught. "So what did my visit accomplish?" she asked the teacher.

Yet Nehama was aware that the phenomenon of personality cult existed. She even used people's interest in the "great individuals of previous generations" with whom she'd had contact, and would bring snippets of gossip from Agnon, Buber, or her brother to illustrate a point. She could also relate her impressions of the Beilis trial, which took place in Russia in 1911, or stories from the Russian revolution, or even of the early days in Jerusalem when there was sometimes only one phone on a street.

Idit Izkowitz, who is an outstanding teacher and a disciple of Nehama's, remembers that as a student at Ulpanat Amana, they once brought the whole class to Jerusalem for a seminar. "We stayed at Midreshet Amalia, and they set up lectures with the most illustrious teachers and personalities. In that week we heard the poetess Zelda, and Rav Zvi Yehuda Kook, Rabbi Hadari, and of course Nehama. I'll always remember her shiur – it was outstanding."

But apparently Nehama gave the principal hell. "What is this," she asked him when she heard who else had talked to the high school girls, "an all-star show!" Then she added, "When I was a girl and we went to meet Bialik, I couldn't sleep a week before the visit and a week after it. Here they're getting a concentrated all-star performance in one week!" (intimating that it wasn't balanced or healthy for their spiritual welfare.)

AN OLD-FASHIONED GIRL

In general, Dr. Shlomowitz thinks she was a product of her time and therefore held certain 'old-fashioned' opinions. She maintained negative views, among other things, about the women's liberation movement, ostentatious celebrations dictated by social norms, and tape recordings of her lessons, which she strictly forbade. "If you have the tape you don't have to listen to me," she'd say. She also sustained a high level of social equity. The concept of socialized medicine attracted her because she'd lived in an era when not everyone was able to get medical attention.

Nehama used to say, half-jokingly, to one of her 'steadies': "On May Day at the Communist gatherings I think they could find nothing more appropriate to quote from the speakers' platform than Yaakov's speech to his wives on exploitation of the workers, don't you agree?" She was referring to Yaakov's tirade against the injustices he suffered as Lavan's employee. To her disciple this is another good example of how Nehama 'lived' the Tanach personalities.

She had, moreover, an old-fashioned deference toward educated people, especially doctors. For many years her personal physician was her cousin, Professor Yeshayahu Leibowitz, and despite their family relationship, she regarded him with the highest respect and also followed his instructions meticulously.

Nehama always acted as if everyone with a degree or Torah knowledge knew more than she. She'd say to yeshiva students, "But this is all well known to you, I'm sure." Dr. Zev Hertzberg relates: "She'd always call me Dr. Hertzberg, or introduce me as such to the academic people who visited her. But once when her regular taxi driver came in, she said, 'Haim, this is Zev.' I once pointed out to her that in the chapter on the Akedah, Yitzhak is called *haNaar* (the boy) only once; when Avraham says to the servants accompanying him, 'And Avraham said to his lads, stay here with the donkey and I and the lad will go....' She quite liked the comparison."

MODESTY

But this outmoded humility did not account for her extreme self-effacement. Her cousin, Mira Libes, knows that she was offered the professorship of Tanach at the Hebrew University more than thirty years ago. But she turned it down, saying, "I'm not suited for that position. How can I sit there among all those great scholars!" and it was given to someone whom Ms. Libes considers far inferior to her. Only years later did she accept the position of professor at the Tel Aviv University. Nor did this awe of academicians interfere with her ability to talk on an equal level with workmen, taxi drivers, cleaning women, clerks, and celebrities.

Some people might think her modesty was phony, overdone. But those who knew her well testified that she was consistently unassuming and humble. For a time she gave a Tanach class in the President's Residence, for Rachel Yanai Ben Zvi and many wives of cabinet members and important personages. They would send the presidential limousine to pick her up and bring her back. It was a beautiful, very snazzy car. In all innocence, the first time she traveled in it she asked her companion, "Do you think we should sit differently in such an elegant vehicle?"

Dr. Mordechai Breuer, a close associate for many years, would visit her every few weeks. It was common that she'd get a phone call in the middle. She'd always lift the phone and bark into it, "Nehama," listening expectantly to what would come next. Then after a pause he'd hear, "You want to interview me? What can I possibly add?" After another second she'd shake her head and say, "No, no – whatever could be interesting about me?" and unequivocally turn down the request.

CURIOSITY

Nehama had a childlike curiosity about all aspects of life. She used to grill her visitors on their work, their families, their customs, and their communities. She loved hearing about exotic places or unusual incidents. With Dr. Samson she was fascinated about his work as a surgeon, working with various kinds of scopes to investigate and even treat patients. "What an amazing thing," she'd say. "With instruments you can actually see what's going on inside the body!" Dr. Samson says, "She even made me excited and wonderous about my work."

Similarly, even though she objected to people going abroad, she accepted the need to do so for academic reasons. Thus when her good friend, Dr. Shaul Yedgeh, went overseas on several occasions for his research, she not only refrained from giving him her 'musar smoose' (tirade against leaving the Land), but she actually was very curious about his work and wanted to be told all about it.

"When you talk about Nehama," says Dr. Bryna Levi, her faithful student, "you have to mention her unquenchable curiosity. She was amazed at so many things – the number of seminaries that have opened for students from abroad, the fact that so many youngsters come to Israel to learn Torah, and even that people buy her books and actually read them."

Rivka Davidowitz recalls Nehama's fascination with an everyday scene. They were taking a Shabbat afternoon stroll when Nehama noticed someone working an automatic banking machine. She couldn't stop raving over the wonder. "Imagine, drawing money out of the wall!" she repeated to everyone she met that day. People especially intrigued her. Gerti Urman of Lavi recalls how interested she was in the groups of Christian German visitors who stayed at the hotel. She wanted to know if they were motivated by guilt and what subjects interested them and where they visited. "Everything was a focus for her inquisitive mind," says the kibbutznik.

PEOPLE-ORIENTED

She was well up on the news and latest fads, even knowing what goodies children liked to eat. Hadassah Zalkin, who studied with Nehama in the '30s, maintained contact with her all these years. "If I visited her or called up, we wouldn't necessarily discuss philosophic subjects. She'd be interested in what was happening with the children; and she'd tell me about her own life. She remembered so many details about people – it was uncanny."

Nehama had an extraordinary range of contacts. Shoshana Brayer, who took her out for walks frequently, sometimes played a game with her. "Let's see if we can get back to your house without meeting even one of your former students," she'd say. "Once we almost made it back," recalls Shoshana. "On the doorstep of her building an elegantly dressed woman came over and said, 'Nehama, I haven't seen you in years. I was once your student sixty years ago.' The woman didn't know why we both laughed. Another time when we were almost successful in getting home without seeing an acquaintance," Shoshana mentions, "a taxi driver pulled up and yelled, 'Do you remember that I used to drive you to …'"

"She was completely people – oriented," says Wendy Bar Yakov. "It's amazing the kinds of contacts Nehama had. She was interested in everything, even mechanical things attracted her, and she always found subjects to talk about with her visitors." Bracha Ashual, her neighbor, relates how Nehama took a personal interest in all her associates. When Bracha was thinking of changing professions after being a teacher for many years, Nehama argued forcefully with her for over an hour. Then early the next morning she called her up to apologize for being overzealous. Later when Bracha decided to study library sciences, Nehama very graciously offered to help finance her studies.

She truly cared about people. Dr. Barry Samson saw in her a kind of tenderness for children and the common people, workmen, taxi drivers, and housewives. "She was less forbidding and somehow sweeter as time went on, especially with them." Barry thinks there are two reasons for her humane outlook. "She had a beautiful soul, but also she had this powerful intellect, which perceived infinite amounts of details. So she saw the richness in everyone; she saw everyone in their best light."

She was very good at getting people to open up to her. Rivka Davidowitz heard her relate how she met a girl in army uniform standing in line at the university cafeteria. They began to talk. The soldier told her she was going to study Bible when she finished the army. "What made you choose that subject?" Nehama wanted to know. "I had a teacher in high school who taught us Bible, and ever since then I do Parshat Hashavuah faithfully," the young woman told her. "Imagine the influence of one single teacher," Nehama stated later to Rivka with great enthusiasm.

She was approached by another girl soldier, one of her students at the Open University, who asked Nehama for some help with a text. Nehama agreed, but found out thereafter that the tutoring was on army time. She therefore refused to continue teaching the girl. "Now you're in the army and that's what you have to do full time," she said. Only after the soldier brought her written permission from her commanding officer did Nehama relent and continue with the tutoring. When she related the story afterward, she also praised the commanding officer who thought the time spent on Bible study was justified.

At the age of eighty-five, she once asked Rabbi Uriel Kessing, "How many hours do you teach a week?" He thought a moment and then answered, "Twenty-six." "So many," Nehama said in appreciation. "How many hours do you teach?" the rabbi asked her in return. It turned out that Nehama at that stage in life was teaching *twenty two hours* a week – and some of them were even out of town.

Nehama was especially attached to her regular students. In later years if one of her more faithful participants failed to turn up at a shiur she would be sorely worried, almost panicky. "Maybe something happened to him ... Could he be sick?" So the more veteran students would call up if they knew they couldn't attend a shiur and thus saved her anxiety.

NON-FEMINISM

Nehama never saw herself as a feminist, and some of her followers think that that made her even more effective. "She simply did her thing," and her thing was to teach Torah, even in *yeshivot*. She claimed that a lot of women, today, teach Bible. When one of her students, Dr. Ben Hollander, would counter that claim, saying, "Yes, but, Nehama, you were the first," she would wave him off with, "What does it matter?"

Rachel Kosofsky recalls an argument she once had with Nehama. Nehama had seen a picture of a woman praying and wearing a *tallit*. It offended her. Rachel tried to defend the woman and the movement behind her. Nehama was adamant, "They don't wear the tallit for spiritual uplifting," she declared. "They just want to make a feminist statement." Rachel mentioned that for some women wearing a tallit improved their *davening* (praying). "You go to shul to daven, not to get a spiritual uplifting," Nehama retorted. "If you want to get high you take drugs." She thought the whole tumult was just a by-product of American feminism, creeping into the Israeli society.

Rachel pointed out that one of the biggest *poskim* (halachic authorities) in Jerusalem did not unambiguously reject the custom of women wearing *tallitot*. This didn't impress Nehama. She saw it as a first step on the slippery slope to religious deterioration. "Women have enough *mitzvot*, they don't have to wear a tallit to fulfill their commandments," she continued. The issue so engaged her thoughts that she called Rachel up later that night to continue the argument. "My brother goes to synagogue every morning at 5:00 a.m. He doesn't do it to get a high, or to improve his *kavanah* (concentration). He goes simply to fulfill a commandment to pray. I don't have to go to shul at 5:00 a.m. I can visit sick people in the hospital or do other mitzvot."

A close associate went through a "feminist stage." She had had three babies in two years (twins) and felt extremely confined. "So I fell prey to feminist propoganda, and I asked Nehama about some of these issues," the woman admits. Nehama in her usual forceful way dealt with some of the issues.

> Feminist: Look how many women are in the Knesset.
> Nehama: Who would want to be in the Knesset!
> Feminist: Why can't women dance on *Simchat Torah*?
> Nehama: What's more important – learning Torah or dancing with a *Sefer Torah*?

The woman also asked Nehama to give a talk to her religious feminist friends. Nehama refused to give a talk, certainly not about feminism, but she said she'd be happy to give a shiur, which she did – on Rachel's plea to Yaakov, *"havah li banim"*, ("give me children"), and the task of women in the Torah view.

ZIONIST

Nehama was a devoted Zionist. This expressed itself in her refusal to travel abroad, despite repeated invitations to lecture overseas; and this was the reason that she bought only locally made products, even if they cost more. Rachel Kosofsky recalls that on their walks they often stopped at the Shekem (a nearby supermarket) to do some shopping. Nehama examined the prices of each item she bought carefully; but she insisted on merchandise that was made in Israel.

Once Nehama received an invitation to give a three-day seminar abroad and was offered $2,000 a night. The letter stated, "We know that this sum is considerably below your usual fee, but we are unfortunately unable to offer more." Nehama, who often gave shiurim gratis, had a good laugh over this letter and the sum offered. She told one of her regular students, David Bir, "Why should anyone put out so much money for a single shiur?"

Hadassah Zalkin was Nehama's student since 1936. She remembers meeting Nehama on the street one day right after the War of Independence. Nehama was furious. She ranted and raged against a colleague who was leaving Israel because of the harsh conditions. "She simply couldn't fathom how a religious man, a teacher at that, could leave the Holy Land and at a time like this!" David Bir's wife, who had traveled with Nehama on a cargo boat to Israel in 1938, left the country for several years for personal reasons. Nehama wouldn't speak to her for years – even after she returned. "It was almost like a betrayal to her if one left Eretz Yisrael," declares David Bir. Only in recent years had they patched up their relationship.

She also was an avid supporter of *'daber Ivrit'* (the Speak Only Hebrew Movement). Once she was getting a lift with Nachum Amsel. A man came over and asked for directions in English. "Can you tell me how to get to Rehov Jaffe?" he requested. Nehama couldn't get over it. "Why doesn't he ask in Hebrew?" she complained. "In the 1930s if we spoke in German or Yiddish we did it in whispers. We were embarrassed not to speak Hebrew." She also was angry that Nachum's school for girls from abroad was being conducted in English. Despite all of Nachum's explanations, that the girls didn't know enough Hebrew to learn, that it was a process, and so on, she maintained her principles: daber Ivrit!

Nehama always found positive things to relate about Israel or Israelis. She recounted, in typical tone of wonderment, how three guests once came to visit. As usual she served some simple refreshments. A discussion ensued about which *bracha* (blessing) one should recite over wafers. One said it was like cake and required the *mezonot* blessing; another countered that there was hardly any grain in the wafers; a third quoted a famous rabbi, and so it went. "Imagine," Nehama retold the story, "where do you find three hungry people, first investigating which bracha should be made before they put something into their mouths!"

Dr. Bryna Levi says that Nehama was terribly disillusioned after Rabin's murder. She expressed her sorrow that such an event could take place in Israel, among Jews. Then on one of her outings she saw a group of Habad men outside the Egged Bus Station offering to help passersby put on *tefillin*. The sight so encouraged her that her spirits rose and she regained her usual optimistic balance. "She always saw the good part of Jerusalem," says Bryna.

To students from *chutz laaretz* (abroad) she never tired of praising the Land of Israel and telling them overtly or indirectly that they should make their home here. "Where can you find a taxi driver who is so versed in Jewish sources?" she would declare, after telling another moving or humorous experience with a cab driver. Professor David Weiss HaLivni, a well-known Talmud scholar and friend, often got "the treatment." "Subtly Nehama always gave me musar about coming to live in Israel. 'What is a Jew like you doing in the *Galut*?' she'd ask me. At least my son is living here... ," he adds wistfully.

"She had a simplicity of character on the matter of living in Israel," says David Bir. "Why don't American Jews come here?" she would ask in all sincerity. "It's the first time in 2,000 years that we have our own country." Because she was so totally lacking in a materialistic outlook, David Bir thinks, she simply couldn't fathom the things that might keep American Jews from settling here.

Bracha Ashual, who often accompanied Nehama on her small shopping excursions, says that Nehama always bought some sweets and simple refreshments (and only those made in Israel) to serve at the regular classes that were held in her home. "Otherwise," she'd say half in jest, "no one will come to the shiur." Many of Nehama's shiurim were given without any recompense. Those that took place in her home and those that she gave in the kibbutzim where she stayed over *Pesach* and *Succoth* were always free.

KINDNESS

Openheartedness was another quality many praised in her. Junia Ben Sasson, who had been her neighbor in the early years when she still lived in a one-floor house in Kiryat Moshe, recalls, "I would ask Nehama, 'Could you lend me an egg?' and she would always say, enthusiastically, 'Of course, come right in. I'll get it for you.' Then she would go and find out that actually she didn't have any eggs. But her willingness, even eagerness to be of assistance was very heartwarming."

Although she lived frugally, she was very generous with her money. She gave charity freely; no one knows just how much. Certain institutions got regular monthly checks, and so did a number of individuals. Nehama often gave loans. One woman who borrowed IS 700 could only repay IS 30 a month. "I doubt if she managed to repay Nehama before she died," says Bracha.

Her dear friend and colleague, the late Professor Meir Weiss, thought that Nehama's most outstanding quality was her *chessed.* "Everyone talks about her talents as a teacher," he said, "but her Gemillut Chassadim (charity work) was just as outstanding." He, himself, was a beneficiary, when as a Holocaust survivor he came to Jerusalem in 1949 and taught with Nehama at the Beit V'gan Seminary. "When I was a newcomer, just starting out, she helped me, she encouraged me; I'll always be grateful to her."

Techiya Greenwald, a faithful student for many years, was asked by Nehama to get her a checkbook from the bank. It was just before Pesach and several of her regular 'clients' had already written her postcards with 'Seasons Greetings' to remember themselves to her. She understood the hint, but had run out of checks. Techiya called the bank, where the clerks were willing to get her a new checkbook immediately for IL 25. Nehama agreed. "I helped her write the checks that very day, and we sent them out. But Nehama was upset. 'Take a look at those banks. They're holding *my* money, after all, yet they make such problems – for what? For a piece of paper. This bureaucracy, instead of helping people, makes our lives more difficult!'"

One cold, winter day, a social worker received a phone call from Nehama. "I know you're involved with old people. I'm sitting here in my warm house, but I know there must be elderly people out there who can't afford kerosene for their stoves. If I give you some money, could you see that it goes to heat the homes of some unfortunate souls?" Yael Steifel believes this offer stemmed from Nehama's embarrassment at spending money on herself. Heating her own home was such a luxury that she only felt comfortable doing it if others would also benefit.

Another close associate related, "Some time after the big aliya from the USSR, two Russian newcomers came to her door collecting alms. Nehama gave them a valuable silver etrog box. 'Why did you do that?' asked her student. 'I don't have any use for it anyway,' Nehama said with a shrug. Another time a woman came to her door asking for old clothes. Nehama went to her closet and gave her a new dress that she had just bought. A family member who was present at the time said, 'Nehama, you just bought that dress; why don't you give her an old dress?' 'What! I should give a Jewish woman old clothes?' she asked in all innocence."

Zev Hertzberg knows of a woman who told Nehama about her financial straits only a few weeks before her final illness. Nehama paid the lady's long overdue telephone bill to help her out. On another occasion, her onetime housekeeper, Tzipporah Ophri, overheard a cab driver who brought Nehama home mention how he would love to buy the rights to run his own taxi. Nehama asked him how much was involved. When he told her the amount she wrote out a check and lent him the money. "For years thereafter he was her regular taxi driver," says Tzipporah, "and every week he or his wife would come like clockwork to repay part of the loan."

Tzipporah thinks that Nehama's generous nature was inherited. She heard that one night when the Leibowitz children (Nehama and her brother) were sleeping, a poor woman came by and asked for alms. She had two children with her dressed in tattered clothes. Nehama's mother went into the bedroom and brought the woman her own children's clothes. She also gave her a sum of money. "But it wasn't only material help that Nehama bestowed. Once she heard that someone's wife was sick and couldn't find the right treatment. She immediately called a number of her German friends who were doctors and arranged for the woman to be seen by one of them. Later she paid for the woman's medicine, which was imported from abroad. That was Nehama."

The long-term housekeeper has another story to relate that could be titled "The Mystery of the Missing Towels." "One day," relates Tzipporah, "during the time of rationing, I went into town to buy some underwear and towels for the Leibowitz males – Nehama's father and husband. I put them into the cupboard and was very happy to have gotten such a good deal on them. Next morning I went to the cupboard to take out a new towel and couldn't find them. Who could have taken them? I asked the cleaning lady, but she didn't have a clue. I asked Nehama's husband, and he also didn't know. When Nehama came home from her teaching schedule, I wasn't there because I did the shopping on Thursday afternoon. When I got back she'd gone off to another shiur. I went to the cupboard, hoping maybe I'd overlooked the towels the first time, but no, they still weren't there. Finally, when it was getting dark, Nehama came in. 'Nehama, did you see the new towels that I bought yesterday?' I asked. 'Listen,' she told me, 'Last night somebody came around to collect for *Hachnasat Kalah* (to help a bride). I didn't have any money so I gave them the towels.' How could I be angry with her?"

HAREDIM

She penetrated the ultraorthodox world through her books, and a great number of Beit Yaakov teachers, who never met her, use her method in their classrooms. Nehama liked to tell the following story, which indicates her 'partial' penetration into the haredi world. "One day I saw my book in the window of a haredi bookstore." She entered the shop incognito, and commented to the storekeeper, "I see you have that book in your shop." The man answered her defiantly, "If you come to the back of my store, I'll show you I have even worse."

Toward Yeshiva students she held certain preconceptions. She complained that they didn't know Tanach, grammar, or Jewish history. It bothered her that many Yeshiva students didn't serve in the army. Even while she maintained great respect for the ultra-orthodox leaders and *Rashei Yeshivot* (deans of talmudic academies), she did voice her displeasure at their students' ignorance of the Bible. Paradoxically Yeshiva students often attended her classes. At one time the Habad Rebbe in New York sent a group of Habad teachers to study with her. She questioned them about the Rebbe's commentary on Rashi. In most cases they knew less about it than she did.

Rabbi Rafael Posen relates the story of a Yeshiva student who tried to show off by asking Nehama a question. They were studying a commentary by the Ibn Ezra who mentions the Gaon (referring to Rav Shaadiya Gaon). "How did the Ibn Ezra meet the Vilna Gaon?" he asked in all naivete. Nehama was a bit perturbed. "What did you do?" asked Dr. Posen when he heard the story from his mentor. "What did I do?" she answered him. "I sent him to an encyclopedia."

On another occasion she was teaching a group of Beit Yaakov Seminar students. As is her wont she asked them: "From where does Rashi get this explanation?" In all seriousness, one of the participants answered, "*MiRuach Hakodesh Kemuvan*" ("from holy inspiration of course"). Nehama liked to relate this story not as criticism nor even to praise the simple faith of certain people. Her purpose was to demonstrate how different educational systems teach different approaches to learning.

Yeduel Basok is a second-generation student of Nehama's. His mother also was her pupil. Doli recalls visiting Nehama one Shabbat afternoon with his wife and children. She was very cordial and especially interested in the children. "Your grandmother also studied with me," she told the kids. Suddenly in the middle of their chat, Nehama stopped the spontaneous lesson she was giving them and asked Doli sharply, "Were you in the army?" Doli assured her that he served in the armory division and did reserve duty every year. "Only then did she continue to be cordial and friendly."

Doli explains why the army service was so important to Nehama. "If I didn't serve in the army, then there was something not right about my learning," he says in reflection. "One puts into action what one learns, in her opinion." Doli was witness to a similiar expression of principles for Nehama. A student from abroad asked her a question in Tanach. She asked him if he was going to live in Israel. The fellow hemmed and hawed. "I have my family in America; I have a job...." "If you're going back, then why bother to learn Tanach," she said to him harshly, and turned away. She wouldn't answer his question. It was a waste to learn Torah and not carry it out, as she saw it.

SECULAR CONTACTS

Nehama was very open and liberal toward those in non-religious circles. Once she and Chaim Shlossberg were discussing the large number of youngsters who become non-observant after they finish their studies – even if they were once in the State Religious School System. Chaim complained that the educational system was at fault. Nehama demurred. "I meet so many soldiers who don't know a thing about Judaism," she said. "At least those who've studied in a religious school know how to open a siddur; they've experienced a Pesach *seder*...."

She once had a serious argument with one of her regular students about having a Reform student participate in her class. The student was adamantly opposed to having someone in the room who didn't accept mainstream Judaism. Nehama was just as adamantly for allowing anyone who wanted to learn Torah, no matter what his philosophy, into the class. Nehama's view ruled but she called him later that night and apologized, as was her wont, in case she'd insulted him. "What a pity that we wasted three hours on that argument; it would have been much more constructive if we'd learned during that time."

Shimon Ron, her good friend from Tel Aviv, who often accompanied her on her shiurim in that area, likes to recall something Nehama told him once, which greatly surprised him. "I have better contact with you than with many people who pray three times a day, but don't understand what they're saying," she told him. "You aren't dati, but you at least think!" she praised him. Shimon recalls that Nehama was very meticulous about the mitzvot, but she had a liberal outlook. When she came to his house he always made sure that she'd eat from a glass plate, and that the cookies he served her had a *hechsher.* "But I know she also had a frivolous side to her," Shimon reveals. "She'd read detective stories – in the bathroom."

VIEWS ON EDUCATION

Nehama thought the Israeli school system could do with some improvement. For example, she thought teachers "chewed" the material too much for the student – all the work pages they gave out rather than have the students go to the sources. "If you ask a pupil today 'What do you learn?' they'll say '*Dapim*' (pages)," said Nehama. "We used to read the books. Books gave us knowledge, a basis, source material, enlightenment, empowerment ..." Even university students, once they glanced at a book list, would ask her, "What's really essential to read?" Nehama couldn't get over their attitude. "When I was a university student we bombarded our lecturers with questions about *what else* we could read."

Rabbi Uriel Kessing heard a similiar complaint from her. It is common in study circles today to receive *Daf Mekorot*, a source material condensed on one page. "Students should learn from a book," she insisted. It bothered her that children weren't being taught to *think.* "Schools now teach material, not how to think," she'd say.

Nehama objected to having her worksheets computerized. When

Nachum Amsel opened his school for girls from abroad, she gave him permission to translate some of her sheets into English and even put them on the Internet. Very soon thereafter, however, she had second thoughts about the project. "You're making it much too easy for them," she complained to Nachum. "It won't nudge the students to go into depth and really study the text," she reiterated. Nachum pleaded, "But, Nehama, you gave your permission; I've put so much work into the English version already," he said. But Nehama was adamant. In the end she said, "I don't believe in the watered-down program. But after 120 years you can do as you like."

SCHOLARSHIP

Because she lived for an extended period, practically spanning the twentieth century, and because she had the privilege of a well-balanced education that gave her exposure to the best of European culture, Nehama was able to combine Jewish learning with general studies, including classics and world literature. She was extremely well versed and well read. Professor Adler once discussed with her the beginning of the Third Reich. He mentioned a book that he had read as a child in Switzerland by Anna Seghers ("I doubt if there are twenty people in Israel who've ever heard her name"). Not only did Nehama know the author, but she was able to tell the doctor about her background and why she'd written that book. Nevertheless, Professor Adler adds, "But only looking at her as a scholar is missing out on the real Nehama."

Similarly, Rivka Davidowitz was very impressed by a book written by Yaakov Wasserman in the last century. When she told Nehama about it, Nehama quoted a dialogue from the book word for word, without effort. She had read the book over fifty years ago. "She was able to quote midrashim word for word as well," says Rivka, "and state on which page each one appeared. She must have had a photographic memory. When I said to Nehama, 'How do you remember so many details?' she replied in astonishment at my astonishment: 'What do you mean? It's my profession!'"

It has been mentioned that Nehama was a genius. The quality of her memory alone was breathtaking, according to Barry Samson. "If you mentioned a friend, she'd smile and say, 'Yes, I loved his article, which he wrote in 1968.' Her bookshelves were covered wall to wall with volumes on every subject in the world. She knew them all intimately." Nachum Amsel, as a student, once cleaned her books for Pesach. "It was amazing the range and scope of those books," he says. She had original works by nineteenth century commentators; philosophy (Jewish and secular); novels, classics, grammars, medieval texts, and maybe forty to fifty commentaries on Rashi. "The amazing thing is that she knew the contents of them all," says Nachum.

She could argue a subject equally well on both sides. A close admirer recalls an evening when Nehama and her husband stood out in the parking lot discussing the concept of *Kedushat HaAretz* (Israel's intrinsic or symbolic holiness). He was taking her home, but they stood there for hours, discussing the holiness of *things:* the *Kotel*, the Land of Eretz Yisrael, and the People of Israel. The man, just as Nehama's brother, Professor Leibowitz, didn't believe a section of ground as such could be holy. It was only a symbolic, not an intrinsic holiness, a means to make Jews more observant. Nehama (maybe for argument's sake) brought all kinds of quotations to indicate that Eretz Yisrael was special in its own right and hence sanctified. The argument went on all night. "I don't know to this day," says the woman, "what her real view was on the subject."

"Nehama could be very impatient with and irritated by some people," explains Barry Samson, "because she couldn't tolerate misuse of the mind. Like in music," he continues, "she had so much love for the perfect note that it brought her pain if someone was abusive to intellect. She always worked so hard to get that perfect note." Still, there are people who were so insulted by Nehama's harshness and her demand for precision that they broke off contact, or stopped coming to her class – rare though they be. If Nehama heard that someone had been offended she made great efforts to placate them. "She tried very hard not to hurt people's feelings," says one of her most intimate contacts.

PIETY

"She was a very religious woman," said the late Professor Meir Weiss of his lifelong friend and colleague. "She was very meticulous in keeping mitzvot," he says. One student recalls that Nehama took pains to ask a halachic opinion when a dilemma arose. For example she said, "If you want to invite someone for Shabbat but he'll probably drive there, it's imperative to ask someone like Rav Shlomo Zalman Auerbach. He'll give us an opinion based on considerations that would never enter our mind."

An ardent supporter says that few of those people who objected to her use of unconventional commentators, or to the fact that she was a woman, knew how meticulous she was about keeping mitzvot and acting in accordance with the *halacha*. "She might criticize some halachic decision or argue about its relevance, but she'd observe it nevertheless, simply because that was the law," says the disciple.

The late Professor Weiss also mentioned the fact that she was always careful to present the commentaries as true to their meaning as possible. Some scholars, however, accused Nehama of taking liberties in her approach, and brought examples where Nehama's search for moral lessons in the worksheets led her to pick and choose among the sources and emphasize the rare ones that suited her theme. For example, one of them pointed out, in teaching *Parshat Shemot* one year, she brought only parshanim who blame Moses for killing the Egyptian taskmaster. In another gilayon, Nehama brings only those commentaries that criticize Rivka and Yaakov for "cheating" Isaac so as to indicate there is something of just punishment when Lavan cheats Yaakov as well.

Similarly, Nehama was sometimes judgmental in presenting some of the classic commentaries in her worksheets. In one lesson she mentioned a commentary by the Ibn Ezra and labeled it "naive realism"; in another peirush on "*HaShem nisah et Avraham*" ("and God tested Abraham") she called a commentary "narrow-minded." "One doesn't talk like that about the *rishonim* (early commentators)," is the opinion sometimes heard, "nor does one give them 'marks.'" And indeed in later life Nehama was much more discreet in her evaluation of the traditional parshanim.

Professor Adler pointed out that when the classic commentators found fault in each other's writings (sometimes using quite harsh expressions to voice their disagreements), Nehama would explain that their strong criticism stems from *ahavat haemet* (a love for Truth). "Ramban, for example, was really a great admirer of Rashi," she would say, even though he occasionally found fault with his predecessor's line of thought.

Nehama always covered her head and dressed very modestly, even when it was less common for national religious women to do so. Students of Rav Zvi Yehuda Kook mentioned that the rabbi had a very high regard for Nehama. He called her *"gedolat haparshanim b'yameinu"* ("the outstanding Bible commentator of our time"). He made a distinction between Nehama and her brother. "Despite her connection to universities, Rav Zvi Yehuda greatly admired her; he talked about the fact that she dressed very modestly, an issue about which he was very strict," relates Rabbi Yaakov Filber.

AGING AND THE STAGE THEREAFTER

Frima Gurfinkle says she was always impressed by the fact that Nehama never complained about her personal life. "Even though there is something tragic about her life, I never heard her bemoaning her fate," says Frima. Nor did anyone else. "She was always content; never showed us that she suffered," she adds. "I think she represents what is written in *Pirke Avot*, 'Who is happy? He that is content with his lot.' Even in old age she never turned bitter. She sometimes complained about her hearing, but no one ever heard her declare, 'Why do I deserve this?'"

Quite the opposite. Barry Samson thinks that Nehama became sweeter and less forbidding as time went on. "She saw people in their best light, and paid attention to a richness of detail in everyone" he claims. "Each individual was unique and she saw what was special in them. She was very tolerant, even tender, towards taxi drivers, children, people from different backgrounds..."

Bryna Levi mentions that in her later years Nehama preferred to teach rather than publish books. She revealed to Bryna that she found it difficult to finish her last book, *Bamidbar*, that it was harder than in the past. "Nevertheless her recall was astounding," mentions her disciple. "In all Jewish history there was never anyone like her."

Gerti Urman recalls that Nehama's worst nightmare was to stand in front of a class and forget what she wanted to say. "This never happened, as far as I know," says Gerti, but apparently that was the aspect of aging that concerned her most. Idit Izkovitz remembers hearing a shiur based on a midrash that describes Moshe's last hours. Many aspects of aging were included in this legend, and it concludes with Moshe's request not to die but to be allowed to enter the Holy Land. Idit felt that Nehama was also talking about herself in this shiur.

Rabbi Uriel Kessing went to visit Nehama when she wasn't well. "She looked so old and forlorn; it was difficult to look at her," says the veteran teacher with sympathy. "But as soon as we started talking matters of the Bible she changed before my eyes and became the old Nehama. Her eyes shone brightly, she spoke animatedly, and she was as sharp and as challenging as ever."

Rabbi Rafael Posen, who was also a longtime disciple of Nehama, once heard her say, "It's hard for me to pray with the same level of kavanah throughout the prayers – I'm just a simple woman. So I put all my fervor into one blessing *"sheaso li kol tzorchi"* ("who has provided my every need"), which we say every morning. I can say it with all my heart because I'm able to see and to walk and don't need assistance from anyone even though I'm an old woman."

When on occasion Nehama heard that someone she had known well from Kibbutz Lavi or from the university had died, she'd say, "They're all disappearing on me." Bryna Levi thinks that from the time her brother, Professor Yeshayahu Leibowitz, died she prepared herself for her own death. "I don't have anyone," she once admitted to Bryna. "I'm an old woman." "Nehama might have been ready to go," wrote one of her students from America, Schulamith Halevy, after her teacher's death, "but I really think we were not ready to let her go."

Yet many other friends and students feel Nehama maintained a very open, healthy approach to death. She once went to buy some medicines at a pharmacy. She asked the pharmacist, "How long can I take the contents?" He reassured her that it was good for three years. "Three years!" she declared. "I'll be in God's hands before that." She never feared death, and often told her friends and students, "A person's soul continues; this is not the end of a person." She once talked to one of her doctors about death. He was horrified at the time to hear her say, "How great it would be to die in the middle of a shiur." But as he thought about it he understood that for Nehama, teaching was her whole life. He even thought that the shiurim she gave in her latter years *gave* her life.

One of her students had this same positive approach to death. This was a young, non-observant woman from Tel Aviv who first met Nehama in her class at the university. She was married to a man who was in theater. The student became very ill, and when she realized she was terminal, she asked to have a picture taken with Nehama. Nehama agreed and traveled to Tel Aviv for that purpose. After they were photographed together, the woman sighed in relief and said, "I'm glad I had the picture taken now because tomorrow I'll be dead."

Her husband replied, "Don't talk nonsense." But she answered him, "You're not in the theater now, and there's no need to perform. You know as well as I do that I'm going to die soon." After that somber retort they were all silent for a minute. The woman, however, continued. Turning to her husband she said, "I have only one request of you. Promise me at my funeral you'll wear a clean shirt." All three of them laughed and that changed the atmosphere in the room.

There was a time when Nehama became very frail, and her students and relatives worried about her being alone. But Nehama loved her privacy and probably didn't want to 'bother' any caretaker with personal requests. Indeed the few times she did have a *metapelet* around, she rarely asked for anything. When she began to have falls she realized, however, that there was no solution, but who could she hire?

Yael Steifel recalls getting a call from Nehama on this subject. "Yael, don't ask, a true miracle has occurred," Nehama said. It seems that a former housekeeper came by to return a loan of IS 500 that Nehama had given her years ago. "You told me to return the money when I can afford it. Well, here it is," said the woman. "I don't remember," admitted Nehama, "but maybe you're willing to be with me a few hours a day?" she continued. "Yes," the woman said, "I'll be very happy to be of assistance." "However," Nehama confided to Yael, "I really don't have enough for her to do. I can't give her the cleaning woman's work. That woman really needs the money."

So the caretaker sat around unemployed, and even fell asleep while 'watching' Nehama. Nehama told Yael in an aside, "I wanted a cup of tea, but I can't wake someone just for a cup of tea." Needless to say, as soon as Nehama felt a little bit better she gave the woman her walking papers and seemed very relieved to be on her own again.

Dr. Shlomo Feurstein, who was first her student (since 1946) and then her colleague, recalls visiting her the night before her final hospitalization. She was preparing her shiur for that evening on the breaking of the Tablets and *Parshat Ki Tisah* and she conferred with him on the famous explanation of the Meshech Chochma – a rather modern commentator. "Seeing Nehama preparing that shiur, which she must have given hundreds of times, and working so diligently even though she wasn't feeling well, made me think that she was like Rabbi Akiva, whose soul left him as he pronounced the last words of the Shema, "*achad*."

Nehama's funeral, right before Pesach 1997, was one of the largest ever held in Jerusalem. At her request there were no eulogies. Doli Basok points out that many leading religious leaders and even Rashei Yeshivot attended, which is a rare testimony of honor for a woman. As she was childless there was no one who was required to say *Kaddish* for her (although her nephews certainly did), nor to sit shivah. Yet this mass outturning of supporters and admirers was the way these thousands upon thousands showed their respect not only for Nehama but for the Torah she had taught them all her life.

6.

Interpersonal Relationships

Nehama had the unique quality of making contact with people of every walk of life, and learning from every one of them. She tried not to hurt people's feelings, but she could be abrupt or offensive when she felt people were acting incorrectly. Esther Gross, who became very close with Nehama in her latter years, recalls that she first learned with her as a student in 1953. When she returned to Israel in 1972, she met the son of a friend. "Where are you rushing off to?" she asked the young man. "I have a shiur with Nehama Leibowitz," he told her. "Nehama Leibowitz!" said Esther. "I'm coming with you."

When they entered Nehama's house, the shiur was just beginning. Somewhere in the middle Nehama began berating "certain individuals" who come into people's houses without being invited, without introducing themselves, and without requesting permission. Esther wanted to fall through the floor. As soon as the shiur ended, she went up to Nehama and apologized profusely. "I simply didn't have time to ask if I could attend before the class began," she explained lamely. "You," said Nehama, "I wasn't talking about you. I thought you belonged here," she said, jumping over twenty years with ease.

Nachum Amsel relates how in 1977 he became quite close to Nehama as a rabbinic student at the Gross Institute and a *madrich* (counsellor) of BMT students from abroad. When he came to take his leave of Nehama before returning to the States, she was shocked and even a little angry. "Why must you return to America?" she wanted to know. Nothing Nachum said was acceptable. "I'll help you find a job here," she even offered. "I'll be back, Nehama, I'm sure," he said, but she didn't believe him.

In 1988 Nachum made aliya, now with a wife, and immediately went to a shiur that Nehama was giving during the Ten Days of Penitence on the Book of Jonah. "There must have been 500 people at the shiur, and I couldn't get near Nehama afterwards," relates Nachum. "So I left her a note with my phone number and wrote, 'You said I wouldn't come back; well, here I am.' I'm not sure she remembered who I was." Nevertheless the very next day she called Nachum; they chatted and she invited him to her shiurim. He even became her driver for a while and that way reestablished the close relationship he maintained with her until her demise.

Rachel Kosofsky had an embarrassing experience that illustrates Nehama's special brand of caring. She and another 'regular' student requested permission to attend a seminar that Nehama was giving for Jewish educators from abroad. On the second day, Rachel came in late and couldn't find a place to sit. So she stood at the back of the room with a number of other people, holding her open Tanach. Nehama spied her and declared, "I'm not beginning until someone gives that lady in the back a place." Five people immediately got up to give Rachel their seat, and, feeling terrible, she scurried into one of them.

Sometimes people brought her their manuscripts to review. She tried not to hurt people's feelings, because obviously if they invested time and energy in writing a book, and brought their finished product to her for an opinion, they were expecting a positive response. However, if the book was "terrible" or "halfbaked" she was in a dilemma. With her analytic, agile mind she could generally sum up the author's ability. If she felt the writer could do better, she'd point out the weaknesses, argue points of view with those who could "take it," and invest considerable energy in helping the person make important improvements. But if the author was incapable of better, she would send him away with some small comments or excuses.

"She was one of a generation," says Rachel Horowitz, a retired nurse who studied with Nehama. "She characterized the great minds and educational leaders of her period, the '40s and '50s, people like Zuriel and Dov Rapell. Just as there are periods in archaeology, there are also periods in thought and outlook," declares Rachel.

Mrs. Horowitz once asked Nehama, "Why do Hassidim consult with their Rebbe for everything?" Nehama thought for a moment and then answered her, "Listen, God is too distant and lofty for some people. They need an intermediary to connect them with the Higher Being." Then she reminded Rachel of the generation that had left Egypt, participated in the great miracles of the Ten Plagues, the Split Sea, and the Giving of the Law, yet descended to idol worship the minute their spiritual leader, Moshe, tarried. "They too needed an intermediary," Nehama said. Rachel sums up, "Whatever she taught us made a lasting impression. Her lessons were like vitamins; they boosted one's spiritual nutrition."

Shoshana Brayer is another student who often took Nehama for walks. She once gave Nehama a copy of her autobiography, in which she describes her childhood during the Holocaust. That night she got a call from Nehama at 12:30 a.m. "I just wanted to tell you," she heard over the phone, "I couldn't put your book down. It's lucky that I don't have to teach tomorrow, because I couldn't stop reading it." "Imagine," declares Shoshana, "calling me in the middle of the night for that!"

Shoshana once took her shopping for a dress shortly before she was going to Kibbutz Lavi for her annual lecture series there. As usual she bought the same plain, dark blue, long-sleeved frock she always wore. But Shoshana convinced her to also buy a second dress, in a different color. When she came back she mentioned quite proudly to Shoshana how everyone had praised her for the dress. She also told Shoshana that her cleaning lady's daughter was getting married. She was concerned that she was paying too much money for the wedding gown, which one wears only once. Then she revealed that she still wore her own wedding gown every *Yom Kippur* to shul.

Although most of Nehama's closest associates were twenty, thirty, and even sixty years younger than she, she still maintained close friendships with a handful of 'intellectuals' her age. Professor Dov

Heiman, the skin specialist, was exactly her age. He had a library that rivaled hers, and an enviable knowledge of the sources. They would meet on holidays at the Reich Hotel. Nehama once confided to a friend that she hated going to Reich for the holidays because there were only old people there – but she enjoyed her long talks in Yiddish with Professor Heiman.

Professor Mordechai Breur chuckles as he recalls "Two old Litwaks, Nehama and Professor Heiman, discussing the important issues of the world in Yiddish!" And why did the two converse in Yiddish? Heiman, who had lived for many years in England, was a perfectionist, and since his Hebrew wasn't flawless, the two friends talked in *Mama Loshen*. Yitzhak Hershkovitz, the owner of Pension Reich, recalls that Professor Heiman would often tease Nehama, especially if in their discussions they had a difference of opinion. "You have to show me more respect," he'd say with a twinkle behind his white goatee. "After all, I'm two weeks older than you."

Idit Izkovitz had many private discussions on various issues with Nehama, but in Hebrew. "She devoted her life to making the spiritual treasures of Israel available to Am Yisrael," says Idit. Nehama once told her, "I think people are getting fed up with television; they want to return to learning Torah." She related the example of some of her more far-flung students, who had returned to the fold, as examples. "So many people come here [to her house] to learn even though they don't get marks or diplomas or even credit for continuing education courses."

Rabbi Uriel Kessing, as a young man in Holland, studied Parshat Hashavua using Nehama's worksheets. "I had thirty years of gilyonot that she had marked (not necessarily in chronological order). When I came to Israel twenty-five years ago, almost the first person I sought out was Nehama. I wanted to see her in person and hear her give a shiur. I heard she gives a class at BMT at 8:00 p.m. and I made sure to be there on time." Rav Kessing laughs at his European standards.

"At 8:00 p.m. no one was in the classroom. It became 8:15, and then 8:20. A few stragglers started to take their place. I asked someone, 'Isn't Professor Leibowitz giving a class here tonight?' He assured me she was. 'She's probably outside talking to her taxi driver, as usual,' he said. That's exactly what happened. She got caught up in a discussion with her driver. At 8:30 Nehama finally arrived, the room filled up, and the shiur was outstanding," says the Dutch teacher. "I was bewitched." Rabbi Kessing became one of her regular disciples, and he still uses her method of teaching Tanach.

"I never called her Nehama," he admits. "My Dutch education wouldn't allow me such liberties. I don't think first grade children should call their teachers by their first names either, which is common in Israel." In the class Rabbi Kessing attended, Nehama took a personal interest in every single member – and in the welfare of their families as well. But the welfare of the whole nation concerned her most. "Once she told me, 'You're from Holland, right? They are looking for Jewish teachers with foreign passports in Morocco.' I had to admit that I'd given up my Dutch passport years ago."

Rabbi Kessing continues: "I once taught her worksheet on *Chayeh Sarah* to one of my children. He was only nine years old, but he not only understood Nehama's point, but like me, got quite enthusiastic about the way she made it. I decided to call Nehama on Motzei Shabbat to tell her how even a child found her lesson enthralling. But then I thought better of it. 'She has no lack of admirers who call her all the time,' I thought. 'Why bother her with my parental pride!' But my wife pushed me to call and tell her how much father and son enjoyed her worksheet. Not surprisingly, Nehama was more than pleased to hear my report. She kept me on the phone for forty-five minutes. She asked thousands of questions; about my children, about my teaching. She was especially impressed with the fact that my son was only nine years old and kept repeating the fact in wonder.

"I remember as a child in Holland," Rabbi Kessing relates. "We once had a substitute *ba'al koreh* (man who reads the Torah portion out loud) in our synagogue. He made a big impression on me. I said to my grandfather, 'I wish we had that ba'al koreh every week!' My grandfather said, 'Come and tell him that.' I was very shy and tried to get out of approaching the man. My grandfather insisted. I very quietly told the reader that I enjoyed his *leining*. He was very happy to hear a compliment even from a youngster. That's been a lesson to me ever since," continues Uriel Kessing. "No matter how important the person, he'll always appreciate an honest compliment. People don't realize how important it is to give positive feedback. I read in the Torah every week, and nobody ever tells me 'Yasher Koach.'"

Asher Hadad, of Lod, looks back fondly on the lessons he had with Nehama at the Lifshitz Teacher's Seminary. "Eighteen years ago she taught us *Akedat Yitzhak* (The Binding of Isaac), one of her favorite chapters. I told her about the liturgical hymn that is recited in Sephardi synagogues before the reading of this chapter on *Rosh Hashanah*. She told us how much another hymn meant to her, which begins, "*Im Efes Roveh Akim*." 'Nehama,' I told her, 'we recite that hymn daily.' I then rattled it off by heart. She got so enthusiastic and started praising the Sephardi liturgy and services."

"The Sephardi services are much more respectful than the Ashkenazi ones," she declared. "In Ashkenazi synagogues they talk all the time during the prayers. In Sephardi houses of prayer they sing most of the *tefillah* together and they keep *quiet*."

"Nehama's death was very hard for me," continues Asher Hadad. "It felt like a personal relative had died. She used to relate to each of us with respect. I know she loved us and believed in our *tzibur* (community). That's why she invested everything she had in preparing us [the teachers and principals that she taught] for our future. She gave us a heritage – tools with which to learn Tanach and to understand the commentaries."

Several people reported not only a strong friendship with Nehama, but actually a 'surrogate' family relationship. Ariela Yedger, one of her closest associates, enjoyed such a bond. "She felt very close to our children and considered herself a type of substitute grandmother. She was involved in all our family celebrations and always wanted to know what everyone was doing. My husband, Shaul, often helped fix things in the house or took her places in our car. When we lived in Kiryat Moshe we'd visit every Shabbat. After we moved to Har Nof we generally spoke on the telephone, sometimes just to say, 'Shabbat shalom.'

"During the Gulf War the children set up her house for any emergency," Ariela continues. "They often arranged her worksheets for an order or a coming shiur. Right before she was hospitalized we brought my son's fiancee to her, and she was very gracious to the

young couple." Nehama took a great interest in Ariela's thesis on
Sefer HaChinuch. "On the day I finished my thesis she went into the
hospital for the last time. We knew each other for twenty years. My
husband actually knew her even longer. She once said to me, 'I'm
like your second mother-in-law.' We all loved her very much."

One of her oldest friends and colleagues is Dr. Shlomo Feurstein,
who was a senior lecturer at Bar Ilan University on the teaching of
Tanach, and who worked with Nehama for many years preparing
the matriculation exams in Tanach. "I actually met Nehama when
I attended a hachshara in Kibbutz Mecholah in 1946. She gave a
seminar for kibbutz teachers who taught Parshat Hashavuah. Even
though fifty-two years have passed since then, the impression she
made on me from that day has been everlasting."

Later Dr. Feurstein studied at the Beit V'gan Seminary, where
Nehama was a favorite teacher. It was during the War of Independence and the Siege of Jerusalem was on. "We used to draw water
from the seminary well and bring it to her, and sometimes we'd
gather wood from abandoned Arab houses. Of course we'd go to her
house in Kiryat Moshe by foot – there was no other way. Whenever
we'd bring her supplies we were always rewarded with some good
vort, something new that she taught us." Feurstein continued to be
Nehama's student at Bar Ilan University, where she taught briefly, and
at the Tel Aviv University, where he got his M.A. in Tanach.

Thereafter they became colleagues. They served on a committee
for improving the matriculation exam. "We introduced the concept
of 'unseen parts' in the Bible questions," says Feurstein. "From 1975
to 1996 I had the privilege of working with Nehama on the actual
questions that were asked in the *bagrut* (matriculation). We must
have worded over 2,500 questions. We had stormy discussions over
the phrasing; sometimes we'd argue over a single question for weeks.
We never asked the same question twice. I estimate that we worked
for eight or nine months on every matriculation test."

Often when they had argued fiercely over a point, Nehama would
call him late at night to apologize if she'd been too harsh or insulting.
"I think Nehama actually enjoyed working and fighting over these
questions – it turned into a kind of *chevrutah* (study circle) for her.
She didn't want any 'yes men' around her just to accept her words.

As I advanced in my studies, we became more colleague and friend than teacher-student. Nevertheless I never related to Nehama as an equal ... I always looked up to her as my mentor," he says.

In 1958 Nehama gave a weekly radio class on Parshat Hashavuah. She carried on a lively correspondence with Professor Hugo Bergman, who was the head of the Philosophy Department at the Hebrew University at the time (see Appendix J). He was distressed by a midrash she had used in her broadcast on *Parshat Vayishlach*, concerning the relations between Jacob and Esau, as a symbol of tense and ongoing, inter-brethren strife. Bergman, who was a founding member of Brit Shalom, an organization that attempted to build brotherhood relationships between the Zionist Movement and the Arabs of Eretz Yisrael, took Nehama to task for her pessimistic attitude toward our association with other nations. The exchange was published by Aviad HaCohen in *MEIMAD*, that political party's newsletter, in honor of Nehama's first *yahrzeit*, April 1998.

"I was shocked to hear [you read the midrash] that says, 'Everything that happened to our forefather [Jacob] with Esau, will always be our fate with Esau's [descendants]....' Can one perpetuate this terrible anti-humanistic tradition even after the Jewish State has been established?" wrote Bergman in real pain. "Is this the way to nurture the first signs of Redemption into a full Redemption?"

To this Nehama replied: "Dear Professor Bergman, I was surprised to read what you wrote. Had you complained that my words were unacceptable or incorrect, I would have taken your criticism to heart immediately.... I know well that I am an imperfect trumpet for God's Word ... but to intimate that my broadcast is capable of spreading hatred in the hearts of men, is beyond conception.... The fact that we were, and still are, like a lamb among seven wolves, hasn't been changed by the reality of a Jewish State. I don't think it is my task as an educator," continued Nehama, "to ignore the pogroms, the expulsions, the decrees against Jews and the Holocaust of our generation ... just as I feel it's my duty to show my students the corruption, the narrowmindedness, the rot, and the nonsense that ... exists in our own State – and this doesn't interfere in any way with my educating towards loyalty and love for our Land."

After defending her approach, Nehama, as was her wont, ends

the letter as follows: "In any case a radio address is not measured by the intention [of the speaker] but rather by what is heard, and if my words were interpreted as a call for hatred [against the non-Jew], I admit that is not good. One needs to be careful, and emphasize other [approaches]. My thanks and appreciation to you for bringing to my attention what you understood from my words ... and thank you again for your help and guidance. Would that I could teach Torah as it should be taught in this generation, but for that one needs considerable assistance from above."

Several years later Nehama attended a philosophy class given by Bergman at the Hebrew University. At the end of the semester she wrote him a letter of appreciation: "Professor Bergman, my respected and admired teacher ... Permit me to take this opportunity to express my deepest appreciation at being permitted to attend your lectures ... I can't tell you how important and how enriching they were for me, and I'm probably expressing what many who participated with me in the lecture hall, felt. May God lengthen your days and years to give you strength to enlighten His works. In respect and gratitude, Nehama." It is no wonder that Nehama's method of dealing with her dissenters usually turned them into admirers and friends.

Nehama was friends with people from every walk of life. She became very close with the Ron family in Givataim when they invited her to give a Tanach class in honor of their son who was killed during army service. Mrs. Ron was a Bible teacher in the National State School System. Many famous people were invited to teach in this chug: Ben Gurion, Yehuda Elizur, Eliezar Sweid, and others, but Nehama remained the most constant 'guest lecturer.' Her lectures were partially taped by Shimon Ron and formed the basis of the five volume *Haguth B'Mikrah*, which was published independently. "She had a special tie with our family," says Shimon, "even though we're not from her world."

When Mrs. Ron died of cancer in 1985, that tie continued. "I used to visit her at least once in two weeks, until her last days," says Shimon Ron. "Sometimes she'd call me and we'd talk for hours. Once she rang up and said, 'Guess why I called you today. I simply wanted to hear your voice.' I'm not an observant Jew, but we had a common language; we understood each other."

Shimon cherishes a note that he received from Nehama one day with a bouquet of flowers. The note read: "My dear Shimon, when do I have the opportunity to thank you for the close friendship that you bestow upon me…. Today, my last day of teaching at the University, and the first day of my expectations as a pensioner, is a good time to settle accounts. Now I begin a new chapter in my life, the last one … and it's a good chance to send a fine friend flowers. May you enjoy them and good health for many years to come…."

Meira Weidenfeld Bein, the author of many children's books in Hebrew, has a fascinating story to tell about how Nehama, her teacher at the Mizrachi Teachers' Seminary, once offered to adopt her. "As a child I always thought of myself as different," relates Meira. "My father came from a religious family in Poland, but he became non-observant as a young man, and moved to Austria. There at a Revisionist meeting he met my mother, who wasn't Jewish. She was studying speech therapy, and the teachers sent the class to hear Jabotinsky give a speech – that's how impressive the Zionist leader's rhetoric was considered.

"Although non-Jewish my mother became a Zionist, and for my father's sake she converted (without really learning anything about Judaism) and they came to Israel in 1927. We lived on King George Street. When my father became seriously ill he started laying tefillin again, and he sent me to a religious school, Ruhama. There I remember feeling out of place because my mother didn't know anything about Judaism, and even was amused at our religious observances. My father and I had a kind of coalition against the 'goyeh' who didn't understand anything.

"When I was eight years old my father died, and no one even told me. I didn't attend his funeral and I just picked up the news but refused to admit it even to myself. When someone would ask me about my dad, I'd say he's seriously ill, and leave it at that. One day when I was ten or eleven years old, a Mandate policeman caught me crossing the street illegally. 'Hey, little girl, you can't do that. Where's your father? I'm going to report you.' And he grabbed my arm and tried to walk me home. I don't know what got into me. Maybe from fear, maybe from frustration, maybe to keep him away from my house, I burst out crying. Something broke inside me. I started beating on the policeman's chest and yelling hysterically, 'He's dead! He's dead! He's dead!'

"He was a very understanding policeman. He calmed me down, and we actually became very good friends. Whenever he'd see me after that he'd always give me a big hello, and sometimes he even let me ride on his police horse. I always tried to keep people away from my house, away from my 'secret.' I didn't want anyone to know I was an orphan and that my mother wasn't Jewish and didn't know Hebrew. To support us my mother took in boarders, once my father died. I was embarrassed about that as well, even though we hosted Knesset members, famous authors, and other leaders of the *Yishuv*.

"When there was a parents–teachers meeting I'd go by myself to talk to the teachers and make up all kinds of stories to explain why my parents couldn't come. Someone once asked me if we were related to the famous Rabbis Weidenfelds. At that time I answered 'no,' but the idea quite attracted me and gradually I built up a mythical rabbinic genealogy, which I began passing around and developed for myself a distinguished family tree. After eighth grade I signed myself up for Seminar Mizrachi, and it was there that I first met Nehama.

"From the first day we were all enchanted with her lessons. I was especially attuned to her way of teaching, to her logic, and even before she would ask the expected question, I would know what she was going to say. I understood her approach and could almost anticipate when she'd ask, 'What's bothering Rashi? I'm sure she, too, noted that I was on 'her wavelength.' Once she accompanied us on an outing to the Kotel. She walked next to me and asked me, 'Meira, I sometimes watch you when you pray, and you seem to have such fervor. How do you do that?' I answered her as teenagers sometimes do, to shock her. I said, 'I don't actually believe in God and I don't know how to pray to Him. So what I do is I give some personal meaning to all the prayers. For instance, when I say *"Refaenu"* (Give us good health) I think of my father who is very sick (this was eight years after he'd died) and who I so much want to get better. Or when I say *"Barech Aleinu"* (Bless our land), I hope with all my heart that there will be peace in Palestine. When you want something very badly you put your whole heart and soul into that wish – but don't think it's because I believe in a Higher Being.'

"Nehama didn't say anything at that time, but a few days later she came up to me and said, 'I talked to my brother, Shaya [Professor Yeshayahu Leibowitz, who later was my professor at the university] about what you told me and he said, 'That's the best way to pray when you don't believe. It's a great "patent"; very deep and it shows extraordinary self-control.' I was chagrined that she should discuss my nonsense with her distinguished brother, and that she even took my stand seriously, when all along all I wanted to do was show her how bad I really am. Nevertheless today, thinking back, I think my strong prayers were motivated by the fact that I was unhappy and had suffered. Out of my own needs I found a practical application and poured out my fervor in prayer.

"In 1942 our boardinghouse was taken over by a platoon of the Polish underground army. Most of the men were devout Christians and the house was full of crosses and rosaries. If girlfriends ever came over to visit or do homework with me I always received them on the porch – never in the house, lest they meet my mother or see our living conditions. One day when I wasn't home Nehama came over to give me a message to relate to the whole class, since I lived closest to the seminary. Maybe she was also curious about my background and the mystery that surrounded me. My mother couldn't talk much Hebrew so they conversed in Russian. Nehama quickly sized up the situation. She saw the Polish soldiers, she realized why I was hiding my mother, and with her usual charm and forthrightness she made a plan.

"Standing up in our hallway, holding her satchel in one hand, she told my mother what a good student I was, and what potential she saw in me. Then she became personal. 'You know I don't have any children, and I'm not likely to have any. Without talking first to my husband, I want to make you an offer. I'd like to adopt your daughter. She has a very sensitive soul, and no doubt she suffers from the conflicts in her life. I can offer her a good family name, a comfortable life, and all the educational opportunities that she deserves.' I don't know what my mother must have thought at that moment. She did feel a certain inferiority complex living in the Land of the Jews, not really understanding them or their language. She must have sensed that I was ashamed of her. Her answer to Nehama was simply, 'It's very kind of you to make this generous offer. I'll ask Meira what she thinks and I'll do what my daughter wants.'

"When I came home shortly thereafter and heard that Nehama Leibowitz, my beloved teacher, had been in the house, I almost fell through the floor. But when I heard what she had offered I was mortified. I was so busy being deeply insulted that I didn't think how noble her offer actually was. I felt very bad for my poor mother, who must have felt inadequate as a parent. For three days I wouldn't go back to the seminary, and when I did, I couldn't look at Nehama, much less talk to her. I never heard a word from Nehama about the issue, and gradually our relationship returned to its original level. I continued to be a beloved, clever student, and she for me, to this day, was undoubtedly the most significant educator I have ever met in my whole life.

"Why do I say that? Nehama taught me how to think logically. Whenever I analyze something, whenever I have to make a decision, I find myself using her rules of reason. Nehama also taught me how to pass on information, which I've used all through my teaching, broadcasting, and writing careers. I remember she used to teach us at the teachers' seminary, 'We start with two entities – the material and the listener. If you don't find the best way to get the material [the knowledge, the story, the information] across to the listener [the reader, the students], then never the twain shall meet: the material remains material and unaccessible, and the listener remains the listener and an uninformed one at that. It takes skill, thought, and especially enthusiasm to get the one across to the other.'

"Another thing I learned from Nehama is the importance of getting the whole picture. I'll never forget the example she used to give us of a man she saw behind a stone wall. Only his head could be seen and it kept bobbing up and down. 'I thought the guy must be crazy lifting and lowering his head repeatedly. Then I stepped behind the wall and saw he was pumping a bicycle tire. As long as I didn't see the scene in its full context I got the wrong impression, and thought he was a *meshuggener.*' This need to understand all sides of an issue or an argument has made me super-tolerant, but it can also get me into trouble. Once I was almost thrown out of a taxi because I said I can understand what motivated the murderer Goldstein.

"Nehama taught me various subjects, not only Torah. When I learned history with her it was the first time that I really studied that subject. She taught the Enlightenment Period. I must admit that everything before and after that period is one big black hole to me, but everything she taught us about the Enlightenment I still remember and I take an interest in anything that comes my way from those years. My whole outlook on life has been influenced by Nehama. Maybe she ruined me a little. I don't make an effort to remember things that haven't been presented in an interesting way. It's a detriment.

"Nehama never put one off for questioning religious dogma. I once dared to bring up an oft-quoted dilemma – the success of the witch who managed to raise Samuel when Saul went to her for help. 'How is it possible that she used sorcery successfully if the Torah claims there's no such power?' I asked. Nehama said, 'I could give you the pat reply, that God can make anything happen if He so wishes. But I think there's another approach.' Then using her best theatrical talents (and she had many), she got up, and I can still see the scene, as in her brown beret with a wisp of gray hair sticking out, she said: 'If I get up in front of you all, put my hands on my hips and say energetically, "Well, show me, dear Witch, what you can come up with," she wouldn't be able to show me a thing. But if a king comes in the dead of the night, to her dark hovel, trembling with fear that he'll be discovered and thinking constantly of the confrontation he will be having on the morrow, I can assure you he'd be able to see Samuel, the Prophet, on a broomstick.'"

Over the years Meira Bein became famous in her own right as a radio producer and director and as a writer. Despite her enthusiasm for her beloved teacher, she didn't maintain contact, even when she became a teacher herself in the same Ruhama grade school where she had studied. "At first I was too much in awe of her to just visit with her socially," she explains. "In class I was able to be open with her, but I didn't have the courage to do so outside." Then when Meira became non-observant she was afraid Nehama would be disappointed in her. "I know she had many, many non-religious students and friends, but I felt that from me she wouldn't have expected the switch.

"I didn't even attend her funeral," concludes Meira, "even though I loved her very much. I don't go to funerals generally. Don't forget, I missed the biggest funeral of my life, my father's."

Frima Gurfinkle was another of Nehama's many students who became very close to her. Frima was a doctoral student in comparative literature when she first attended a shiur by Nehama. "It was an unbelievable experience," she recalls. "At the time I hardly knew how to read Hebrew. But I became convinced that hers was the way I wanted to take; I wanted to be her student." Frima began attending as many of Nehama's classes as possible. "I tried to stay on the sidelines; I was afraid she'd check my answers and at the time I didn't know how to even look up a text."

Once Nehama asked her to read aloud some passage. Frima feigned eyesight problems, claiming she'd left her glasses at home. Gradually the Russian immigrant got to know Nehama's style and was able to be more actively involved. "I was amazed how Nehama could give the same shiur to different groups of people, and how she adapted the same verses and the same commentaries to different audiences.

"I don't remember when the relationship with her went from fear and awe to close, personal interaction," says Frima, who now is a renowned Tanach teacher for Russian immigrants. "I used to dream about her." Whenever Nehama would see Frima she would ask about her teaching, her students, and her views. "She had a few standard subjects of discussion with me," says Ms. Gurfinkle. "She had very strong convictions about teaching Bible in a foreign language, and she'd often ask me in what language I taught, just in order to get an argument going."

Nehama also asked her about socialism. "Only later," says Frima, "I realized she wanted to know where I stood on these subjects – my views changed over the years as I distanced myself from the Soviet Union. She also wanted to compare my Communist-nurtured indoctrination with her own beliefs in social justice, views that she'd absorbed in her youth, and that were prevalent in Israel in the early days of the State.

"Over the years," Frima continues, "we had less formal contact. I used to visit her occasionally or called, but she was always in the back of my mind. Whenever I went to Russia I felt I had to report to her upon my return. In the last twenty years she was a very important part of my life – much bigger than just the personal contact. It's love, but it's more than that really. It's missing her, which I did even when she was alive; it's a 'soul connection' and it's all mixed up with the incredulity that a person like her actually existed. We used to have an expression among ourselves (the regular students) *"Zot Nachmateinu"* ("she is our comfort").

7.

Tales of Nehama

When Professor Nehama Leibowitz died, Israel lost one of its leading Bible scholars, and a doyenne educator – someone who changed the lives of everyone who came in contact with her. "Nehama," as she was fondly called by all, was a master teacher who used a variety of pedagogical methods, which were designed to involve the student in the learning experience. It mattered little whether the pupil was an elementary school youngster, a budding teacher in a seminary, or any one of the many thousands of adults all over the world who followed her shiurim or learned Parshat Hashavuah from her books or gilyonot.

She was concerned that everyone should understand the text of the Bible, be able to compare how various commentators explain the meaning, and state concisely what in fact was "bothering Rashi." To highlight her lessons, she liberally used stories, an age-old way to make one's message clear. She made ample use of folk tales, midrashim, and world literature, but especially tales from her everyday experiences.

Whatever Nehama did, or wherever she went, she made contact with people; she got them to open up, she held long, philosophical conversations with the taxi drivers who took her to her classes, and she engaged in lengthy correspondence with those who filled out her weekly "sheets." All these experiences, as well as her personal history, were richly woven in her teaching, as stories that form the basis of this chapter: "Tales of Nehama."

What Do I Know About Little Children?

In one of her visits to Kibbutz Berot Yitzhak (in one version to Kibbutz Lavi), one of the mothers asked if she could teach the kindergartners (in one version the second and third graders). "What do I know about little children?" said Nehama. But in the end she agreed. However, she wouldn't let any of her adult students be present.

The subject she taught, one of her favorites, was the sale of Yosef. She got to the sentence, "We are guilty because we didn't hear [our brother] cry out and beg us [when we threw him into the pit]." One bright lad asked, "That's not right! It doesn't say that Yosef begged his brothers when they threw him into the pit!" Nehama was delighted. She explained that even if the fact is not mentioned specifically, it's logical that he cried out to his brothers. Many times the Torah doesn't detail every act and every sentence spoken. Using one of her most popular methods, she asked the class, "What do you think he yelled when he was in the pit?" The answers were many and varied. They revealed quite a lot about the personality of each child.

One boy said: "I'm cold. It's dark down here, I'm afraid."

Another one declared: "Yosef shouted, 'What will you tell our father?'"

A third child said simply: "I-ma!"

One lad said: "He pleaded; he cried: 'I won't tell any more dreams, I promise.'"

And finally one stated: "No, none of those are right; he yelled, 'Just wait, just wait 'til I see you in Egypt.'"

Nehama asked him, "But he didn't know he would be going down to Egypt."

The boy answered emphatically, "Trust Yosef."

Nehama Was a Great Actress

Nehama was a great actress. When she told a story she often used dialect, or acted out the dialogue in a way that made the tale live. In one of her famous taxi driver stories, she related: "Once I finished teaching at the university, hailed a taxi, and asked to be taken home, to Rehov HaZvi 10. The driver didn't really look at me. But he did know that address. He said, 'There's an old hag who lives in that house who teaches Bible. Do you know her?'" Nehama answered innocently, "No, no." The driver came back: "You should, it'd be worth your while."

The Most Famous Taxi Driver Story

Another famous taxi driver story that she repeated often, showed her empathy for the simple faith of "the people." She began her narration with background details that always add authenticity to a story. "I came out of the Jewish Agency one day, and took a cab that was waiting there. We were about to pull out, when another cab driver came over to my driver. 'Listen, Moshe,' said the visitor, 'I have a great job for you, to take a tourist couple up north; I can't make it.' 'When is it?' asked Moshe with interest. 'This coming Shabbat,' answered his friend. 'No, sorry, I don't drive on Shabbat,' said my driver.

"'Listen Moshe,' said the other driver, 'this is a real opportunity, believe me. You can make IL 300 for one day.' 'I told you,' said Moshe, getting a little upset, 'I don't drive on Shabbat.' 'Forget that nonsense,' said his friend. 'They'll probably stop over in Caesaria, and invite you to lunch at the Rimonim, at their expense. It's a real opportunity. Don't be a fool, Moshe.'"

Now Moshe was getting really angry. He started the motor. 'I've told you, I don't drive on Shabbat! Now get out of my way, this lady has to go to an important meeting.' Now Nehama, in a dramatized aside, whispered, "I didn't say a word; I kept out of it." Nehama continued, "As we drove away, Moshe muttered to himself, 'IL 300 is a lot of money! Lunch in Caesaria too, that would be nice. But I don't drive on Shabbat.'"

"What do you do on Shabbat?" Nehama asked the driver, to be friendly. "On Shabbat I go to the synagogue; I take my tallit with my *siddur* and I go to prayers, and I'm together with my Maker." "As he said that, he took his hands off the wheel and held them together to show solidarity with his Maker – we're lucky we didn't have an accident. But as he said those words, Moshe was actually beaming. 'Together.'"

The Talpiot Maabarah

Another classic story took place in the *Talpiot Maabarah*, right after the State was established and the mass immigration began. There were 22,000 tents in that camp in 1951, according to Nehama, and she taught there. It was a terribly rainy winter and the authorities made a public request on the radio, asking every Jerusalem family to take in a child or two, so that these youngsters at least would be spared the hardships of living in the maabarah that winter.

There were so many children and so few classrooms that they conducted school in shifts. In this setting she remembers teaching the story of Rivka and Eliezer at the well to a group of Yemenite children in fifth grade. She and the children figured out how many jugs of water little Rivka had to lug from the well in order to water Eliezer's camels. It took about 360 minutes, or six hours, quite an achievement for the gracious girl.

The children were duly impressed. "Ah, *tzaddikah* (righteous girl), our mother Rivka," they said. One little boy raised his hand to ask a question. "If she left at six in the evening, 'at dusk' according to the text, and came back at midnight, didn't her father whack her?" Nehama says she was stunned. She knew the cultural background of the class, so she didn't know what to say. "What does a teacher do when she doesn't have an answer?" she asked rhetorically. "She asks the children." Sure enough, another little Yemenite boy had the solution. Quoting from a well-known axiom, he said knowingly, "For a *mitzvah* it's permitted [to come home late]."

"Receiving Guests is Greater Than Receiving the Divine Presence"

Nehama liked to tell a story based on the verse, "Receiving guests is greater than receiving the Divine Presence," which we learn from Patriarch Avraham at the beginning of *Parshat Vayerah*. Avraham interrupted his visit from God when he saw the three "guests," it will be recalled, and her tale was about a music lover.

There was once a poor man who loved Beethoven but couldn't afford to attend a concert. His friend lent him a radio and told him, "Avi, in three days' time there's going to be a Beethoven concert on the radio. I know how much you'll appreciate it, so here's my radio." Every day Avi marked off another day, until the evening of the concert. On the day of the concert he warned his wife and children to go into another room and be very quiet. Then he sat close to the radio, waiting for it to begin half an hour early.

The concert begins. Avi is in heaven. The music washes over him with its beauty. Suddenly there's a ring at the door. It's his neighbor, who has to bake a cake for tomorrow. "Could you lend me two eggs?" asks the neighbor. Avi receives her nicely, gives her the eggs, and returns to his radio. But again the doorbell rings. "Sorry to trouble you," says the neighbor again, "but I see I don't have milk either." So Avi gives her milk, and asks if she needs anything else.

Meanwhile the music that he's been waiting for for three days is playing on the radio. "Well, as a matter of fact, I could use some oil, and a bit of sugar," says the neighbor. Avi continues to give her everything she wants. He doesn't tell her, "Go to hell," or even, "Come back later, I'm listening to a concert." He misses very beautiful parts of the concert, and he does it smilingly. "And," added Nehama with a significant smile, "that was only Beethoven!"

The Dramatization of Avraham and the King of Sodom

Nehama was supervising a student teacher, who organized the dramatization of Avraham and the King of Sodom. One little girl in the second grade, who was playing Avraham, wanted to stand on the teacher's chair, to increase her height. She thought she needed to be taller than the King of Sodom so that she could spit in his face, as the Patriarch refused any recompense for his deeds. "I thought that showed a good grasp of the subject," said Nehama.

The Obvious and the Obscure

During the riots of 1935–39 many Jews were killed. The British didn't interfere too much, because it gave them justification for remaining in power. Still, when the situation got too hot and threatened to get out of hand, they would send in their bloodhounds, and the dogs often smelled out the terrorists.

Two residents of Tel Aviv were discussing the ability of the dogs to find the culprits. "It's truly one of the wonders of God, how these bloodhounds can find the murderers from a distance of several kilometers," said one. "What wonders of God!" said his friend, sarcastically. "It's purely the dogs' instincts," and he didn't even realize he was saying the same thing.

Another version of the same theme concerns two children standing under an umbrella, during a heavy storm. One of the children stands in wonder as the lightning and thunder follow each other. "Look at that storm. What a lot of rain! God must really be angry," he says to his friend. "Silly," says the other. "The rain doesn't come from God, it comes from the clouds."

Mekarev et Hager

A young girl once came up to Nehama and asked her to help tutor her in preparation for conversion to Judaism. It turned out the young woman was marrying a Jewish boy and lived in Kiryat Moshe, her neighborhood. Nehama agreed and the two set up a learning schedule.

One day the fiance's father called Nehama and said very angrily: "You shouldn't teach my son's girlfriend Judaism," he yelled. "You should influence her to leave my son." "Why?" asked Nehama in all innocence. "Isn't she a good girl?" "Yes, she's a very good girl," admitted the father, "but I don't want my son to marry a convert."

"But the Rambam tells us we must *mekarev et hager* (to bring the convert close)," said Nehama. "I know very well what the Rambam says," declared the man. "You don't have to tell me, lady. But that's good for the Rambam, not for me." In the end the young couple were married in Nehama's house, and as fairytales end, "lived happily ever after."

Do You Believe the Bible is the Word of the Lord?

Nehama on occasion met with spiritual leaders of other religions. They often sought her out. She held long theological discussions with some of them. One priest visited her home and she asked him, "Do you believe the Bible is the word of the Lord?" The priest answered in the affirmative. "We do too," she said. "But why then do you pray to a statue?"

The priest answered as follows: "The Church, in its infinite wisdom, knows that 'Man is not made so.'" Three times he repeated his maxim that people can't pray to an indefinite Being – they need an intermediary. Nehama, however, pursued the subject. "But we see that many do pray to an unseen God," she said. "Four hundred million Moslems and thirteen million Jews do so daily." "That's not prayer," was the priest's response.

On another occasion she had a discussion with a Jesuit seminary supervisor who attended her class at the university. He admitted that his students used to sin with prostitutes, and afterward would gain forgiveness at the confessional. "We know that people cannot overcome their baser needs," he declared. "We're not like you Jews who think you can overcome the evil inclination."

This same supervisor did not eat with the seminary students because they spoke about forbidden subjects and he didn't think he could get them to "clean up their language." "I know you Jews try to improve, and rise above man's baser nature." In his opinion, the task of an educator was solely to instill belief into his students, not to change their nature. "We know we are all worthless scum; you Jews are proud; you think it's possible to rise above original sin!"

"Thou Shall not Steal"

Another taxi driver story in Nehama's own words: "I was in Rehavia and ordered a taxi. They said it would take seven minutes. He arrived after twenty-five minutes, without a word of apology. At the end of the ride he requested IS 10.80. I didn't realize I handed him an IS 100 bill. He said sarcastically, 'Lady, you gave me an IS 100.' 'Oh, very nice, very nice,' I said. 'Why very nice?' he asked. 'It says "Thou shall not steal" somewhere; I don't know where, maybe in the Book of Leviticus.' That's Jerusalem for you," concluded Nehama.

Hidden Meaning

Leah Goldberg, the famous Hebrew writer, complained that too often people look for hidden meaning when there is none. "Some parables are not to be taken literally; nor is there an analogy to every detail." Once she taught one of her stories and brought in the alienation of urban society. One of the students perked up. "That's why the hero in the story slammed the door shut, right?" she said with a question mark in her voice. "No," Leah Goldberg answered her, "he shut the door because he was simply cold!" To which Nehama added two maxims of her own: (a) Don't force meaning where the author meant none; and (b) There isn't always a moral to every parable.

"Kosher Sandwiches Will be Provided."

Nehama made fun of her fame. Once she was invited to give a short weekend seminar at the YMHA in New York. To get her to come and overcome her longtime resistance to travel abroad, her former students tried to convince her by saying, "You don't have to stay too long. You can talk on Thursday and get back home in time for Shabbat." The notice that the organizers sent to her house read, among other things: "Kosher sandwiches will be provided." "That's great," said Nehama. "That means I don't have to bring my own from Jerusalem." She didn't go.

Honesty

Nehama Leibowitz was as straight and honest as a ruler. She often quoted Rabbi Shmuel Salant, who came to Jerusalem as a youngster. In Europe he had been a weak and sickly child. In Israel he gained strength and lived well into his nineties. He also became a renowned Torah scholar and eventually the first Ashkenazi Chief Rabbi in Israel. Rabbi Salant lived in the Hurva Courtyard and was extremely careful about "stealing" from the public.

For example, he never took even small items for personal use. He claimed that even a page of his Yeshiva's letterhead was equivalent to a *pruta* (less than a cent) so that he would be a thief if he took one. "If someone takes public property that is worth less than a pruta it may be permitted, but it won't make Torah scholars happy with him."

Prisoner of Zion

One of the famous Prisoners of Zion was accused by the KGB of dealing in drugs. They needed 'evidence' to 'put him away.' Their agents planted drugs on his desk and on Friday night 'witnesses' entered his house and testified that they saw him smoking it.

Because the Prisoner of Zion was newly and strictly religious, his defense lawyer was able to state that this claim was simply impossible – his client did not smoke on the Sabbath. The prosecuter quickly spoke up. "Perhaps the witness can correct his testimony. When did you see the accused smoking pot?" "Yes, of course," the witness replied. "It happened on Saturday night; that's when I saw him smoking," and with that the man was sentenced and sent to Siberia for ten years. Today he is a happy resident of Jerusalem.

The Lab Technician

Her students were found in all walks of life and in every corner of the world. Once when Nehama was in the hospital she had to have blood tests every day. When the lab technician came around, she simply held out her arm in expectation. But that day it was another worker and he told her, "I'll only take blood from you if you explain a Rashi that's been bothering me." "How do you know that I can interpret Rashi?" she asked. "Nu, really … ," said the lab technician and explained what was bothering him.

'Telephone Interruptions'

On innumerable occasions the students in her Thursday night class would be sitting in her house for the weekly class in Bible. The students were crowded around the ancient desk, which always held her most useful reference books, notes, and pens with which they would be writing answers to her queries, as well as articles and brochures people had sent her. In addition some modest refreshments were laid out on the desk. There would be a ring, and one of the students would answer the phone and hand it to her. "Nehama here," was the way she replied. As she listened she would shake her head up and down and then say into the receiver, "Listen, we're in the middle of a class right now; call back in half an hour." Then, as she hung up, she would sigh happily and explain, "Someone in Alaska (or Texas, or Belgium) wants to know how to understand a commentary in Ramban."

The Taxi Driver and the Yom Kippur Question

The day after Yom Kippur, a taxi driver told her, "I didn't sleep all night, and it's not because I overate. I know you're not supposed to eat a lot after a fast." "So what was the problem?" asked Nehama politely. "I'm *brogus* (angry) ever since *Mincha*. Tell me, did He forgive the people of Nineveh, yes or no?" Nehama, puzzled, answered, "Yes, He did forgive them."

"Then why is it written," continued the driver, "'I won't forgive Nineveh'?" "Ah," replied Nehama, "it's not a statement, it's a question." It took a while for the driver to absorb her explanation. "Oh," he finally said, "in that case it should read 'And I won't forgive Nineveh?'" "Imagine!" said Nehama with pleasure, "it really bothered him."

Nehama's Childhood

In her later years Nehama spoke more and more about her childhood, her parents, and her illustrious brother, Shaya (Professor Yeshayahu Leibowitz). "When I was ten years old I decided to be very, very good during the Ten Days of Penitence. When my mother called me, I really came right away. One day I even ran to get my father's cane and galoshes. He was surprised at my uncharacteristic behavior, and said, 'Listen, it's more important to be good from Yom Kippur to Rosh Hashanah than from Rosh Hashanah to Yom Kippur.'"

"Where are You?"

Nehama liked to tell the story of the original Lubavitcher Rebbe, who was imprisoned for some time. One day the warden asked him, "You're a wise and learned man, maybe you know the answer to a question that's been bothering me in the Bible. How can it be that the All-Knowing God asks Adam, 'Where are you?' God knows all, so why does he ask this?"

The Rebbe asked the warden, "How old are you?" The man answered, "Forty-six, why?" The Rabbi answered, "What have you done in those forty-six years? Every day He asks you, 'What have you done; what have you contributed in your forty-six years? Every day God asks us all, 'Where are you?'" According to folklore the warden was so impressed he eventually became a Jew and a very learned Torah scholar.

Taxi Driver's Dilemma

One of Nehama's cab driver stories went like this: "On my way to the university one day the taxi driver asked me, 'Can you tell me why it says in Jeremiah 9:22 "Let not a wise man glory in his wisdom; and let not the strong man glory in his strength; let not a rich man glory in his wealth. But let him that glories, glory in this: that he understands and knows Me.'"

Nehama, in measured voice, gave an answer that could be understood by a taxi driver. But the man wasn't satisfied. "No, no, that's not what I meant." She very patiently again explained the simple meaning of the verse. "The prophet is teaching us that the things important to people – wealth, strength, and wisdom – are not all that central." But the driver persevered. "I know all that, but why does he [Jeremiah] write, 'A rich man, *a* wise man,' but '*the* strong man'?"

Nehama was flabbergasted, or pretended to be as she related the incident in class: "What an interesting point. I'd never thought of it! And from a cab driver!" She loved getting examples of folk wisdom from simple people or children. It illustrated the universality of the Torah's wisdom.

The Childless Couple

A young Yemenite woman came up to her after class to get some advice. "My husband and I are married ten years," she said, "and we have no children. We don't know if we should get divorced and try to raise a family each with another spouse. What do you think, Nehama?" Nehama replied, "I'm not qualified to give you an answer. You should consult a psychologist or a marriage counselor."

The woman persisted. "No, I want your opinion, Nehama. I respect your view." "No, no, I'm a teacher, this is not my field," she replied. But the woman wouldn't take no for an answer, so Nehama reluctantly asked her: "Do you love your husband?" "Very much" was the reply. "Does he love you?" "Yes, very much!" "Well, if you love him, and he loves you, I think you should continue the marriage and may HaShem grant your wish."

A year later (no, it's not the happy ending you expect), Nehama met the woman in the university library with a big smile on her face. The woman right away told her, "Nehama, do you remember the problem I discussed with you last year? Well, we decided to go to the Rebbe (the Habad leader) in Brooklyn. We saved up the whole year and we finally went." Nehama said, "How exciting. What did you do in New York?"

"No, we didn't do anything except consult with the Rebbe. We didn't do any sightseeing or visiting. The Rebbe received us at two a.m. one morning." "What did he say to you?" asked Nehama. "He was very friendly. After we told him our dilemma, he asked my husband, 'Do you love your wife?' My husband said, of course, 'Yes.' Then the Rebbe asked me, 'Do you love your husband?' and I also answered, 'Yes.' Then the Rebbe said, 'If you love her and she loves you, you should be married and not divorced. May HaShem fulfill your wishes.'"

Nehama told the story with humor and empathy, adding, "Faith in the Rebbe is a powerful thing, a powerful thing."

Dr. Bonchik, who relates the story that he heard from Nehama herself, added his personal comment. "This is a tale of love, respect, and concern for a fellow Jew. I remember thinking, as I drove home that night after hearing this story, neither Nehama nor the Rebbe has children. They know both the pain of childlessness but also the power of love. Their deep-seated love has blessed them both with thousands of 'children' throughout the Jewish world."

The Truth is Impossible to Burn

Nehama gave a very inspiring shiur on Jeremiah to a group of women from Kfar Maimon. She described to them very vividly how the King sat next to his furnace in winter trying to keep warm when they brought him the prophet's proclamation. As he read it, he got more and more upset. In the end he threw it into the fire. "I taught this chapter during the end of the Mandate Period in a broadcasted shiur over Kol Yisrael. There was a British censor who sat through each program and he had to approve whatever we said. It was the day after the Palestine Post building had been burnt down by Arab terrorists, perhaps with British support. When I finished describing how the prophet's proclamation was burnt, with one eye on the censor sitting outside the broadcasting room, I added, 'But the truth is impossible to burn.' He looked daggers at me (because this hadn't been in my script) but it was too late to do anything about it. Wherever I went that week, people all over Jerusalem gave me a smile and repeated: 'But the truth is impossible to burn.'"

Torah L'Am

The fact that citizens from all walks of life often referred to traditional sources in their daily pursuits made her very happy. She was ever tolerant of the mix-ups they made in quoting incorrectly or mistaking their reference to the Bible. For example: "Once I was in a taxi and the driver got very upset, because another car was trying to overtake him illegally. 'What's a-matter with that guy,' he snarled. 'Doesn't he know the biblical saying: 'Who is a strong man? He who controls his *yetzer*'?" (The phrase comes from *Pirkei Avot*.)

Once she was sitting at the seaside enjoying the scene and the good breeze. A mother and her two children sat next to her. One of the children was playing with a kitten, and pulled its tail and ears, inadvertantly hurting the animal. "Don't do that," the mother admonished her youngster. "It's not nice to hurt the kitty. The Torah tells us that Moshe Rabeinu always looked after the animals. Once a little goat he was looking after kept running away from the flock. Moshe ran after it, but as soon as he almost caught the kid, it danced off again. Moshe got a little angry, but the goat ran over to a spring of water and began drinking long gulps. 'Oh, I didn't know you were only thirsty,' Moshe apologized to the tired little animal. He then put the kid on his back because he thought it must be very tired and walked back to the flock. That's what's written in the Bible. That's how you should treat animals." (The story is actually a midrash, but Nehama was pleased at its application.)

A third example of *Torah L'Am* (Popular Torah) that she told took place after the Six Day War. She was waiting at a bus stop, near a building site. She had to wait a long time because many buses were still at the front. She had ample time to listen to some workmen who were on their lunch break.

The men were exchanging war stories. One man told his comrades about the Egyptian front where he fought. "We were supposed to move forward, when suddenly we came under terrific fire from the Egyptians. One member of our platoon was wounded, but nobody could crawl out to get him, because of the shooting. We couldn't even lift our heads. It was pitiful to hear his cries for help. Finally the medic crawled out of the bunker and went to get the wounded man."

Munching on his sandwich the worker said, "That medic! He's not a man, he's a super-being! To go out in that fire! He jumped into 'the fiery furnace.' He's not a man!" Nehama added, "You think the workman at that building site made up that metaphor? That's ingrained in him. It comes from Avraham who, according to the Midrash, was thrown into a fiery furnace." That's what she thought of Am Yisrael.

Kal V'Chomer

A little girl came up to her and asked to help carry her heavy basket. She explained that they had learned that week the commandment, "If you happen to see a donkey fall down under its load, you must surely help it." "I did a '*kal v'chomer*' (a ruling that if this is true, then under this circumstance, it is even truer)," the little girl continued in full innocence, "and I thought I could help you." Many people in the class who heard the story laughed, but Nehama shut them up immediately. "You're laughing; I have tears in my eyes. I wish I had such success with my shiurim. Here is a teacher who did such an excellent job in conveying not only the written text, but in internalizing the principle behind it, that her student went looking for a way to act accordingly. Isn't that an achievement!"

"They Didn't have Television or Videos Then…"

Nehama often explained biblical texts with modern references – she made the material relevant by using examples from her audience's daily lives. Once she said to a group of students from abroad. "How did Rivka have the time to water all those camels? Today if you ask someone for directions, they practically knock you down as they move along – they're in such a hurry." Everyone laughed or nodded. Then as an afterthought, Nehama added, "Well, they didn't have television and videos then…."

Similarly in explaining how the elders gradually disappeared as Moses and Aaron approached Pharoah's palace for the first time, she said: "One suddenly discovered that he had to help his wife today; one had a dentist's appointment; one got an awful headache ... and soon there were none."

On Abraham, who left his homeland, his kin, and his family to come to Israel as he was commanded in *Lech Lecha*, she often said in mock astonishment: "Imagine, he came all that way, without a pilot trip, without a shaliach, without even immigrant benefits!"

"Not so Difficult"

In another taxi driver story, Nehama related that she once asked a driver to wait several minutes for her. She left some of her latest gilyonot on the seat next to him. He started filling one out. When she came back and saw him busy at work, she asked him, "Do you find it difficult?" The man answered her, "Not particularly," and drove her home.

"It Won't Hurt You"

Once she was asked to teach at an army camp near Gush Etzion. Nehama was really very proud of these opportunities. She was picked up by an army vehicle and brought to the commanding officer. He welcomed her formally and called over a military escort. "Yosie, take this speaker to the hall; see that she gets everything she needs. Make sure the soldiers all arrive immediately, and that the mike works properly. And, Yosie, while she's giving the lecture, go in and *listen*. It won't hurt you." Nehama got a big kick out of, "It won't hurt you."

What is a Lie?

To make moral dilemmas clear, Nehama also used common, everyday incidents, such as the following: "I saw a group of children playing hopscotch one summer evening. Yosie was especially engrossed in the game. 'I could jump from here to Tel Aviv without stepping on the lines,' he proclaimed to his friends. Just then his mother called him from the window. Apparently it wasn't the first time she'd called him. 'Yosie, didn't I tell you to go to the grocery store and get a loaf of bread!' It was Yosie's turn to jump. He clearly didn't want to stop and go to the grocery store. He yelled back to his mother, 'Ima, the grocery store is closed,' and quietly, under his breath added 'on Shabbat.' Nehama used this story to initiate a discussion: What is a lie: what is heard or what is intended?

An Erlicher Yid

Esther Gross, one of Nehama's 'faithful,' relates a story she heard frequently from her. Nehama was on an intercity bus and listened to two passengers talking in Yiddish. One was a *Yerushalmi* and the other was an American tourist. The tourist had come to visit his son, who was studying at a yeshiva.

"The *Rosh Yeshiva* asked me to let my son stay another year. He said, 'He'll learn another 500 *blat* (pages) of gemara; it's worth his while. Then you can take him back to America and put him in your business.' I told the Rosh Yeshiva that I wasn't so sure it made that much difference. He argued with me. He said, 'Look, he doesn't have to learn in a kollel his whole life; just another year; those 500 blat of gemara are important.'

"I said to the Rosh Yeshiva," continued the father, "Forget about the 500 blat of gemara. I just want him to be an *erlicher Yid* (an honest Jew). Can you promise me that?" The tourist turned to his friend. "He didn't answer me. The Rebbe didn't even reply to that, what do you think?"

The Yerushalmi nodded his head. "It is a question, yes indeed."

"Oi, Bist Du A Soicher"

For every chapter in the Bible she had a good story or example to relate to make the material clearer. Some sections were her favorites. One of them was Kerem Navot (Navot's Vineyard), which King Achav coveted. Nehama taught this chapter to a class of new immigrant adults in the early years of the State. Even though the students had a very limited vocabulary at the time, she knew that she had gotten the chapter across to them, because when she asked in careful Hebrew, "How did Achav's wife, Jezebel, react to her husband's disappointment," one of the men answered in Yiddish, "She put her hands on her hips, she shook her head, and said to him, '*Oi, bist du a soicher.*' (You sure are some businessman)!"

119

The Famous Ganav Story

Nehama often related her famous *ganav* (thief) story. In fact Chana Tubal, one of her close students from Meretz, tells the story (as she heard it) in three chapters. When Nehama was teaching in the teachers' seminar in Beit V'gan shortly after the State of Israel was founded, there was a close feeling of comradeship and trust among the students and the staff.

However, one day some money was taken out of a student's purse. The next week a valuable pen was missing and shortly thereafter one pupil's watch was gone. The seminar was in an upheaval. Was it possible that there was a thief in the close-knit group? The principal had no other recourse but to call the police. One day while Nehama was teaching the fifty students of the seminar, the principal came in with an elderly policeman to start the investigations. Nehama asked if she should leave the class. "No, no, what I have to say is no secret. Everything is open and clear." Then he turned to the students. "I'm a very experienced policeman. I started my career in the days of the British Mandate. I've already investigated hundreds of cases like this one. It's clear to me that this is an inside job – someone among you is a thief and he knows it."

The old policeman continued: "Now I want to talk to the thief who's sitting here in this room. Only you know who has stolen things from your fellow students three times – only you and God Almighty. You've succeeded three times; maybe you've succeeded in getting away with it in the past several times. Let me tell you, from experience, once you've succeeded in getting away with stealing you'll continue – and probably you won't get caught."

He looked sharply at all the group, but continued talking to the thief. "You'll see that it's not so difficult, and you'll continue. You'll be rich, you'll have money and jewelry and watches and other nice things that other people don't have. And you won't get caught, because we know in the police force very few robberies get solved. You might become respected, wealthy, and a person of prominence, but ... *you'll be a thief all your life.* You'll never be able to clear yourself of that fact.

"Now I'm going to make a suggestion. It's now 12:30. We're all going to go home, because it's *Erev Shabbat.* Between 1:00

120

and 2:00 at the latest, put the things you stole in some open place where they can be found – and you'll be absolved, you'll no longer be a thief." The policeman took his briefcase, put on his coat, said Shabbat Shalom, and left the room. Everyone was in shock. Nobody spoke. Nehama and the principal left the room in silence and went home. So did the students.

At the bus stop Nehama met the policeman waiting for the bus. "How do you know your idea will work?" asked Nehama. "What if nobody returns the things that were stolen?" The policeman looked at her and asked, "Lady, how long have you worked for the police?" and got on his bus.

An hour later, Nehama relates, she was at home preparing for Shabbat, when she got a phone call from the principal. Very excitedly he told her that the money, the pen, and the watch were all sitting on the table in the main corridor; someone had quietly placed them there for all to see. End of Act I.

About ten years later Nehama gave a ten-minute talk on the radio for a program called "The Most Interesting Man I've Met." She told this story and how the wise policeman had saved some young person from becoming a thief. A week later she got a call from a teacher in a girls' school. This is the story she heard: "We were organizing a class outing to the Galil. Every girl had to bring IL 5. (In those days you could still go somewhere for IL 5.) I counted the money in front of the class and we all saw there was IL 150."

At the end of the day before she left the classroom, she decided to count the money again. To her amazement she found only IL 140. The teacher continued: "I counted again and again, but it was clear that IL 10 was missing. On my way home, very upset, I suddenly remembered the radio program you gave. I decided to use the same tactics. The next day I told the girls that I had counted the money once again before I went home and IL 10 was missing. I looked everywhere and I counted many times and I came to the sad conclusion that there obviously was a thief among them. I also added that, because she'd been successful, that girl would continue to steal; and it was even likely that she wouldn't be caught – ever. But that girl would *remain a thief all her life.*"

The teacher went on with her report to Nehama: "Then I distributed thirty envelopes and told the girls to put a piece of paper in each one after school and return them the next day. I said that the thief could put the money inside the paper and no one would ever know who she was. The next day I collected the envelopes. Sure enough, one of the envelopes had the missing IL 10 in it. I can't tell you how grateful I am to you, Nehama. And oh, incidentally, it was a wonderful outing!" End of Act II.

Another five years passed. One bright day, Nehama got a letter from the principal of a youth village near Beer Sheva. "I want to meet with you as soon as possible; please let me know when you can give me an appointment." Nehama answered immediately and the man came to her house, obviously very upset.

"I've been the director of the X Youth Village for many years, but I never had an incident like this. Over the period of several weeks eight ballpoint pens disappeared (in the days when ballpoint pens were still a novelty). I remembered your radio program several years ago, and I called an assembly in the dining room. More or less like that policeman you described, I told all the children: 'There's one person in this room who knows he's a thief – that he's taken eight pens, and maybe we'll never discover who he is. But one bad deed leads to another; he might be successful, and he might never be caught, but he'll *be a thief all his life*, no matter what else happens to him.'"

The director told Nehama that he announced that the teachers' room would be left open so that the thief could return what he'd stolen when no one was around. A week passed and nothing happened; two weeks and still no reaction. "I was really disappointed," said the director, "but gradually forgot about the whole thing. One day, while I was in the teachers' room reading, a little boy came in with the eight pens in his hand. With lowered head the boy put his treasure on the desk."

"Tell me," asked the director, "what took you so long? Why did you wait three weeks to return the goods?" The boy explained that until now there were always other kids around waiting to see if and when the thief would show up; now they had gotten tired of watching. Then the director thought: "He must have something else on his mind; otherwise why did he bring back the pens while I'm in the room?" So he waited.

122

He waited, and at last the boy said with some hesitation, "Perhaps the *menahel* will give me some way to do penitence; the director knows how one does *teshuva*?" "I was astounded. I said, 'The fact that you returned the pens shows that you've done penitence.'" "No, no," the boy insisted, "I have to do something. I did something bad, so now I have to do something good in its place." "Like what?" asked the director. "Well, like going to the blind institute across the street after school twice a week to read to the blind children," said the boy. "O.K.," said the director, "why don't you do that?" End of Act III.

And Nehama, as was her wont, used the story, or one chapter of it, to illustrate the explanation of Malbim on the verse in *Devarim* 11:21: "Behold I set before you this day a blessing and a curse. The blessing *that you* obey ... The curse *if you* don't obey...". It should say "The blessing *if you* obey" just like it says in the next verse, "The curse if you don't obey." To this the Malbim explains: "The very act of doing God's mitzvot is a great blessing; whereas performing the sin itself is the biggest punishment that can befall the sinner."

How Nehama's Commentary Got Bracha a Reduced Parking Fine

Bracha was one of her faithful students since her university days. She relates: "I had been to Nehama's class where we discussed the Rainbow that God sent as a sign to humanity that He would never again destroy the world with a flood. The various commentaries discuss whether the Rainbow has a concrete meaning [e.g., an upturned bow to indicate a sign of peace in primitive times], or was used arbitrarily, as an agreed-upon sign – something like a string around one's finger to remember something, or like traffic signs.

"That week I parked my car near the university library. There was a traffic sign that indicated no parking, but the usual two lines were horizontal instead of slanted. This I took to be a sign that the area was free parking. I even thought, 'How clever of them to use the no-parking-sign idea to indicate 'here you may park.' How wrong I was. It turns out there is no free-parking sign. Someone had simply hung the no-parking sign askew. Sure enough, I got a ticket.

"In Israel you can either pay your fine or go to court. I decided to go to court, fortified by my conviction and using Nehama's shiur as my backing. The whole experience was extremely interesting. When my turn came I explained my misconception to the judge, who listened sympathetically. Then I added Nehama's view on signs – the traffic sign obviously held an 'arbitrary' not a 'concrete' meaning; hence I could be excused for misinterpreting its placement. "Everything was very quiet in the court. I'm not sure if that was the only time Nehama's studies were used as evidence in a traffic court. The judge quite liked the explanation, I could see. He turned to one of the people near his desk, whispered something in his ear, and reduced my fine by half."

The Absurdity of Fanaticism

Nehama couldn't stand intolerance. Gerti Urman of Lavi tells the tale Nehama used to show the absurdity of fanaticism. In the Temple they were preparing a sheep for a sacrifice. All the priests were gathered around, getting ready for the slaughter. One of them stumbled and somehow fell on the knife. He started to bleed profusely. All the others ran toward him, but not to help. They wanted to see if the knife had been contaminated. "This is indicative of too many Jews in our generation," she'd say sadly.

"Students Remember Nothing!"

One of Nehama's most common expressions was: "In my experience, students remember *nothing!*" Doli Basok, one of her disciples, relates the following tale that she used to illustrate this phrase. Nehama once gave a course to army officers at their base. At the end of the first lecture one of the participants came over to tell her how much he had enjoyed the shiur.

"I love Tanach," the young man told her. "When I leave the army I'm going to study it at the university." Nehama was interested. "How did you come to that decision?" she asked. "When I was in high school I had a Bible teacher who really opened the world of the Tanach for me." "What book did you learn with him?" asked Nehama. "Oh, all of them," answered the officer. "Which one made a big impression on you?" Nehama continued. "Uh, I remember the book of Job," he replied.

"I made a big mistake," Nehama said afterward. "I opened the book of Job and asked him, 'Explain something that your teacher taught you.'" The officer turned pale and then red. He took the Tan-ach and turned page after page in *Sefer Iyov*. He went over it again and again, but he couldn't recall a thing to say. "To this day I'm sorry I put him on the spot," said Nehama afterwards. "All he could manage as he handed the Tanach back was, 'I don't remember much, but I recall all of life is in that book. It's very deep, very deep.'"

A Special Lecture
Once Nehama was invited to give a lecture at an army base in the Gush Etzion area. It was the beginning of the Intifada. An army vehicle was sent to pick her up. At the checkpoint near the base, a soldier stopped them and said, "Sorry, you can't continue on this road now." "But I have a lecturer here who's been invited to give a talk at the base tonight," said the driver. "Sorry, I have instructions not to let anyone through," answered the guard. "But it's Nehama Leibowitz who has to speak," insisted the driver, pointing to Nehama in the back. "Oh, Nehama Leibowitz, why didn't you say so?" said the soldier on duty, and quickly opened the barrier to let them through.

Always Complaining
To show that *B'nei Yisrael* were always complaining and ungrateful during their forty-year trek through the desert, Nehama described two of them who were present at the miraculous splitting of the Red Sea. As they were walking through the seabed, one turned to the other and said, "Nu, Shimon, what do you think of this?" "What do I think!" answered Shimon as he delicately picked his way through the wet seabed. "There we had *bohts* (mud) – in Egypt, and here we have bohts – what's the difference?" Then Nehama related a conversation she heard between two Jews on the bus shortly after the State was established. It was the time of severe rationing and economic restrictions. "What a State, eh, Shimon?" said one to the other. "With the amount of taxes we have to pay nowadays we can't even buy margarine to put on our bread." "What margarine?" said Shimon in disgust. "We can't even buy bread."

The Israeli Supreme Court Judge
Nehama was proud of her correspondence with Supreme Court

125

Judge Zvi Tal, who wrote to her as a private citizen (but she never-theless recognized his name). The letter by mistake was sent out by his secretary in a court envelope rather than a blank one, as he had requested. The letter goes as follows:

> Dear Professor Leibowitz,
> First of all permit me to express my appreciation for your undertaking in the *Studies* and especially for the latest publication. [All] the *Studies* enlighten and deepen one's understanding of the *Mikrah* (the Holy Text)....
> I found interesting and maybe even surprising support for your approach in explaining midrashic dialogue as being [an expression of] inner thought. In Tractate *Chulin*, p. 7, a story is told of Rabbi Pinchas Ben Yair who [seemingly] argues with the Ginay River ("Give me of your waters … you are going to perform God's will …"). The Tosphot on p. 5 says: "Perhaps the waters' guardian angel answers him thus. Alternatively (the words) could be an expression of Rabbi Pinchas' aspirations…. In a similar fashion, one can explain the first chapter in Tractate *Avoda Zara*, p. 17, regarding Rabbi Eliezer ben Durdai who declared, "Heavens (and mountains) plead for mercy on my behalf."
> Thus the conversation with the river and with heaven is explained as the heart's desires.
>
> Sincerely,
> Zvi Tal

To this Nehama replied in a warm, emotional way, only a few days later…

> To the Honorable Supreme Court Judge, R. Zvi Tal,
> When I received your letter and saw the words 'Supreme Court' on the envelope in clear letters, I got scared and I thought: "What did I do? Did I reveal any State secrets? Did I smuggle State treasures abroad? etc." Then when I opened the envelope and read the contents, my eyes lit up and I was never happier … not since I was honored with the Israel Prize in 1957, to the present date. Who am I, after all, that a Supreme Court Judge should take an interest in my words, and should even find time to write to me

and to praise me and bring support for my words and indicate that, without me even being cognizant of it, I have followed in the ways of the 'Gedolim.' For I, being ignorant of the Rabbinic Sources, wasn't acquainted with the reference you took the trouble to copy out for me, [and] for which you have my deepest thanks.

Of course I looked up the two sources you pointed out (Tractates *Chulin* 7 and *Avoda Zara* 17). In the latter reference I found a Reitva (commentator) that says: "It's not the mountains that beg for mercy, rather the author of the Breita (the saying) wants to state: He muses in his heart, 'To whom shall I turn? To the mountains, to the heavens?' They themselves need mercy (as the Marshal (another commentator) points out: For the whole world is transitory). If [the mountains or heavens] had a mouth they would tell him that.... Several other references with the same message exist where the mountains don't actually talk; rather we assume that if they could talk they would say something like that. Similarly in Judges 9 it's written: "And the vine says to them, 'I have ceased to produce my grapes which give enjoyment to man and God, and I've gone to climb on treetops.'"

(Not that I'm such a scholar of the Reitva, but I have a good publication of the *Ein Yaakov* (published in Jerusalem by Am Oved, 1961) which gives different explanations of the legends, among which is the Reitva.)

[Then, after this learned discussion, which shows Nehama wasn't so ignorant of the source after all, she continues on a more personal note.]

If in our childhood in the Diaspora at the beginning of the century (after all, I'm ninety years old), someone would have told me that we would be privileged to witness in Jerusalem a Supreme Court and a Supreme Court Judge who would write talmudic references, my late brother and I would have thought [then] that that's just an *Aggadah* (a legend), like the whale that will be eaten by the righteous in the World to Come. We would have believed that our dear father was telling us the tale to strengthen our Jewish and Zionist education. Yet lo and behold, this is no legend from *Ein Yaakov*. The envelope is actually in my hand and it says "Supreme Court." The fact that we have been thus privileged only strengthens in me the belief that you, the honored judge, will yet sit in the Sanhedrin of 71, and all the Jews from the four corners of the earth will reside with us here and will await your further pronunciations.

Thank you, thank you, thank you for your letter, With blessings, appreciation, and much honor,

Nehama Leibowitz

Leaving Israel

Rabbi Dr. Rafael Posen is another disciple of Nehama's who studied with her over the years and often visited her. As director of the girls' high school in Kfar Eliyahu he had occasion to invite Nehama to give shiurim to the students. She never refused him.

He also consulted with her on didactic problems and educational issues. However when he told her that he was being sent to Canada with his family for several years to direct a large yeshiva high school there, she was opposed and even angry that he was leaving Israel, where there was so much to do.

After a few months Rabbi Posen wrote to Nehama and stressed all the important things he was doing in Canada, awakening congregants to their heritage, sending youngsters to schools of higher education in the spirit of Bnei Akiva, and sometimes even to Israel. He expected to get a letter of encouragement. Instead he got a *spactel* (a tirade). "How can an intelligent, learned man so deceive himself, that his place is not in Eretz Yisrael. How can he go on and on describing what he's doing, but it doesn't mean a thing? How can he take his own innocent, susceptible children and expose them to the dangers of chutz laaretz, where twice a year they recite '*L'shana habah beYerushalayim*' ('next year in Jerusalem'), at the end of Yom Kippur and at the Passover Seder, and not a one of them really mean it … and their children know that." It really bothered her that Rabbi Posen and his family were out of Israel.

A Child's Imagination

Once Nehama was teaching a class of children who are classified in Israel as *teuneh tipuach* (disadvantaged youth). She had been teaching them the Exodus, and wondered how she was getting through to them. After ten minutes of reading the text she called for a break. "I want you all to write on a piece of paper," Nehama said on the spur of the moment, "what you want to be when you grow up."

The children all set to their task with enthusiasm. One of the youngsters wrote: "I'd like to be a kiosk owner in the Paran Desert." Nehama couldn't contain her curiosity. "What do you mean?" she asked the child.

"Six hundred thousand people passing through the Paran Desert ... all they have to eat all day long is manna. They must be good and tired of it. I'll be a millionaire!" Nehama told the story over and over again. She was impressed for two reasons: "Just see how great a child's imagination is," she said. She also was happy at the internalization of the material she had taught from the Torah, which the student's choice of profession showed.

Do a Good Deed Every Day

Nehama's general knowledge was no less impressive than her command of Jewish studies. On several occasions she related a little-known fact about the Boy Scout's ritual. When Baden Powell founded the Boy Scout movement in the last century, he established a set of rules, the prime one being: Do a Good Deed Every Day. He looked for some symbol that would constantly remind the scouts of this maxim. Powell was a devout Christian and knew the Bible well. The mitzvah (commandment) to wear *tzizzit* gave him his inspiration. Every Jewish male is required to wear a four-cornered undergarment with fringes as a reminder of the mitzvot.

Just as wearing the tzizzit reminds the Jew of the commandments he must keep, so Baden Powell chose the Scout kerchief as part of the Scout uniform to remind his members of their duty. The kerchief was subsequently adopted by every youth movement in the world, including those in Israel. It is doubtful if today's HaShomer Hatza'ir or even Bnei Akiva members are aware that the *Tnua Anivah*, each with its distinctive design, color, and accessories, originated with the nineteenth-century founder of the Scout movement, and he in turn adopted this symbol from the mitzvah of tzizzit!

"Ki Marim Heim"

Nehama had a "great" story to illustrate the famous verse describing the bitter waters that the Children of Israel drank in the desert: *"Ki*

129

marim heim" ("for they are bitter"). Nehama pointed out that *they* could be the waters or the people. Two elderly people were standing in a long line in the post office to get their monthly old-age pension. The first one, a cranky old man, came up to the clerk complaining about the long wait, the heat in the post office, and his sore leg.

"Please show me your identity card," said the clerk. "Why must I bring my identity card?" said the old man. "I left it at home. What kind of a State is it that makes its old people take their identity card wherever they go!"

"O.K., O.K.," said the tired clerk. "Just tell me your identity card number, and I can write it down here. Then you can get your pension."

"I don't know my identity card number. Why should I remember things like that! What's a-matter with you people? Why can't you give a man his just rights?" After ranting and raving a few more times and arguing with the poor clerk, the man left in a rage, fuming at the government and its inflexible workers.

Next in line was a little old lady with a basket in her hand. She went up to the desk and said "Shalom." As she happily handed over her I.D. card, she praised the State for providing for its senior citizens. She collected her money and said thank you to the clerk. He noticed she was looking for something. "Can I help you?" asked the clerk. "I'm looking for your charity box," said the old woman. "There's always one here and I'm used to giving my *maaser* (tithe) on the spot." The clerk picked the charity box up from the floor where it had fallen, watched while the lady put in some coins, and said good-bye with a smile.

That's how Nehama described "*Ki marim heim*" ("for *they* are bitter").

"Shabbat with Nehama Leibowitz"

Several years ago Dr. Gaby Cohen attended a conference in New York. On the bulletin board of a synagogue on the West End in Manhattan he saw an invitation that read, "Shabbat with Nehama Leibowitz." Gaby was amazed. Was it possible that after all these years, Nehama had succumbed and agreed to travel abroad – against all her principles? "And how is it," he thought, "that she didn't tell me,

130

when we're so close?" Dr. Cohen quickly found out what was behind the invitation. Three of Nehama's former students were organizing a *Shabbaton* of Torah learning based on Nehama's method. "And indeed that was a Shabbat *with* Nehama," says Gaby Cohen. "Just as there's a Shabbat with Rashi, or a Shabbat with the Malbim ... so Jews will continue to learn *with* Nehama Leibowitz..."

"Here We Have Noah"

The last story was told on Nehama, not by her. On one of her visits to Kibbutz Lavi she saw that a certain lecturer was giving a shiur in Tanach and decided to go. When the lecturer saw her enter the room, he immediately asked her to give the class in his stead. "No, by no means," said Nehama and sat down expectantly. The embarrassed lecturer was somewhat flustered. He began his lesson with a story: Once the Mississippi flooded and many towns were wiped out. In one state only one man survived. He decided to spend the rest of his life going from one end of the country to the other, telling people about his experience.

After 120 years the man died. When he got to heaven they asked him, "What did you do in life?" He told them, "I went from town to town telling people how I survived the great flood." They told him, "O.K., you can do that here too, if you want to. But know ye, here we have Noah."

131

Appendices

Whenever Nehama was asked for an interview she would refuse, replying, "Write about what I teach, not about me." A book on Professor Nehama Leibowitz would be incomplete without samples of her work, her gilyonot, the *Studies* and even isolated chapters on subjects of interest.

Very little is available in English, because after all Nehama wrote for the Israeli student or teacher whom she met personally. However, she had great rapport and respect for students from abroad, and she readily agreed to have her gilyonot translated not only into English but also into several European languages as well. Similarly certain *Studies in the Weekly Sidra* were issued in English by the World Zionist Organization's Department of Torah Education in the Diaspora.

Organizations as varied as the Hadassah women's organization, the Eliner Library of the Jewish Agency, and newspapers in Israel and abroad have, over the years, produced excerpts of her works or commentaries on her style of teaching. Samples included herein give only a very partial grasp of her range and depth of teaching, but hopefully will act to whet the reader's appetite for more.

Studies in the
Weekly Sidra*

The Torah Department of the World Zionist Organization was among the first to recognize the importance of Nehama's gilyonot and made some of them available to students from abroad, first in English and then in Spanish, French, and other languages, beginning in the early 1950s. I remember my first contact with the *Studies*, when as a student at the Machon L'madrichei Chutz LaAretz, we tried first to study the Portion of the Week and decipher them in Hebrew, and what a relief it was to then turn to the English, which made it so much easier. On my return to the United States to be a madricha, I took a whole set of Nehama's *Studies* with me and used them for many, many years thereafter.

– L.A.

> 3rd *Series*
> *By Nehama Leibowitz*
> *Translated and adapted by Aryeh Newman*

---

* World Zionist Organization, Dept. for Torah Education and Culture in the Diaspora, P.O.B. 92, Jerusalem

MIKETZ

And Joseph knew his brethren, but they knew not him and Joseph remembered the dreams which he dreamed of them and said unto them, Ye are spies; to see the nakedness of the land ye are come.

(Genesis XLII, 8–9)

Joseph's conduct towards his brothers has puzzled our commentators. For what purpose did Joseph falsely denounce them? Abarbanel formulates the difficulties in the biblical account as follows:

> Why did Joseph denounce his brothers? Surely it was criminal of him to take vengeance and bear a grudge like a viper. Though they had meant evil, God had turned it to good. What justification then had he for taking vengeance after twenty years? How could he ignore their plight in a strange land and that of their families suffering famine and waiting for them, particularly his aged father gnawed by worry and care? How could he not have pity on him and how could he bear to inflict on him further pain through the imprisonment of Simeon?

Modern non-Jewish biblical scholars, particularly those moved by animosity to Judaism, have cited this as a proof of the moral superiority of Christianity. They claim that here we have a clear example of vengeance, of unforgiving and even sadistic conduct, apparently approved of by the narrative. Even Joseph's own brothers after the death of his father suspected that he would "hate us and will certainly requite us the evil which we did unto him" (Genesis L, 15). But let us recall here Joseph's reply:

> Fear not: for am I in the place of God?
> But as for you, ye thought evil against me;
> but God meant it unto good…
> Now therefore fear ye not.

(Ibid. 20, 21)

134

Joseph could therefore not be accused of being inspired by feelings of vengeance. At any rate when he had a golden opportunity of paying off old scores he not only refrained from doing so but allayed his brothers' fears "comforted them and spoke kindly unto them" (Ibid. 21). Moreover, the tears that he could not hold back and that forced him to clear the room do not support the theory that Joseph was a sadist who enjoyed inflicting pain on his brothers.

A closer study of the text bears out that Joseph is not meant to be depicted as taking vengeance. This is certainly not the plain sense of the Scriptures. Though the exact motive for his denunciation of the brothers is not recorded, the Torah gives us a clue to his mood and the train of thought prompting his conduct. The text does not read "and Joseph remembered all that they (the brothers) had done to him, how they had cast him into the pit ...," or "how he had entreated them but they had not hearkened." Rather it reads:

And Joseph remembered the dreams which he dreamed of them.

(Genesis XLII, 9)

From here Nachmanides and others (including the famous novelist Thomas Mann in his *Joseph and His Brothers*) conclude that Joseph acted in accordance with the path marked out for him by Providence in his dreams. He did not feel himself free to do as he liked, but considered that he was destined to play the part of saviour and leader of his family. This had been the significance of the dream where he had seen:

For behold we were binding sheaves in the field and lo, my sheaf arose and also stood upright; and behold your sheaves stood round about and made obeisance to my sheaf.

(Ibid. XXXVII, 7)

Here is how Nachmanides explains the function that Joseph felt he had to perform.

The text states that when Joseph saw his brothers he remembered

135

his dreams and noted that not one of them had been properly fulfilled on this occasion, since he understood from the first dream "where we were binding sheaves," that all his brothers had first to bow down to him. The second dream alluded to a second occasion on which the "sun, moon and eleven stars," i.e. his parents and brothers would bow down to him. Noting that Benjamin was absent at this first meeting, he schemed to bring Benjamin along and thus effect the realisation of the first dream, where just the brothers – all eleven of them would bow down to him. Consequently he did not reveal his identity to them and ask them to bring his father along as he did later, for then his father would have undoubtedly come immediately. After the first dream had been fulfilled and Benjamin joined them to make the brotherly circle complete, he revealed his identity in order to effect the realisation of the second dream. Otherwise we would have to conclude (i.e. if this were not the real explanation of Joseph's conduct) that Joseph committed a grave sin inflicting pain on his father and allowing him to suffer an unnecessarily prolonged bereavement for him and Simeon. For even if we agree that he wished to make his brothers suffer, he should, at least, have had pity on his father's old age. But Joseph carried out everything in the appropriate manner in order to fulfill the dreams knowing that they would really come true.

This explanation of Nachmanides was strenuously opposed by later commentators including R. Isaac Arama in his *Akedat Yitzhak:*

> I am astonished at Nachmanides' explanation that Joseph did what he did in order to make his dreams come true. What did this benefit him? And even if it profited him he should not have sinned against his father. As for the dreams, leave it to Him Who sends them to make them come true. It seems infinitely foolish for a man to strive to fulfill his dreams which are matters beyond his control.

We may certainly repudiate Arama's suggestion to leave it to Providence to fulfill the dreams that He communicates to man. Gideon (Judges VII, 14–15), did not leave it to Providence to fulfill the dream that foretold that he would deliver Midian into the hands of Israel.

Rather he immediately made practical preparations to further the success of Israel's armies. Similarly, though Jeremiah foretold that God would restore the Jewish people to their land after seventy years of exile in Babylonia, the leaders of the Babylonian exile did not wait for it to come to pass. But before the seventy years were up Zerubabel and Jeshua the son of Jozadak (their leaders) went up to the land "with forty-two thousand three hundred and three score" (Ezra II) of their fellow Jews. But there is another objection to Nachmanides' explanation. Could not Joseph have accomplished the realisation of his dreams without making his brothers and his father suffer?

For this reason another explanation is to be preferred. It is also alluded to by Nachmanides himself as well as other commentators. The house of Jacob was guilty of a serious iniquity in the wrong that had been done to Joseph. How could this iniquity be atoned for and the unity and spiritual honour of the Chosen Seed be restored? In this connection let us cite Maimonides' prescription for genuine repentance, basing himself on the Talmud, *Yoma* 86b:

> What constitutes complete repentance? – He who was confronted by the identical thing wherein he transgressed and it lies within his power to commit the transgression but he nevertheless separated himself and did not succumb out of repentance, and not out of fear or weakness. How so? If he had relations with a woman forbidden to him and he was subsequently alone with her, still in the full possession of his passion for her and his bodily vigour unabated and in the country where the transgression took place; if he separated himself and did not sin, this is a true penitent.
>
> (*Code*, Teshuva II, 1)

In other words, a man must be brought into the same temptation to which he succumbed previously. If he stands the test and resists, he has proved his mettle. How could this be effected in the case of Joseph and his brothers? Whatever affection they might show to their brother in Egypt now, would be no indication of their true remorse. With Joseph as the vice-regent of Egypt they could, in any case, do him no hurt and whatever they would do would constitute a reform prompted by "fear and weakness." How could Joseph test them and

137

give them the possibility of achieving true repentance? Indeed, Joseph arranged everything appropriately, as Nachmanides has observed.

He had to arrange for his other brother, Benjamin, the son of his mother Rachel, and like him, the beloved of his father, to be brought into a similar situation. This time the brothers would find themselves really faced by a valid excuse for leaving their brother to his fate. For how could they fight the whole Egyptian empire? If, in spite of that, they would refuse to go back to their father without Benjamin and would be willing to sacrifice their lives as indeed Judah indicated when he said:

> Now, therefore, I pray thee let thy servant abide instead of the lad, a bondman to my lord; and let the lad go up with his brethren –
>
> (Genesis XLIV, 33)

Only then could the brothers be considered true penitents and Joseph would be able to make himself known to his brothers and the game would be over.

ACHAREI MOT

After the doings of the land of Egypt, wherein ye dwelt, shall ye not do;
and after the doings of the land of Canaan, whither I bring you, shall ye not do;
neither shall ye walk in their statutes.
My judgements shall ye do, and My statutes shall ye keep, to walk therein: I am the Lord your God.

The children of Israel, who had left and were about to enter a highly civilized environment after their long wanderings in the desert, were particularly susceptible to the cultural attractions, or rather as the Torah terms it, "defilements" and "abominations" of their past and future neighbours. We know today, only too well, how the technical achievements of civilization do not always reflect similar advancement in the field of ethics and morality. The Jewish people was therefore warned, in the above passage, against preferring the outward attractions of civilization above the purity of personal conduct. The author of the work *Berot Yitzhak* comments as follows on the above quotation:

> The passage should be interpreted in its plain sense. If you copy the practices of the Egyptians – for what purpose did I bring you out of Egypt? If you copy the practices of the Canaanites, why should I expel them for your sakes? On this condition did I bring you out of Egypt and on this condition did I drive out the Canaanites – that you should not emulate their deeds.

The children of Israel were admonished rather to follow the "judgements" and "statutes" of the Torah. Our Sages distinguished between these two types of Divine ordinances. The "statutes" were those ordinances the reasons for which were not apparent. The judgements were precepts, the motivation for which was obvious to the human mind.

> "My judgements shall ye do" – these refer to the commands stated in the Torah of right. If they had not been stated, they should have been.
> "And My statutes shall ye keep" – these are the commands constituting royal decrees about which the evil inclination raises the objection why we should at all observe them, and regarding which the Gentiles taunt us, such as the eating of pork and the wearing of shatnes.*
>
> (Rashi)

Rabbi David Hoffman notes that this distinction is not adequate and cites another view. The judgements refer to the laws governing the relations between man and his fellow, in society, in business relations. The statutes belong to the sphere of man's relations with himself, the demand for purity in his personal and sexual life.

The passage we are studying speaks of both the statutes and the judgments:

---

* Garments woven of linen and wool: Deuteromony XXII, 11

Ye shall therefore keep My statutes, and My judgements, which if
a man do, he shall live by them...

(Leviticus XVIII, 5)

The prophet Ezekiel repeats the sentiments of this verse:

And My judgements did I make known to them, And I gave them
My statutes,
which if a man do, he shall live by them.

(Ezekiel XX, 11)

The last phrase in the above quotation lends itself to different
renderings. The Jewish Publication Society version cited here takes
the phrase to imply that the Divine precepts provide a means for living: "he shall live by them." This is similar to the "live *through* them"
of the Buber-Rosenzweig version. The King James version translates
the phrase: "he shall live in them," implying that "life" will be the
reward for observance of the precepts.

But whichever rendering we adopt, this does not tell us what is
meant by the words: "he shall live." What kind of "life" does the passage refer to? Some commentators have seen here an allusion to the
Hereafter, the eternal life after death, as indeed the Targum Onkelos
takes it. Here we cite the views of Albo in his Jewish philosophic
classic *Sefer Haikkarim:*

The material rewards promised in the Torah are held out not to
the individual but to the nation as a whole. The personal reward
accruing to every individual is not alluded to explicitly in the Torah,
neither in the spiritual nor material field. It is indirectly hinted at in
a few places, one of them in *Acharei Mot* in the passage "according to the practices of the land of Egypt wherein ye dwelt shall
ye not do...." This is undoubtedly a warning directed at both the
nation as a whole and the individual, calling on the Jew to keep
the Divine laws "which if a man do, he shall live by them." Here
we certainly have a reference to the spiritual, personal reward
accruing to the individual. Though the Divine laws were more difficult to observe than those of the Egyptians and Canaanites, and
though the latter nations achieved material advancement through

them, nevertheless, the individual will not achieve spiritual perfection and eternal life, as he would, if he kept the laws of God. He should keep them, though they were difficult, since they brought the individual eternal life: "he shall live by them." It cannot refer to material life, as if to say that by observing the Torah a man will live a more prosperous life than if he observed the laws of the other nations. The falsity of this is evident to all, but here we are speaking of the life of the soul and not that of the body.

It is doubtful however whether the plain sense of the Scriptures alludes to the Hereafter. According to some commentators, therefore, the passage merely registers an emphatic protest against the practices of the surrounding nations, to which the Jews might become addicted. Here is the view of Nachmanides:

> You shall observe the judgements I have outlined in the Torah. Their performance will ensure a peaceful and orderly society in which no man will harm his fellow.

Nachmanides however did not wish to limit the laws of the Torah by a purely utilitarian definition and adds:

> Know that man's experience of the commandments is conditioned by his approach to their observance. There are those who perform a command out of an ulterior motive in order to gain thereby a material reward. They live in this world a long and prosperous life. There are others who perform the commandments in order to merit the World To Come, who serve God out of fear for Him. By their approach they merit to be delivered from the suffering inflicted by the wicked and their soul will fare well. Those who perform the Divine precepts out of love, as they should be observed, side by side with their everyday pursuits, will merit a comfortable life in this world and earn a perfect portion in the World To Come. Those who completely divorce themselves from material cares, forgetting as it were the existence of their bodies, all their thoughts being concentrated on their Creator alone, will gain eternal life in body and soul. The Torah's reward for the observance of its precepts "that thy days may be long," "that ye may live" is intentionally ambiguous and includes all levels of "liv-

ing," in accordance with the differing spiritual standards achieved by each individual.

All the interpretations quoted above have one thing in common, that they interpret the concluding phrase: "he shall live by them" to be one of purpose. Man is bidden keep the Divine law in *order to* attain a particular standard of living, whether in the physical or spiritual sense. Our Sages, however, did not regard this phrase as a subordinate clause of purpose. They understood it as a conditional clause, implying: "Man should observe the Divine precepts on condition that he can live with them." But if their observance entails a danger to life, he must not go through with them.

> How do we know that danger to live overrides the Sabbath? Said R. Yehuda in the name of Samuel: Since it is written: HE SHALL LIVE WITH THEM ... and not die through them.
>
> (Talmud, *Yoma* 88b)

Maimonides elaborates on this theme in his Code on the Sabbath Laws:

> The Sabbath is overruled wherever danger to life is involved, just as in all other precepts. Consequently we may attend to the needs of a sick man who is in danger as prescribed by the physician, and we may violate, on his account, even a hundred Sabbaths, so long as he stand in need and is in danger, or the matter is in any doubt. We may kindle for him the lamp and extinguish it, slaughter for him, bake, cook, and heat water for drinking or washing purposes. To sum up: The Sabbath is regarded as a weekday as far as the needs of the dangerously ill are concerned. When we perform these duties for him we may not do them through the medium of a non-Jew or a minor, but through the medium of the scholars and saints of Israel, and it is forbidden to delay in any way in violating the Sabbath to help the dangerously ill, as it is said: "And he shall live by them," and not die through them. You see then that the laws of the Torah do not breathe vengeance but rather mercy, loving-kindness and peace. Regarding those unbelievers who consider this to be a violation of the Sabbath and forbidden, the prophet Ezekiel stated (XX, 25): "Wherefore I gave

them also statutes that were not good, and ordinances whereby *they should not live....*"

We cannot conclude our *Studies* this week without referring to yet another valuable lesson which our Sages learnt from our passage. Why is there a sudden reversion from the second person to the third person? At the beginning, God addresses the children of Israel and warns them: "*ye* shall not do ... *ye* shall not walk ... *ye* shall observe...." Suddenly, in verse five, the third person is introduced "which if a man do *he* shall live by them" instead of "which if you do, you shall live by them." Here is the explanation of our Sages:

R. Jeremiah used to say: Whence may you learn that even a non-Jew who keeps the Torah is to be regarded as equal to the high priest? The Torah states: "Which if a man do..." Similarly it is stated "open ye the gates that the *righteous* nation that keepeth faithfulness may come in" (Isaiah XXVI, 2). It does not say that "priests, Levites, and Israelites" may enter. Similarly it is stated "this is the Gate of the Lord's." Priests, Levites, and Israelites are not mentioned, but rather "that the *righteous* may enter in." Similarly it is stated "exult in the Lord" (Psalms XXXIII). It does not say, "Priests, Levites, and Israelites" but "exult in the Lord O *ye righteous*" (Psalms CXXV, 4). Similarly it is stated: "Do good O Lord." It does not say to "priests, Levites, and Israelites," but "do good O Lord unto *the good.*" From this you may learn that even a non-Jew who observes the Torah is equal to the high priest.

(*Sifra*)

143

Post Nehama Studies
of the Weekly Portion

After Nehama died there were several organizations that began putting out her gilyonot in English, with the addition of answers. Yitzhak Reiner and his team contacted many former students and gleaned interesting corrections and comments by Nehama that assisted them in publishing these 'updated' worksheets.

– L.A.

> From the Keren Kayemet Religious Dept. Series,
> Jerusalem 1999

VAYESHEV
Genesis 38 Tamar
Gilyonot on the weekly portion
by Nehama Leibowitz

A. From the Midrashim

1. *Midrash Rabbah* Genesis 85:1 – "About that time Judah went down from his brothers" (Gen. 38:1): R. Samuel b. Nahman commenced as follows: "For I know the thoughts that I think towards you, said the Lord" (Jer. 29:11). The ancestors were taken up with selling

Joseph; Joseph was taken up with his sackcloth and fasting; Reuben was taken up with his sackcloth and fasting; Jacob was taken up with his sackcloth and fasting; Judah was taken up with finding a wife; and the Holy One, blessed be He, was taken up with creating the light of the Messiah, as it says, "About that time Judah went down..." "Before she travailed, she brought forth" (Isa. 66:7), implying that before the first to enslave Israel [i.e. Pharaoh] was born, the last to redeem Israel was born [David, descendant of Judah].

    a. What is the problem that this midrash tries to explain?

    b. Explain the underlying idea of the midrash.

2. Midrash Rabbah Genesis 85:9 – "And Judah sent [her] the kid of the goats" (Gen. 38:20). R. Judah b. Nahman quoted in the name of Resh Lakish "Laughing [Heb. *m'saheket*] in His habitable earth" (Prov. 8:30), "Laughing always before Him" (ibid., verse 30). The Torah laughs (*m'saheket*) at mankind. The Holy One, blessed be He, said to Judah: You deceived your father with a kid of goats; by your life, Tamar will deceive you with a kid of goats!

    a. What is the meaning of laughter in this midrash?

    b. The midrash attempts to connect our chapter with the preceding one. Find other ways, in the same vein as this midrash, in which our chapter is connected to the story of Joseph.

3. Midrash Rabbah Genesis 85:11

The Hebrew here is: *"Hu mutzet vehi shalhah el hamehah."*

    "As she was being brought out (Heb. *Mutzet*), she sent this message to her father-in-law" (Gen. 38:25). R. Judah said: They [the signet, cord, and staff] had been lost, and the Holy One, blessed be He, brought out (*him tzi*) others in their place, the word [brought out, *motzeh*] having the same meaning as in the verse "or found (*matzah*) that which was lost" (Lev. 5:22). [The midrash interprets *mutzet* (she was being brought out) as *motzet* (she finds)]. Rav Huna interpreted the verse "As he was being brought out" (Gen. 38:25) to mean "S/he should have been brought out." [The word for "she" – *hi* is actually written *hu*, which means "he," thus deducing that the Torah hints that if there were guilt, they both shared it.]

"She sent this message to her father-in-law, saying: 'I am with child by the man to whom these [signet, cord, and staff] belong.' And she added, saying: 'Identify [Heb. *haker na*] these'" (Gen. 38:25). He wished to deny it, whereupon she said to him: "Identify" your Creator in these, for they are yours and your Creator's. "Identify whose signet this is." [As stated in the beginning of the midrash, she had lost the originals and the Creator had brought out others.]

    a. What is the problem that Rav Huna addresses?

    b. What is the importance of the statement of Rav Huna in assessing the behaviour of Judah?

    c. Where does the midrash find a basis for saying that Judah wished to deny it?

• • d. What indication is there in the verses that led Tamar, according to the midrash, to remind Judah of his Creator?

B. Tractate *Sota* 10b – R. Johanan said in the name of R. Simeon b. Yohai: Far better for a man to cast himself into a fiery furnace [even as Tamar was ready to be burnt to death] rather than shame his fellow in public. Where do we learn this from? From Tamar.

Rashi on Gen. 38:25:
"As she was being brought out" – to be burnt:
"she sent this message to her father-in-law" – she did not wish to put him to shame in public by saying: "It is by you that I am pregnant." But she said only: "by the man to whom these belong." She thought: "If he is to acknowledge it, let him acknowledge it voluntarily, and if not, let him burn me and let me not put him to shame in public." From this passage our Rabbis derived the teaching: Far better that a man should let himself be cast into a fiery furnace rather than shame his fellow in public.

    1. Explain what is the difference in style between Rashi and his midrashic source.

    2. Some sages post the following challenge: "From where do we know this? Perhaps Tamar did not expose Judah because she had not yet been brought to the fire; but if the fire were burning around her, she would have shamed [Judah]!?"

How could you answer these skeptics?

C. Gen. 38:26: "And Judah identified them, and said: '*Tzadkah mimeni*', inasmuch as I did not give her to my son Shelah'" [*tzadkah* can mean "she is more righteous" or "she is more in the right": *mimeni* can mean "than I am" or "from me"].

Tractate *Sota* 10b – "And Judah identified them, and said, 'She is more righteous than I am (*mimeni*)'" – That is what R. Hanin b. Bizna said in the name of R. Simeon the Pious: Joseph, who sanctified the heavenly Name in private [resisting Potiphar's wife], merited that one letter should be added to him from the Name of the Holy One, blessed be He, as it is written, "He appointed it in Joseph [Yehosef] for a testimony" [in Ps. 81:6, the letter *hey* of God's name is added to Yosef]. Judah, however, who sanctified the heavenly Name in public, merited that the whole of his name should be called after the Name of the Holy One, blessed be He [*Yehudah* contains the four letters of the Tetragrammaton].

Rashi on Gen. 38:26: "*Tzadkah*" – she is more in the right in what she has said: "*mimeni*" from me, she is pregnant.
Our Rabbis, of blessed memory, explained this to mean that a Divine voice [*bat-kol*] came forth and said the word *mimeni*, i.e., from Me and from My authority did these events unfold.

Rashbam on Gen. 38:26: "*Tzadkah mimeni*" – She is much more righteous than I am, since I commanded her to wait in her father's home until Shelah would grow up. She kept her part of the arrangement, but I did not keep my part of the implied promise, since I did not give her to my son Shelah. For similar usages see: "[Job] *tzadko nafsho mi* – Elokim" (Job 32:2), meaning "Job justified himself rather than God"; and "*Tzadik ata mimeni*" (I Sam. 24:17), meaning "You are more righteous than I am."

Ramban on Gen. 28:26 – "*Tzadkah mimeni*" – "*tzadkah*" she is more in the right in what she has said: "*mimeni*" – from me, she is pregnant.

147

Our Rabbis, of blessed memory (*Sota* 10b), explained this to mean that a *bat-kol* came forth and said the word *mimeni*, i.e., from Me and from My authority did these events unfold. Until here the words of Rashi.

The correct interpretation is that it is similar to the verses: "Men more righteous and better than he" (I Kings 2:32); and "He [Saul] said to David: 'You are more righteous than I, for you have rendered unto me good, whereas I have rendered unto you evil'" (I Sam. 24:17). Here, too, the meaning is: She is more righteous than I, for she acted righteously, and I am the one who sinned against her by not giving her my son Shelah. The purport of the statement is that Shelah was the brother-in-law [hence he was the first designated to marry her, and if he did not wish to take her as his wife, his father is next in line to act as the redeemer, as I have explained above [on verse 8] when I discussed the law of marrying a childless brother's widow.]

- • 1. Does one of these three commentators agree with the view of R. Simeon the Pious?
  2. Copy the words *tzadkah mimeni* four times, and each time put in punctuation marks according to the explanations of Rashi; the explanation of the Rabbis cited by Rashi; Rashbam; and Ramban.
- • 3. What is the difference between the explanation of Rashbam and the explanation of Ramban?
  4. Why did Ramban add at the end of his explanation: "the purport of the statement is that Shelah..."? What difficulty did he want to resolve by that addition?
  5. In the explanation of the Rabbis cited by Rashi, the phrase *tzadkah mimeni* is broken down into a statement by Judah and a statement by the *bat-kol*. Where do we find in other explanations of Rashi that he treats a midrash similarly, and what is the reason he does this in that case?

See answers on p. 151–154.

A riddle

"And Er, Judah's firstborn, was evil in the eyes of the Lord"

(Gen. 38:7)

Note that Er in Hebrew is *ayin-resh;* evil in Hebrew is *resh-ayin*.
Bechor Shor – The beauty of the holy tongue is that some words can be read forwards and backwards; that is, Er can change into *ra*.

Where else do we find a similar example of the "beauty of the holy tongue" in Genesis?

• Indicates difficult questions   • • Very difficult questions

Study guide for gilyonot on the weekly portion by Nehama Leibowitz

Genesis *Vayeshev* 38

This chapter, especially the first portion, was discussed in the gilayon of *Vayeshev* 5708 – 1947. This is, in effect, a continuation of that gilayon.

This chapter abruptly interrupts the events of the episode of Joseph, and only in chapter 39 does the story line of Joseph in chapter 37 continue. In order to pick up the threads (see Rashi on 39:1: "When Joseph was taken down to Egypt") the commentator U. Cassuto tries to demonstrate that our section is a direct continuation of the preceding episode about the sale of Joseph (see his essay, "The Episode of Tamar and Judah," *Tzionim*, Festschrift in memory of Y. N. Simhoni, Eshkol Publ., Berin 1929, 93–100). We will quote some portions from that essay which enable us to understand the purpose of the midrashim cited in question A:

> What in particular has brought us around to the view that our chapter cannot be separated from what preceded it is the fact that there is a kind of internal connection between the episode of Tamar and Judah and the episode of the sale of Joseph. This is reflected in the correspondence of a number of details in one episode to details in the other, and becomes quite clear when we examine a number of corresponding idioms which are used in both episodes.
>
> In our chapter we have: "... she **sent** this message to her father-in-law, saying ... And she added, saying: '**Identify** these: whose signet, cord, and staff are these?' And Judah **identified**

them, and **said:** 'She is more in the right than I am'" (verses 25–26).

And in chapter 37 about Joseph: "And they **sent** the ornamental tunic … and they said: 'We found this. **Identify** it; it is your son's tunic or not?' And he **identified** it, and **said:** 'It is my son's tunic!'" (verses 32–33).

It is difficult to imagine that this correspondence is accidental; it is most certainly narrated intentionally. On the suggestion of Judah (37:6) Joseph was sold. In order to disguise this Judah and his brothers took Joseph's tunic, slaughtered a kid of the goats, dipped his tunic in blood, and sent it to their father, saying, … "Identify it" … and in his immense misery, from incomparable depths of grief, their elderly father looked at the tunic and said, "It is my son's tunic!'"

The Judge of all the world paid Judah back measure for measure for the misery he caused Jacob, for it was Judah who advised them to sell Joseph.

Immediately after the sale of Joseph a chain of events ensued which were to bring Judah the punishment he deserved. Just as Judah and his brothers **sent** their father the ornamental tunic and asked him to identify it, thus the various articles were **sent** to Judah and he was asked to identify them. Just as he and his brothers forced their father to identify the tunic, thus bringing upon him tremendous grief in acknowledging the death of his son ("And he **identified** it, and **said:** 'It is my son's tunic!'"), thus Judah was also forced to identify, to his great embarrassment and utter shame, the articles which were sent to him, and he had to acknowledge that the one who sent them to him was more in the right than he ("And Judah **identified** them, and **said**…").

At this point Cassuto adds a comment:

> The talmudic sages have already pointed out the correspondence between the repeated use of the expression "*haker na*" (identify it/them). (See *Sota* 10, and *Bereshit Rabbah*, sections 84 and 85.) Perhaps an additional point of correspondence should be added: the kid of the goats (37:31) and the kid of the flock (38: 17–20) (*Genesis Rabbah* 85), as well as other details.

On question A-2 about *Midrash Rabbah* 85:9 we might add the additional insight that the same "kid of the flock" symbolizes the crime and its punishment, measure for measure. Jacob had preceded Judah in using a kid of the flock for wrongdoing, and the midrash elaborates on this:

Torah Shelemah *Vayeshev* (181) from a midrash in the Schechter Genizah collections: "They slaughtered a kid of the goats" (Gen. 37:31) repays man measure for measure, and even the righteous of the world must pay measure for measure. The patriarch Jacob deceived his father using the skins of kids of the goats (Gen. 27: 16–17). Subsequently his sons deceive him with the same animal, as it says, "they slaughtered a kid of the goats and they dipped the tunic in the blood."

Answers to gilyonot of Nehama Leibowitz on the weekly portion by Yitzhak Reiner

Genesis *Vayeshev* 38

A. 1. a. The most precise formulation of the problem is that of Rashi on our verse, "About that time" – "Why is this section [about Judah and Tamar] placed here, thus interrupting the section dealing with the history of Joseph?" The Torah hints that the two sections are indeed related by opening with the phrase "About that time," thus joining the timing of the second section to that of the first [the sale of Joseph]. (See Rashi on Gen. 38:1 and the Study Guide.)

    b. Man's viewpoint, which is limited to seeing many details, cannot equal the comprehensive view of the Holy One, blessed be He – all inclusive as it is – which explains details in a macrocosmic plan, and weaves new connections which take on meaning when seen in this perspective. In Nehama's words: "Humans are busy with their own concerns, and see only the matters nearest to them. They don't know how their small concerns fit into the larger picture of the whole of history, which is guided by the One and Only."

    2. a. The meaning of God's laughing is that He returns measure for measure, and providentially guides history. (The Hebrew *m'saheket* implies a rueful, rather than a malicious, laughter. It also contains intimations of playing/toying with man in the sense of confounding man's attempts to get away with misdeeds – trans.)

b. Compare verses in chapter 38 with verses in chapter 37.
"She **sent** to her father-in-law" (38:25);
"They **sent** the ornamental tunic" (37:32).
"And she said**: Identify** them" (38:25);
"They said: **Identify** it" (37:32).
"And Judah **identified** them, and said…" (38:26);
"And he **identified** it, and said…" (37:32).
"And she **took off** her widow's garb" (38:14);
"They **stripped** Joseph of his tunic" (37:23).
"So he **returned** to Judah and said: '**I could not find her**'" (38:22);
"When Reuben **returned** to the pit and saw that Joseph **was not**…" (37:29).
See also the Study Guide.

3. a. There is a difference between the way in which the Torah is read in Hebrew (*kri*) and the way it is written (*ktiv*). The word for "she" is read as *hi* but it is written as *hu*.

b. R. Huna emphasizes Judah's struggle within himself, and against this background we can better appreciate his intention.

c. The word "saying" appears twice in the verse. "She sent this message to her father-in-law, **saying**: 'I am with child by the man to whom these belong.' And she added, **saying**: 'Identify these…'" When the Torah indicates that there is a repetition of the words of the person who is speaking and in between the two quotes there is no pause or response from the listener, then this is an indication that there was indeed a response but it is not explicitly stated.

Tamar: "I am with child by the man to whom these belong."
Judah: (Denies it, but his response is not recorded.)
Tamar: "Identify these."

See similar examples in Gen. 15:5 and Num. 32:3,5.

In addition, the language of beseeching, *haker na,* which literally means "Identify, **please**," indicates that she implored him to admit and acknowledge his role.

    d. The verbal phrase "identify these" (*haker na*) in the phrase "Identify these: whose signet, cord, and staff are these?" is superfluous. It would have been sufficient had she said "I am with child by the man to whom these belong. Whose signet, cord, and staff are these?"

In her reference to being "with child" there is a veiled reference to the Creator, who is a participant (along with the father and mother) in the creation of a child.

B. 1. The difference is in the order of presentation. Rashi bases himself on the verse, explaining a difficulty in the verse itself, and eventually generalizes about personal ethics: "From this passage our Rabbis derived the teaching."

On the other hand, the Gemara opens with a generalized rule of personal ethics, and then cites the verse to substantiate the rule.

Rashi – is a commentator, an explainer who comes to resolve difficulties in the verses.

The **Gemara** – often rules on points of law, and the verses serve as examples or proofs for the law.

    2. It says, "As she was being brought out," and does not say she was brought to the fire. They interpreted the Hebrew word for "she was brought out" *mutzet,* to be instead related to the phrase for "light a fire" – *hetzit esh.* That is, she was already burning in the fire; they had already lit the fire, *hetzitu esh.*

C. 1. Rashi: it was *kiddush HaShem* (sanctification of God's name) in that what came to light was not only part of the truth [as in the Joseph episode], but the full truth.

    2. Rashi: "She is more in the right; from me [she is pregnant]."

In Hebrew: "*Tzadkah, mimenu.*"

The Rabbis: "She is more in the right" (*bat-kol:* – "From Me").

In Hebrew: "*Tzadkah*" (– "*Mimeni*"*!*)
Rashbam: "She is more in the right than I am."
In Hebrew: *Tzadkah mimeni* (*yoter*).
Ramban: "She is a more righteous person than I am."
In Hebrew: "*Tzadkah mimeni.*"

3. According to Rashbam, there is a conditional agreement between two people. She fulfilled her part of the agreement, but I did not fulfill mine. She is right and I am not.
    According to Ramban, from our viewpoint as persons, she is a righteous person (*tzadeket*) and I am a sinner.

4. In what way did Judah err in not letting Shelah wed Tamar, and what did Tamar do that was righteous? Ramban explains that the subject here is the precept of levirate marriage (*yibum*), and Judah was obligated to give Shelah to Tamar in order to exempt himself from the obligation.

5. Rashi says on Gen. 37:20: "We will see what becomes of his dreams" – "The Holy Spirit (*Ruah Hakodesh*) said this latter part of the text." Then Rashi explains why he says this: "It is impossible that they would have said: 'We will see what becomes of his dreams,' because as soon as they would kill him, his dreams would be of no effect." Another example is Rashi's comment on Gen. 37:22. It is clear to Rashi that part of this verse is not said by Reuben, because it is in the third person, "from their hands" instead of "from your hands," and "to his father" instead of "to our father." Additionally, it is not logical that Reuben would reveal to his brothers his plan to return to save Joseph. Finally, if these were Reuben's words, in what way would this be a way to save Joseph, since he would perish from hunger or from snakes?

Answer to the Riddle:
Gen. 6:8: "Noah found favor..." Note that the two letters of the name Noah are reversed in the Hebrew word for favor:
nun-het (Noah)
het-nun (*hen* = favor).

MIKETZ
Genesis 41
Gilyonot on the weekly portion
by Nehama Leibowitz

A. Gen. 41:1: "After two years' time."

1. *Midrash Rabbah* Gen. 89:3: "Happy is the man who makes the Lord his trust" (Ps. 40:5) – this is Joseph. "Who turns not to the arrogant" (ibid.) – by his saying to the cupbearer: "But think of me ... and mention me," two years (in the prison house) were added for him: "After two years' time."

2. Rashi Gen. 40:23: "He forgot him" – afterwards, because Joseph had relied upon him to remember him, he had to remain a prisoner two additional years, as it is said, "Happy is the man who makes the Lord his trust, who turns not to the arrogant" (Ps. 40:5) – and does not trust the Egyptians, who are called "arrogant."

3. Targum Jonathan ben Uzziel Gen. 40:23: Because Joseph abandoned Divine mercy and relied upon the cupbearer, the servant of flesh-and-blood, for this the cupbearer did not remember Joseph but forgot him, until the time had come from the Lord for him to be freed.

- 1. Explain whether this midrash is in conflict with the view of *Akedat Yitzhak* on the portion of *Vayishlach* (see the Gilayon for *Vayishlach* 5715 – 1954*) and the Rabbinic midrashim cited in support of this view, or is there no contradiction between the above passage from *Genesis Rabbah* and the interpretation of *Akedat Yitzhak*?
- • 2. Explain the wording "this is Joseph" in *Genesis Rabbah*, which poses a difficulty for all the commentators.

B. the text narrative (verses 1–6)		**Pharaoh's narrative** (verses 17–24)	
v. 1(1)	standing by the Nile	v. 17	I was standing on the bank of the Nile
v. 2(2)	when out of the Nile there came up seven cows, handsome and sturdy	v. 18	when out of the Nile came up seven sturdy and well-formed cows
(3)	and they grazed in the reed grass		and grazed in the reed grass
v. 3(4)	But presently, seven other cows came up from the Nile	v. 19	Presently there followed them seven other cows –
(5)	ugly and gaunt		scrawny, ill-formed, and emaciated
(6)	and stood beside the cows on the bank of the Nile		—
(7)	—		never had I seen their likes for ugliness in all the land of Egypt
v. 4(8)	and the ugly gaunt cows ate up	v. 20	And the lean and ugly cows ate up
(9)	the seven handsome sturdy cows		the first seven cows, the sturdy ones
(10)	—	v. 21	but when they had consumed them, one could not tell that they had consumed them, for they looked just as bad as before

Haketav Vehakabbalah comments on this comparison:

Haketav Vehakabbalah (Gen. 41:17) *"Ba-Halomi hineni omed"*: The Torah spoke at length about the relating of Pharaoh's dream to Joseph, and did not speak in a concise and general manner: "And Pharaoh said to Joseph, 'I have had a dream,'" as the verse says of his speaking to his magicians and his wise men: "and Pharaoh told them his dreams, but none could interpret them for Pharaoh." It seems to me that this narrative comes to inform us of the greatness of God's providence over those who fear Him, because even though Pharaoh changed several things in the telling of the details of his dream, the meaning of which does not relate to its interpretation, nevertheless, this was caused by the Lord, may He be blessed, to inform Joseph of its interpretation as Pharaoh actually saw it, even though this does not coincide with his telling of his dream.

1. Explain, according to this, the reason for some of the changing, especially the omissions (verse 19) and the additions (end of verse 19, verse 21) that Pharaoh inserted in his telling of the dream.

   (For this manner of changes in the "telling," as opposed to the "event" itself, compare with the gilyonot: *Miketz* 5709 – 1948; *Vayehi* 5711 – 1950; *Pinchas* 5711 – 1951; and especially *Chayeh Sarah* 5712 – 1951; *Vayeshev* 5707 – 1946.)

2. Compare the following commentaries:

Abarbanel:
Now Pharaoh related his dream to Joseph, changing things, shortening the text in one place and lengthening in another, as matters required.

Radak on Gen. 24:39:
In truth, he managed everything as they were. We cannot give a reason for all the incompletions and completions, because they are many…. The repetition of these matters contains changes in wording, but the meaning is the same, because it is the practice of Scripture when repeating something, to **preserve the meanings**, but **not the wording.**

On Gen. 41:17, "*Va-yidaber Paro el Yosef*": We have already written, that when a person repeats something, he adds, detracts, or changes, and takes care only that the content remain the same, as is the case in this narrative of the dream.

Rabbi S. R. Hirsch:
It is interesting to compare what Pharaoh says he dreamt with the description above of what the dream actually was. Above, we heard an objective description of the dream, while here we see how it is reflected in the soul of Pharaoh.... When God wishes to tell somebody something in a dream, His speech, even when He speaks in metaphors, is always clear. But Pharaoh left out essential details.

Ha'amek Davar:
"Ba-halomi hineni omed": Scripture did not have to retell the story of the dream, but merely to say: and Pharaoh told Joseph his dream. Rather, this was done because it contained new things, precise details that had not been clarified the first time, and each detail has its own interpretation, as will be explained below.

(a) Explain the two methods of interpreting such repetitions, and what is the advantage of each method.
(b) Do you agree with the principle that "Scripture preserves the reasons, and not the words"?

3. Can you find a reason other than that offered by *Haketav Vehakabbalah* why the Torah spoke at length in relating the details of Pharaoh's dream in Pharaoh's speaking to Joseph (verses 17–21), and was not concise as in Pharaoh's speaking to the magicians (verse 8)?
See also Gen. 24:34-48, in comparison with 24:66.

• Indicates difficult questions   • • Very difficult questions
See answers on p. 162.

* The commentary of *Akedat Yitzhak* is appended to the Study Guide; see p. 160–161.

Study guide for gilyonot on the weekly portion by Nehama Leibowitz
Genesis *Miketz* 33:1–11

Although one gilayon is usually not related to another, and each examines a separate topic and raises a different question, in accordance with the Torah portion and the section selected from it, this time question A in the current gilayon is nevertheless connected with question A in the *Vayishlach* gilayon (see p. 160–161). Here as well, as in that gilayon, we discuss the question of the bounds of human activity, as opposed to "Cast your burden on the Lord" (Ps. 55:23). It is probably worthwhile to begin the lesson with a perusal of the commentary of *Akedat Yitzhak* that was cited in the *Vayishlach* gilayon, to be followed by the midrash in *Genesis Rabbah* quoted in the current gilayon (question A). Is there a contradiction between the two? Can it be that what *Akedat Yitzhak* seems to find praiseworthy in the actions of Jacob, Samuel, and David – human effort and "diligence" – are denigrated by the midrash?

The students are to examine these instances and see if there is a difference between their behavior and that of Joseph; or perhaps there is no difference, and do these sources present two different philosophies?

The lesson should possibly begin with question B, because it is not concerned with a single verse, but rather encompasses the first half of each chapter. The verses are printed in the gilayon in a manner that emphasizes the differences, thus avoiding the need for excessive page turning. The teacher of the lesson should not provide an explanation for the changes until the students themselves have voiced their opinions. In every study circle, even among young pupils, there will surely be someone who will offer an explanation for the additions in Pharaoh's statement in verse 19 (the seventh line on the right), and for the additions in his words in verse 21 (the last line). The teacher should not be hasty in giving his answers but should wait patiently, perhaps the students will be able to put forth a reason, why Pharaoh used so many adjectives in his description of the lean cows (line 5). The students' intellectual satisfaction is always greater if they themselves succeed in discovering something. The teacher must be patient and allow his students **of all ages** to search, to feel their way, to hypothesize, to offer logical arguments, until they weary of this pursuit. Only then should the teacher offer his explanation.

The teacher who possesses gilyonot from past years would be well advised to bring to the students' attention at least some of the references mentioned above in the current gilayon, to show the students that changes of this type (which are always made in reference to the **speaker** or the **audience**) are a normal occurrence in the Torah. It is especially recommended to draw to the students' attention the gilayon for *Chayeh Sarah* 5712 – 1951. If this gilayon is not available to the student, he should at least examine the difference between Genesis 24:22–23 and 24:47, and Rashi loc. cit., "*Va-eshal va-asim*"; and the difference between verses 1 and 35 in that chapter.

This is to be followed by an examination of the two schools of interpretation, that of Abarbanel, Hirsch, *Ha'amek Davar* (which is consistently followed by Malbim as well), on the one hand, and that of Radak, on the other (question B.2). The students must decide: Does Radak, who is usually regarded as providing a literal interpretation, to be so regarded in this instance as well? In the light of all that we have seen, does the lack of precision regarding each word and ignoring the search for a reason for the change constitute a method leading to an understanding of the literal meaning of the text?

Incidentally, if the students reveal interest in this methodology, then they should also read the commentary of **Ibn Ezra** on the Ten Commandments (Ex. 20:1), from "Abraham said: It is the practice of those employing the Holy Tongue" to "and many others, only a single reason will be found for different wording," and so afterwards, from "We will now speak about *Zakhor* and *Shamor*, know that the reasons are preserved, and not the words" to "and thus did Moses."

*Vayishlach 5715 – 1954 [for comparative study]

A. Akedat Yitzhak, in his introduction to the portion of *Vayishlach*: "Truly the eye of the Lord is on those who fear Him … to save them from death" (Ps. 33:18) – but effort and diligence are of greater avail for them, because the absence of effort and the lack of diligence where necessary is a sin. As the Rabbis explained in *Midrash Shohar Tov* on Ps. 23:

"Indeed, the Lord your God has blessed you in all your undertakings" (Deut. 2:7). Rabbi Eliezer ben Jacob: "Has blessed you" – one might think, that this also applies to one who sits idly by? The verse teaches you (otherwise): "In all your undertakings." If one acts, he is blessed; and if he does not (act), he is not blessed. What is the meaning of "He has known (*yoda*) your wanderings" (Ibid.)? *Hilukhekh* (your waking, that is similar in sound to) *likhluhekh* (your dirtiness), the trouble you encountered in (earning) your livelihood.

(Note especially: the midrash understands "**yoda**" as similar to the wording in Genesis 18:20: "I will take note (yodati): see Rashi ad loc.)

Discernment is to follow both of these: if in the direction of his actions, for them always to be pleasing to the Lord; and if what he discerns as a purpose in his affairs, what is possible, and that he not abandon diligence and effort as one who is assured of his merit or (conversely) as one who despairs, rather he must act **to the limit of his abilities**. He should not, however, expect that he will attain his heartfelt desires other than by the Divine will of the One who possesses all, and Who encompasses all. As the wise man said, "A man may plot out his course, but it is the Lord who directs his steps" (Prov. 6:9).... Every person must regard himself as one whose effort will be of avail to him (and not rely upon his merits), and one like him who heeds the words of God, who said to Samuel: "Take a heifer with you, and say, 'I have come to sacrifice to the Lord'" (I Sam. 16:2).

... And who do we have who is as great and beloved by his God as our master David, who was assured by the prophet who was faithful to the Lord and to all Israel, but nevertheless was not deterred from exerting every possible effort to extricate himself from the hands of all his enemies and from the hands of Saul? He did not rely upon His promises, because he knew that the salvation of the Lord and His promises would be given only to the one who **does his part** in his human activities, to the extent that his intellect allows. This is what obligated him to conceal his good sense, to feign madness, and to let saliva run down his beard (see I Sam. 21), even though this was revolting, contemptible, and repugnant, because he had the possibility of doing so, and this was one method of rescue, even though despicable. As he said there: "I turned to the Lord, and He answered me; He saved me from all my terrors" (Ps. 34:5). After he had (seemingly) changed his nature and done all that was possible, he asked that the Lord rescue him, and then He responded and saved him from all his terrors – which would not have been appropriate to do if he had **not** done everything humanly possible to ensure his success.

This is what is explained by his prayer in the cave (Ps. 142): "Look at my right and see – I have no friend; there is nowhere I can flee, no one cares about me. So I cry to You, O Lord; I say, 'You are my refuge' … listen to my cry … free my soul from prison…." He said that he had already turned hither and yon, to be aided by all possible effort from human actions, but he found no (succor), neither in terms of fleeing to any friend or supporter, because he had no friend; nor mental flight, because he could not escape; nor by means of reconciliation and appeal, because no one cared about him. When every possible form of effort had been exhausted, what was left for him? Only his outcry and his prayer. It is to this that he refers when he says: "listen to my cry … free my soul from prison."

Answers to gilyonot of Nehama Leibowitz on the weekly portion by Yitzhak Reiner

Genesis *Miketz* 41

A. 1.   There would seem to be a conflict here. The midrash on this verse says: Await the salvation of the Lord, and do not turn to the aid of humans. *Akedat Yitzhak* says: Make all possible human efforts, but nevertheless await the salvation of the Lord. This contradiction may be resolved as follows: Joseph, who saw that his entire way in life was miraculous (the dreams, the interpretation of the dreams), and was subject to constant Divine Providence, did not have to ask for special aid from this Egyptian.

Another possible method of resolving the contradiction:

Joseph, in whose mouth the name of God was familiar (see Rashi on 39:3), and who said to the courtiers, "Surely God can interpret!" (Gen. 40:8), did not mention God's name in reference to his rescue, which he attributed solely to the Egyptian: "so as to free me from this place" (40:14). He thereby deviated from the rule given by Akedat Yitzhak concerning the correct proportion in which a person should direct his efforts. The Netziv writes about the midrash: "This is Joseph, who, by his saying, 'But think of me,' had two years added for him": This is the punishment that we have heard was given to Joseph, who had never turned to the arrogant among humans, and was accordingly punished, for having changed his regular attribute. This is a general rule, that when a person customarily has a good quality, this becomes as a vow for him, and if he later violates this, he is punished. (See the Netziv on Gen. 32:26, *Beherhev Davar*, n. 1, and also on the current verse, *Beherhev Davar*, n. 1.)

2. "This is Joseph" – this refers to the specific event that befell Joseph (that is, that in this instance he turned to the arrogant).

B. Before reading our answer, take another look at the Study Guide, on the importance of personal exertion in the discovery of an explanation in general, and for the changes in the case before us. After having made this effort, here are additional criteria that you may not have thought of, for examining what is added or missing in the two versions.

a. Within a dream, the dreamer does not critically examine what he sees, there are no thoughts regarding the dream, and no questions are raised; none of this is possible. When one awakens and relates the dream (to himself or to another), then responses arise: "Wonderful!", "How beautiful!", "This is impossible" (lines 7, 10).

b. A person describes at length things that made a strong impression on him, and will be concise in his depiction of regular events. (He therefore spoke at length and added details in the portrayal of the bad ones.)

163

c. If a person does not comprehend the meaning of the dream, he will not pay attention to details that are of significance only to the one who understands the interpretation of the dream. For example, line 6: "and they stood beside the cows on the bank of the Nile," i.e., the lean years will immediately follow the bountiful ones.

d. As for line 1, Pharaoh omits the main emphasis: "by the Nile," not understanding that this is the key to the interpretation of the dream. Egypt's power and wealth lie in the Nile, and its harvest is dependent upon the river. In his narrative, the Nile is incorporated in the landscape.

2. a. Radak represents the school of thought that sees no significance in stylistic changes. The other commentators, in contrast, ascribe importance to every change, i.e., additions or omissions. In your efforts to answer question B.1, you undoubtedly dicovered intellectual wealth and a plethora of meanings that emerged from a comparison of the versions. On the other hand, we are liable to "get lost" and build castles in the air if we do not place limits upon our imaginations.

b. No. This principle is simply incorrect. If you say "Please don't talk" or if you were to say "Shut your mouth!" you have not said the same **thing** (= "preserve the meanings"), merely in other words, you rather have said two different things. We have before us two different worlds, each with its own atmosphere.

3. The only significance to the interpretation by the magicians is the fact that they were unsuccessful in interpreting the dreams. The details are of no intrinsic importance. This is not so regarding the interpretation by Joseph, who found the correct associations, and with G-d's help completed what was missing in the description; in this case, the content of the interpretation and the way of reaching it, despite the "misleading" elements – the omissions and additions, this is the message of the Torah.

VAYIGASH
Genesis 45:25-28; 46:1-6
Gilyonot on the weekly portion
by Nehama Leibowitz

A. Gen. 45:2: "But when they recounted all that Joseph had said..."

Ramban Gen. 45:27: "But when they recounted all that Joseph had said"– It seems to me that the literal interpretation is that Jacob was not told his entire life that his brothers had sold Joseph. He rather thought that he had been wandering in the field, and that those who found him had taken him and sold him to Egypt. His brothers did not want to tell him of their sin, for they feared for their lives, lest he become angry and curse them, as he had done to Reuben, Simeon, and Levi (49:3–7, below). Joseph, who possessed a good nature, also did not want to tell him. It therefore is said, "So they sent this message to Joseph. 'Before his death your father left this instruction ... "Forgive, I urge you, the offense and guilt of your brothers"'" (Gen. 50:16–17). If Jacob had known of this, they should have beseeched their dying father to command Joseph from his own mouth, so that he [Joseph] would look directly at him and not disobey him and they would therefore not be in danger and would not have to fabricate things.

1. Explain why Ramban saw fit to give this explantion for this verse. What difficulty in this verse is explained by his commentary?

2. Can any verses be cited from *Vayehi*, from Jacob's blessing, that will either prove or refute Ramban's interpretation?

B. Gen. 46:1: So Israel set out with all that was his..."
Gen. 46:2: "G-d called to Israel in a vision by night..."

Can you explain why he is called "Israel" here, and not as in 45:25,27, and in this chapter, verse 5?

(For questions of this type, see *Miketz* 5706 – 1946, question A: *Chayeh Sarah* 5713 – 1952, question B.)

165

C.   Gen. 46:1: "So Israel set out with all that was his, and he came to Beer-sheba, where he offered sacrifices to the God of his father Isaac."
Rashi Gen. 46:1: "To the God of his father Isaac" – a person has a greater obligation to honor his father than his grandfather: [the sacrifices] are therefore associated with Isaac, and not with Abraham.
1. What difficulty did he have?
• • 2. The supercommentaries on Rashi raise the objection to his interpretation: "But these are not the words of Jacob, rather Scripture calls him 'the God of his father Isaac'?" Respond to their question, and remove the objection against Rashi's interpretation.
3. Can you resolve the difficulty in this verse, with the help of Gen. 26:2?

D.   Gen. 46:3: "Fear not to go down to Egypt...."
Abarbanel asks: Why did the Holy One, blessed be He, have to tell Jacob: "Fear not to go down to Egypt," since he did not fear this: before this statement, he said: "I must go and see him before I die," and he had already set out, as it says, "So Israel set out with all that was his"?
Try to answer his question.

E.   Gen. 46:4: "I Myself will go down with you to Egypt and I Myself will also bring you back [literally, I will bring you back also (*gam*) bring back]...."
1.   **Rashbam** Gen. 46:4: "[I] Myself will also bring you back," that is, I will go down with you, and I will also bring you back, similar to: "And may you bring a blessing upon me also! [literally, may you bring a blessing also (*gam*) upon me]" (Ex. 12:32).
• • What is the difficulty common to this verse and to the verse from Exodus, and what is Rashbam's method of resolving such a problem? (Make use of Rashbam on Gen. 29:30, "*Vaye'ehav gam et Rahel.*")
2.   **Rashi** Gen. 46:4: "I Myself will bring you back" – He promised him that he would be buried in Eretz Israel.
Sforno Gen. 46:4: "I Myself will also bring you back

[*a'alakha gam aloh*, literally... bring you up]" – after I bring you up and bring you forth from there, you will have an advantage (*ma'aleh*) in addition to what you had before you went down there, as it is said: "and to bring them out of that land to a good and spacious land."

a. What difficulty does each commentator have with this verse?

b. What is the main difference between their responses? (See the gilayon for *Chayeh Sarah* 5715 – 1954. B.1.2.)

3. **Mechilta**. *Beshalach, Masechet De-Shirah* 3 (on the Song at the Sea). "This is my God and I will glorify Him":

The Rabbis say: "And I will glorify Him" – I will accompany Him until I come with Him to His Temple. This is comparable to a king whose son went to a faraway land, and he set forth after him and stood by him. He went to another land, and he went forth and stood by him. So too, Israel: when they went down to Egypt, the Divine Presence was with them, as it is said: "I Myself will go down with you to Egypt." When they came up, the Divine Presence was with them, as it is said, "I Myself will also bring you back." They went down to the sea – the Divine Presence was with them, as it is said, "The angel of God, who had been going ahead of the Israelite army, now moved and followed behind them" (Ex. 14:19). They went forth to the wilderness – the Divine Presence was with them, as it is said, "The Lord went before them in a pillar of cloud by day, to guide them along the way" (Ex. 13:21).

How does the interpretation of our verse by the Mechilta differ from the above interpretations?

F. Gen. 46:4:... and Joseph's hand shall close your eyes."

Ibn Ezra Gen. 46:4: "... and Joseph's hand shall close your eyes" – upon your death, as is the practice of the living with the dead.

Sforno Gen. 46:4: "... [his] hand shall close your eyes" – you will not need to open your eyes to attain what you desire, because Joseph will labor on your behalf, without your attention. You will not have to deal with the Egyptians, who are not worthy to approach you.

Ha'amek Davar: This contains a wonderful promise for the very existence of the nation in Egypt, and the meaning of "your eyes" is Jacob's desire and the special attribute that Jacob provided for this. It is interpreted in the portion of *Vezot Haberachah* (Deut. 33:28) "Thus Israel dwells in safety [*betah*], alone [*badad*] is Jacob's abode [*ein*, literally, eye]," in which "*ein Yaakov*" means to dwell in safety, alone with **betah** meaning to be at peace and with the attribute of love between man and his fellow, and **badad** means not to intermingle more than is necessary with the non-Jewish nations.... As regards **badad,** Joseph endeavored with all his might that Israel not assimilate among the Egyptians. (See the gilayon on *Vezot Haberachah* 5711 – 1951, question C.)

1. What weakness did Sforno find in the interpretation of Ibn Ezra, that seems to be the meaning of the text, and forced him to offer a different interpretation?

2. Can you find in the portion of *Vayigash* support for the commentary of *Ha'amek Davar*, that Joseph attempted to keep Israel isolated in Egypt?

3. Can you find in the commentary of *Ha'amek Davar* any indication of the period of the commentator (the Netziv Rabbi Naphtali Zvi Judah Berlin, last third of the nineteenth century, notably the period of Hibbat Zion)?

• Indicates difficult questions   • • Very difficult questions

* ***Pesikta Rabbati*** 3: see the quotation from the *Pesikta* in the Study Guide.

Ha'amek Davar: The interpretation of "**betah**" consists of metal tranquility, love between man and his fellow, without competition with the other nations of the world; while "**badad**" means: without excessive intermingling with the non-Jewish nations in friendship and in marital ties, rather *badad* – separated and by themselves. These two attributes are "*ein Yaakov*" – Jacob's nature and desire was that his sons would act in this manner.

See also: Gen. 17:6–8: "and make nations of you ... I give the land you sojourn in to you and your offspring to come, all the land of Canaan":

Ha'amek Davar: "And make nations of you" – that you will teach knowledge to the nations, like the matter that is written in Jer. 1, "I appointed you a prophet concerning the nations." i.e. that he would prophesy to them as well. This is the interpretation here, that you make wise and impart knowledge to the non-Jewish nations. Verse 8: " I give the land you sojourn in": so that Abraham would not say that this alone is Israel's purpose, to wander among the nations and to make them wise; if so, they would not have title to settle in the world **to live an independent state life**. Consequently, it restated and explained that at the end of all this would be: "I give to you all the land of Canaan."

Study guide for gilyonot on the weekly portion by Nehama Leibowitz

Genesis *Vayigash* 45:25–18; 46:1–6

Before the students begin to answer the questions in this gilayon, they must first read all of Chapter 41, beginning from the moment when Joseph reveals himself to his brothers, to Jacob's departure from the land of Canaan. Close study should be devoted to Joseph's meeting with his brothers, which is replete with conciliatory and placatory statements to his brothers, words of peace, forgiveness, and encouragement. Above all, they contain an explanation of everything that has befallen him, both ascents and descents, his brothers' hatred of him and his sufferings, in the words: "it was not you who sent me here, but God." He then shifts to a description of the mission to his father and his invitation to Jacob to come down to Egypt. The lengthy treatment afforded this subject by the Torah is not purposeless, because at this point the time of our forefathers' descent to Egypt is drawing near. The arrival of the brothers in the land of Canaan is to be followed by a reading of Ramban's commentary on verse 27 (question A), which constitutes a sort of preface and explanation for all that will come to pass until the death of Jacob. For those who do not have the *gilayon* for *Vayehi* 5711 – 1950, we will cite the *Pesikta*, which strongly supports the view of Ramban:* *Pesikta Rabbati* 3: "Some time afterward, Joseph was told: 'Your father is ill'" (Gen. 48:1). Who told him that his father is ill? According to one opinion, he saw this with Divine Inspiration. According to another view, Bilhah, who attended Jacob, informed him; when he fell ill, she came and told Joseph. According to yet another opinion, Benjamin disclosed this to Joseph. But, was not Joseph worthy of praise because he was so exceedingly respectful of his father and went in to him all the time? And if others had not come and told him that his father was ill, he would not have known this? This rather teaches you of his righteousness, that he did not want to be alone with his father, lest Jacob say to him: "Is this how your brothers have treated you?" and curse them. Joseph said, "I know my father's righteousness, and everything that he says comes to pass ... and I will come and tell him to curse them?" He therefore did not go in to his father all the time.

Regarding question A.2, the students may bring a proof to refute Ramban from the commentary of Rashi on 49:7, *"Ikru shor"*; Rashi on 49:9, *"Mi-teref beni alita"*; and Rashi on 49:23, *"Va-robu."* It should be explained to the students that Rashi consistently followed another view, but all three verses (7, 9, 23) may also be explained well in accordance with the commentary of Ramban, and they do not contain any proof that Jacob did indeed know of the sale of Joseph by his brothers. The student must also be aware that the general language of this verse (45:27) lends itself to different interpretations, since "all that Joseph had said" could be interpreted as **all** his statements in this chapter, beginning with verse 2, or everything that he sent to say to his father, beginning with verse 9.

A. 1.   The students' attention should be drawn to Ramban's comment on "**Joseph, who spoke only well**," and to his proof from 3:16–17.

Question B.2, which is concerned with the name change from Jacob to Israel, cannot be easily resolved. Let the students try their best. Attention should also be paid to this change among the two names in the portion of *Vayeshev*, chapter 37, between verse 2 and verse 13, the verse in which our forefathers' descent to Egypt begins.

The importance of this question lies in inculcating in the minds of the students the understanding that nothing in the language of the Torah, either major or minor, is incidental. The change of a name or appellation is always significant. If the teacher sees that the students are interested in this question (or that they find it strange that such a minor detail as a name change is actually of significance), he should direct their attention to Gen. 42:1–6, in which Joseph's brothers are called in five verses: "Jacob's sons," "Joseph's brothers," "Benjamin's brothers," "the sons of Israel," and once again "Joseph's brothers," with the reason easily understandable in each case. They might also peruse Rashi on 42:3, *"Ahei Yosef"* (and Rashi on 19:1, *"Ha-Malakhim"*), and the interchange of appellations between "servant" and "man" in Gen. 24.

The citing of many sources such as these to clarify a certain interpretive rule is appropriate only for advanced students, who possess the expertise to be quite familiar with these passages, because the taking of examples from different places is liable to only confuse other groups of students. The teacher must therefore properly evaluate the ability of his audience to absorb such information.

Question D is suitable to all students. In this case, they can consider Jacob's condition when he left his land – the land promised to Abraham, to Isaac, and to him – and provide an answer.

Incidentally, here too the teacher **can** show his students parallel passages. Each of the Patriarchs was promised with the wording "Fear not": Abraham – 15:1; Isaac – 26:24. In these other two passages as well no mention is made what, or from what, the Patriarch feared, and the commentators have given many answers.

The last part of the lesson must concentrate only on

question **5.2–3.** The students must understand that verse 4 is not only God's promise to Jacob on the eve of his going down to Egypt, but also the words of the Lord **to Israel** as they go forth to exile and to all the lands of their exile. The promise "I Myself will also bring you back" was not given to an individual, but to the nation. Of great importance here is the comparison with what we learned in the gilayon to *Chayeh Sarah* 5715 – 1954. B.2. The observation taken from the Mechilta was stated in different language in *Megillah* 29a. If the lesson is held in a synagogue or study hall where copies of the Talmud are to be found, the version of the Gemara should be read, beginning from "It has been taught: Rabbi Simon ben Yohai says, Come and see how beloved are Israel before the Holy One, blessed be He," because these words are of inestimable importance, and they explain the secret of our existence to the present.

Answers to gilyonot of Nehama Leibowitz on the weekly portion by Yitzhak Reiner

Genesis *Vayigash* 45:25–28; 46:1–6

(Note: pay close attention to the Study Guide on this portion; the answers complement what is written in the Guide.)

A. 1. Is the word "all" in the verse "But when they recounted all that Joseph had said" to be understood literally, implying that they also told him about the sale? (45:4, 5, 8)

Or, does the word "all" relate only to Joseph's instruction in 45:9: "… and say to him: Thus says your son Joseph…." If they had spoken as the first alternative suggests, why was there no response by Jacob to this?

2. It would seem that there was some response. Verses 49:9: "Judah is a lion's whelp; on prey, my son, have your grown" – see Rashi, "*Beni alita*"; 49:23: "Archers bitterly assailed him" – see Ibn Ezra on this verse: "They already bore a grudge against him; this alludes to his brothers, who sold him"; see the Study Guide, beginning with "Regarding question A.2, the students may bring proof to refute Ramban…"

B.   Israel, the father of the nation, because here we are on the threshold of a decisive turning point in the annals of the people of Israel, on the eve of the Egyptian bondage. It should be added that the name Israel teaches that Jacob was in full command of his spiritual powers at that time, after having been informed that Joseph was alive.

    See Rabbi S. R. Hirsch on Gen. 45:28, and the analysis of Rashi on 46:2, "*Yaakov Yaakov.*"

C. 1.   He had difficulty in understanding why Jacob did not mention Abraham as well, since he had mentioned him in his prayer in Gen. 32:10: "Then Jacob said, 'O God of my father Abraham and God of my father Isaac.'"

   2.   The text speaks here from the perspective of Jacob.

   3.   Jacob offered sacrifices to the God of his father Isaac because Isaac was forbidden to go down to Egypt, and Jacob, as he relates to that event, presumably asks permission from his God.

D.   When Jacob is informed that Joseph is alive, he reacts as a father, and wants to see him immediately. On the other hand, during the preparations for the journey to Egypt and the Divine revelation "in a vision by night," there is an allusion to the visions of exile. In the addressing of "Jacob, Jacob," and not "Israel," the harsh meaning of his going down is revealed to Jacob, from which his fear ensues. Regarding this, the Lord says to him: "Fear not to go down to Egypt."

E. 1.   Why "also" in addition? And as in Exodus, "also" Myself – who else? Gen. 29:30: most instances of "gam [also]" in the Torah relate to a different syntactical position in the verse. Consequently, in Exodus the blessing "also" of me means: also bless me, and here as well, "I Myself will bring you back also."

  2. a. Rashi's problem: but Jacob did not come up to Eretz Israel?

Sforno's problem: the repetitious language: *"a'alakha gam aloh."*

b. Does the Holy One, blessed be he, speak to the personal Jacob, the individual, or does He address Jacob the people, the descendants?

3. The emphasis is upon "and I," as if to say, I will be with you also, and also in the other places to which you will go. According to Rashi and Sforno, "I Myself will bring you back also" is an additional promise, while the Mekhilta regards this wording as the continuation of the promise in the first part of the verse: "I Myself will go down with you," and I will be with you afterwards as well.

F. 1. In the sequence of prior promises that speak about life, this promise, which talks about death, seems to be exceptional.

2. Joseph makes no effort to obtain positions for his brothers in the palace of Pharaoh. Consequently, he advises them to present themselves as shepherds; since sheep were an abomination to the Egyptians, this would keep them apart from the latter. Also, he arranged for them to live in the distant region of Goshen.

3. The Netziv fought the desire to assimilate and was aware of the Jewish mission to be a light unto the nations. This task could be fulfilled if we will be "a people that dwells apart" (Num. 23:9) in its land and homeland.

And thus the Netziv interprets Gen. 17:6: "I will make nations of you" – that you will teach knowledge to the nations, like the matter that is written in Jer. 1, "I appointed you a prophet concerning the nations," and afterwards he is promised: " I give the land you sojourn in to you and your offspring to come." A further interpretation: so that Abraham would not say that this alone is Israel's purpose, to wander among the nations; if so, they would not have title to settle in the world to live an independent state life. Consequently, it restated and explained that at the end of all this would be: "I give to you all the land of Canaan."

Nehama Leibowitz
Teacher of Torah

This beautifully written and comprehensive article on Nehama was written by Dr. Gabriel Cohen, himself a distinguished educator and scholar who was closely associated with Nehama for many years. He manages to put all the subjects covered in this book into one short essay.

– L.A.

BDD *Bekhol Derakhekha Daehu*
Journal of Torah and Scholarship, No. 6 – Winter 1998
Editor Cyril Domb
Sub-Editors Yehuda Friedlander and Daniel Sperber
BAR-ILAN UNIVERSITY PRESS, RAMAT-GAN

AN APPRAISAL IN COMMEMORATION OF HER FIRST YAHRZEIT, FIFTH OF NISAN 5758

In this article on Nehama Leibowitz, written to commemorate her first Yahrzeit on the 5th of Nisan 5758, the author outlines features which account for her uniqueness. He suggests three basic reasons for her phenomenal success as a Torah teacher: her warm and interesting personality, her pedagogical grasp and didactic skill, and her ability to translate classical Jewish exegesis into the language of our generation.

The article describes how Nehama Leibowitz succeeded in adapting the Yeshiva method of learning Talmud to the study of Tanach, and how she thereby transformed Torah study into an intellectual, emotional and moral challenge.

Special attention is paid to her contribution to increased study of Jewish commentators among various groups of Bible scholars. We focus particularly on her revelation of the P'shat aspect of rabbinic Midrashim, which form the basis of Jewish exegesis through the generations.

Nehama Leibowitz was probably the greatest Torah teacher (in the plain sense of the word Torah) in our generation. For almost 70 years she taught Torah, and attracted an enormous number of students – old and young, religious and secular, Israelis and foreign students, *Talmidei Hachamim* and *Amei Ha'aretz* – who came to study Torah with this world renowned teacher.

Many of us ask ourselves what made Nehama Leibowitz such an outstanding teacher, what made her contribution to Torah learning so remarkable. I think three components made the life and work of Nehama Leibowitz so unique: her personality, her teaching abilities, and her special approach to the exegesis of the Bible. These three traits were strongly interwoven in the activities of Nehama Leibowitz, and they influenced one another in a most creative way.

1. Personal Student – Teacher Relationship

One must first mention the charming and warm personality of Nehama Leibowitz. Despite her remarkable pedagogical skills, Nehama could not have captured the hearts of so many disciples had it not been for her personal relationship with each individual. This was clearly manifested in the personal discussions which she conducted with her pupils. Her genuine interest in their daily activities and in their spiritual environment created a cordial bond between her and her students. The very fact that she requested all her friends and students to address her simply as "Nehama" created, at the outset, an atmosphere of intimacy.[1] Her outstanding simplicity – her apartment contained only bare necessities and her appearance bespoke modesty – facilitated a direct relationship with her.

In Israel it was also well known that Nehama was prepared to travel to any place where her presence would increase Torah learning; she was never deterred by the amount of effort or time needed for the journey. In contrast, Nehama refused to travel as a guest speaker to the Diaspora, despite many attractive invitations. She suggested to those who issued these invitations that they should come to participate in her shiurim in Jerusalem. As a result, Nehama did not leave Israel for an unbroken period of more than 60 years.

Moreover, the whole system of worksheets (gilyonot) which she innovated was based on a personal bond with each student. Thousands of people regularly replied to her questions on the weekly *Sidra*, and she related to each and every one individually. For the correction of the replies she never made use of an assistant in spite of her professorial status.

The following story illustrates the extent to which Nehama was personally involved with those who answered her worksheets. Shimon Bar Chama, the Vice Principal of the famous Reali High School in Haifa, used to send her answers regularly every week during the 1940s. During his military service he participated in a long army course, and his coded address was "The Convalescent Home, Ein Hashofet." On the first occasion Nehama responded to the new address she added "How nice it is that even in a convalescent home Torah is studied"; but when he continued to send his answers from there she posed an anxious question: "Are you unfortunately unwell that you are obliged to spend such a long period in convalescence?"

The worksheets were specifically designed to cater for the needs of students at different levels (using the letter X to indicate harder questions). Also, in lessons that she taught to various groups Nehama obligated each person to participate actively. Anyone who had not brought a text to the class was not allowed to come into the lesson. She was not prepared to accept a situation in which two students shared a text. From time to time she posed questions the answers to which every student was required to write on a sheet of paper in front of him, while Nehama walked around the room examining each answer and commenting on it. Even when, after much hesitation, the books of *Studies* were published, she always included at the end of each study questions for further thought, which she encouraged her pupils to answer.

2. Personal Student – Text Relationship

The basis of Nehama's approach as a teacher and expositor of Torah was the demand that she made on students to wrestle with the text. She presented her students with a range of commentaries on a particular verse and asked them to analyse these commentaries and relate to them.

But her great innovation was not that they should study Rashi and other commentaries, but that they should study *with* Rashi. At Nehama's shiurim one could imagine all the commentators (midrashic, medieval, and modern) seated around the table and contending with the meaning of the text. In practice, what Nehama did was to adapt the Yeshiva method of studying Talmud. Just as in the Gemara, *Tanna'im*, *Amoraim*, *Saboraim*, *Rishonim*, and *Aharonim*, deliberated upon the sugiah, so too in Torah study commentators from different generations participate in an intensive and continuous symposium.

This is how the late Rabbi J. B. Soloveitchik describes the adventure of Gemara learning which Nehama adapted for Torah study:

> When I sit down to study, I immediately find myself in the company of the scholars of the *Mesorah*. The relationship between us is personal. Rambam on my right, Rabbenu Tam on my left, Rashi sits at the head and explains, Rabbenu Tam queries, Rambam decides, Raavad challenges, they are all in my small room sitting around my table. They gaze upon me with affection, chatting with me about logical reasoning and Gemara, encouraging and fortifying me like a father. Torah study is not just a didactic process, involvement with Torah texts is not just a technical and formal matter which is accomplished through the existence and exchange of ideas. It is a powerful experience of "comradeship" with many generations, a marriage of spirit with spirit, a unification of soul with soul. Those who handed down the Torah and those who received it enjoy hospitality at the same historic Inn.[2]

Indeed, by analogy with Yeshiva learning, Nehama demanded that her students wrestle with Rashi and find answers to the questions. Thus, Nehama asked not only what Rashi said, but also sought to clarify "what bothered Rashi"; what was the textual basis for his comments and what is the essential meaning of his interpretation. Nehama dealt with other commentators such as Ibn Ezra, Rashbam, and Ramban similarly.

In addition, her students were then given the task of comparing two interpretations to decide which of them was closer to the simple meaning of the text, linguistically and in its general context. In this way each student indicated the choice which appealed to him from among the traditional commentators. The personal struggle of the student with the Torah text and its commentators converted the study into a powerful intellectual challenge, and each of the students saw in the text his own Torah. In this respect, Nehama based herself on the observation of Ludwig Strauss that the understanding of a piece of literature depends not only on the writer but also on the reader who approaches it with his own spiritual essence. Through the constant thrust and parry of debating with the text and its commentators the student adopts the Torah for himself and identifies with it. He also fulfills the requirement that a person should see himself in the very situation to which the verse refers. This is how Nehama defined this educational aim in connection with Psalms.

> My purpose is not that you should read these Psalms as documents relating to days gone by, but as poetry that is timeless. The "I" who speaks in these chapters is not the "I" of King David or Assaf or the Sons of Korach, the "I" who speaks or weeps or pleads, expresses joy and gives thanks for it, is the "I" of the reader at the moment when contemplating the words of the Psalm.[3]

Nehama was conscious of the dangers inherent in this approach, and reflected that it might not be appropriate for youngsters of 15 or 16 to decide which interpretation to accept and which to reject.

> ... If all this is done in a proper spirit, the spirit of serious in-depth analysis of the commentaries – and the purpose of this method is to train the student to analyse, and to deter him from haste and superficiality – there is no disrespect. On the contrary, proper regard for scholars consists of studying in depth what they have written.[4]

3. Jewish Interpretation of Scripture

Nehama was a teacher of outstanding talent, familiar with all the didactic methods of interesting her audience of pupils in the learning of Torah; she also described these methods in her writings.[5] She transformed, as we have said, Torah learning into an intellectually exciting experience. However, we would err if we thought that her contribution to Torah learning was limited to mere pedagogics.

In Orthodox circles the attention focused on study of the written Torah was limited, the emphasis being on the oral Torah. In Haredi circles, it was jokingly noted that verses of Tanach were quoted according to the pages where they appeared in the Gemara. Even in National Religious circles the study of Tanach was peripheral, and usually found its place in religious educational institutions as part of the program of secular studies. In non-religious secular circles Bible study experienced a revival with the Zionist return to the Land of Israel, but the accent was placed on archeology, history, linguistics, etc. The program of study was often guided by biblical research, which was far removed from the classic Jewish commentaries.[6]

Then – and let us not forget that we are talking about a revolution which took place more than sixty years ago – Nehama arrived on the scene, and initiated a variety of activities in the field of classical Jewish commentary. Suddenly wide circles of people, among them many who loved the Bible but were far removed from the world of Mitzvah observance, discovered the real Jewish Tanach. In this context we should remember that the Five Books of Moses and the rest of the Bible led to different lines of interpretation. In days gone by there was a Karaite approach and a rabbinical approach, and even up to our own days, for example, we have Jewish and Christian interpretations of the same texts. To some extent, the Tanach is "neutral" and only the commentaries give it a clear spiritual direction. For this reason Nehama saw it as her main task to teach *Jewish* scripture, and she therefore stressed in the titles of her books that they contain "studies in the footsteps of our early and late commentators."

Thus, to Nehama's great credit, Torah students wrestled with the *Jewish* commentaries, and she chose a wide variety of representatives from among them which penetrated to the heart of the Jewish Torah.

4. Multiplicity of Jewish Interpretations
Even though Nehama always emphasized only the Jewish aspects of Tanach, her students understood that Jewish interpretations are not monolithic; that there are different approaches to the understanding

of Scripture. In the halachic realms of Torah there is a clear line of practical decision making, but beyond this there is delight in enormously creative interpretations, with different opinions sometimes agreeing with, and sometimes contradicting, one another; but all live together peaceably on the basis of the principle of "both these and those are the words of the one living God."

Yet another aspect of learning with Nehama has to be stressed: despite the involvement in rational analysis of texts, anyone who studied Torah with Nehama Leibowitz senses that he/she was not studying Bible or Scripture, but Torah in the profound Jewish sense of the word. When we studied with Nehama we experienced what R. Soloveitchik sensed when he studied Gemara:

> I am not a Kabbalist or a Mystic, and when I talk of the presence of God, I sense it when I study Gemara, I feel as if the Holy One, Blessed be He, is standing behind my back, putting His hand on my shoulder, looking into my Gemara from behind me, and asking me "What are you studying here?" I am not talking about imagination – for me this is a real experience.[8]

Hence, we can understand why, as in Talmudic discussions, almost all her studies begin with a precise and detailed discussion of the text and its commentaries and then – as a result of the fascinating revelation of all the facets of the verse – there emerges a timeless and enduring message of the words of the Torah for all generations.

Let me give just one example: In the seventh study to the Sidra of *Kedoshim*, Nehama deliberates on the verse "And you shall not put a stumbling block before a blind man." As usual she quotes the Jewish commentators of this verse (Lev. 19:14) over different periods from the Midrashim of the Tanna'im and the Amoraim, via Rashi, Rabbenu Behai, and the Maharal of Prague up to Malbim. But, as usual, she is not satisfied with a mere technical explanation of the various possible interpretations but, from the study of the commentaries themselves, she draws clear conclusions about the significance of the Torah command vis-a-vis the personal responsibility of everyone to society of our day.'[9] This method of deep and meaningful Torah study as developed by Nehama exercised an enormous influence on the attitude rekindled in our day towards the study of *Chumash* and *Nach*.

It seems to me that the great increase in the last few years in the study of Tanach in religious circles is, to a considerable extent, the result of the blessed efforts of Nehama Leibowitz. The publication of modern traditional commentaries to the Bible, the establishment of institutes for the study of Scripture associated with the senior yeshivot, the increase of scholarly articles – all crystallized decades after Nehama had started her activities aimed to increase Torah study.

Particularly striking is the influence of Nehama's deductive interpretive method on women's learning in our generation. In most of the institutes of higher Torah education for women which have arisen in the last few decades, the study of Torah and Nach (and not Talmud) forms the core of the program. There is no doubt that the transformation of Torah into a medium for intellectual discussion and moral striving in the religious education of women took place largely as a result of Nehama Leibowitz's activities. It is perhaps ironic that Nehama, who was far removed from any feminist organizations in the religious camp, should have paved the way for serious Torah study by women.

5. Centrality of Rashi

Nehama excelled not only in her individual attitude to her students and in her special methodology, but she also contributed very significantly to the elucidation of the principles of Jewish exegesis, which she presented so vividly to the wider circle of Torah scholars in our generation. In this area, attention should be especially drawn to her creative approach to the commentary of Rashi, and to her innovative – even revolutionary – attitude to the world of Midrash.

Rashi occupied a central role in Nehama's thinking, and she penetrated so deeply into his spiritual world until she was able (in collaboration with Prof. Moshe Ahrend) to organize a course, within the framework of the Open University, devoted solely to Rashi's method of interpretation. This course, embracing 10 chapters and 618 pages, brings Rashi as the Jewish commentator into the framework of general scholarly research.[10]

As is well known, scores of books and articles have been dedicated to Rashi, among them works of penetrating scholarship, as well as more than 300 supercommentaries, but even these did not analyse Rashi's method in full detail. In addition, this Open University course investigates the manner in which Rashi relates to the stylistic rules of the Torah and to his Midrashic sources. In this way students are made aware of Rashi's definitive and precise rules of exegesis, and they are directed into his spiritual world by systematic scholarship.

6. Rediscovery of the Midrash

Furthermore, Nehama was an outstanding guide to the connection between Torah and Midrash. For various reasons, not much attention had been paid to studying Torah together with Midrash. It seems that many people were dissuaded from making use of Midrashim as a tool for understanding Scripture because of their mistaken feeling that Midrash concerns itself solely with drash, while their aim was to understand p'shat. The mere fact that Rashi, who regards himself as providing p'shat, draws 70 percent of his explanations from the world of Midrash demonstrates clearly the p'shat content of Midrash.[11] As a result of Nehama's effort over a period of many years, the Midrash was restored to its rightful place. She frequently made use of the multitude of rabbinic sources, understanding well that Midrash forms the basis of all Jewish exegesis, and anyone who wishes to contribute a Jewish interpretation is obliged to stress its importance. To quote one of Nehama's associates:

> Scriptural study among the Jewish people cannot be conceived without an intimate association with post-Biblical literature and thought, dominated by Rabbinic literature. It is the scholars of the Midrash who selected from the infinite variety of possible directions of development those perspectives of the world of the Bible which constituted Judaism.[12]

The enormous number of extracts from the Midrash which are quoted in the gilyonot shows the extent to which Nehama regarded Midrash as the base of Jewish exegesis. She made use of forty (!) different Midrashic sources and cited nearly 700 (!) references to Midrash in her weekly Sidra sheets – this in addition to 300 Talmudic passages which also have a Midrashic character.[13]

For the Midrash to be understandable and acceptable as a real contribution to interpretation, Nehama was obliged to translate the language of the Midrash to that of traditional exegesis. She did this very skillfully, with the help of the classic commentators on the Midrash

(Maharal, Maharsha, Maharzav – R. Ze'ev Volf Einhorn, Radal, and many more; also the collections and commentaries of *Torah Temimah* and *Torah Shlemah*). She also used modern research, like that of Yitzhak Heinemann (author of *Darkhei HaAggadah*) and Ephraim Urbach in many scholarly articles, and others.

Thus, Nehama explains, for example, that the conceptual is subordinated to the concrete, the precise details of which convey ideas. In this way scriptural verses which deal with a specific incident are used to express eternal truths. For example, the Torah does not say why Cain killed Abel, and the Midrash advances a number of possible scenarios, such as: (a) the brothers divided the world into land (for Cain, the tiller of the soil) and movable property (for Abel, the shepherd); (b) they got into a dispute and quarreled about the location of the Beit Hamikdash – in relation to the bringing of sacrifices; (c) they "fought" over their sister. These scenarios of the Midrash show the murder of Abel as a recurring problem in each generation, and the Midrash wishes to remind us that economic factors, or factors related to human egocentricity, or faith, or reasons connected with the he/she relationships, are some of the causes that can lead to fratricidal wars. It must be stressed that these Midrashim are based on an exact analysis of text and context.[14]

Following another Midrash, Nehama alerts the reader to the parallels between the first test of Abraham, "Take yourself out of your country," and the final test of "Take yourself to the land of Moriah." She explains the Midrash, and the literary comparisons which she presents to us arising from it, as a conceptual expression of the unique torment of Abraham, who with the first test relinquished his past, the house of his father, and with the last test his great dream of the future – namely, the Divine promise of seed. With the support of modern literary methods Nehama converts the words of the Midrash to a faithful rendering of the in-depth p'shat of the text.[15] Similarly, she interprets the apparition of Satan accosting Abraham and Isaac on their way to the Akedah as a projection of inner struggles into the real external world.[16]

There are so many examples that it is not possible to enter into details. It is important to note that in the sphere of halachic Midrashim also, the words of our Rabbis are treated as an interpretation of the

Scripture, where the outstanding concept emphasized is God's justice in the world, the uprightness of the Torah law, and our commitment to fight on its behalf.

7. Foundations of Midrashic Exegesis

It appears that Midrashic exegesis is built on three assumptions which were close to Nehama's heart. Midrash and the classic Jewish commentaries are built on a close, detailed reading of the text – a central feature of Nehama's approach to exegesis.

> The serious importance which they attach to the written word: to every word, not only the major words that possess deep religious, philosophical, and ideological significance (such as *kedushah*, *mishpat*, *tsedakah*, *hesed ve'emet*, or *segulah* [holiness, judgment, justice, etc.], but even to the *vav hachibur* [the prefix meaning "and," "but," "or," etc.]. They took this serious attitude, and paid this serious attention, not only to the gravity of the words but even to their sequence, to the sentence structure, repetition, parallelism; to everything written – and unwritten.[17]

The Midrash, like modern literary interpretation, is also built on the assumption that there are "seventy facets to the Torah," and that it is unnecessary to strive to discover the *sole* meaning of the text. Is this not precisely Nehama's philosophy, that one must pursue the whole variety of possible meanings of the verse, and understand that frequently there are different layers to what has been written and that there is more than one explanation which is appropriate?[18]

The third base on which the Midrash rests, and similarly the exegesis of Nehama, is that translations of words and sentences do not suffice, but penetration into the deeper meaning of the text is essential. It must be repeatedly emphasized that Nehama usually remained anchored to the p'shat of the verses, but succeeded in converting the seemingly dry words into an existential experience.

8. Torah Study and Torah Life

In view of the very creative work of Nehama as a teacher of biblical exegesis, it was suggested by the late Professor Ephraim Urbach more than 40 years ago[19] that Nehama should write a modern traditional commentary to the Torah, a work which many Torah scholars and educators felt to be lacking. Nehama rejected this idea. She did not want to compose a *commentary* on the text of the Torah, but she wanted to promote a method of *studying* Torah using classical commentaries.

It was largely because of Nehama's "exegetical" method that the impact of her work was so enormous. Through Nehama tens of thousands of students (of all ages!) found a genuine personal interest in the active in-depth study of the Torah. Thousands of teachers learned from Nehama how to make the teaching of Torah an exciting intellectual and emotional experience. Thanks to her erudite work, Jewish commentators of all ages were understood by our "modern" minds and they became relevant and meaningful to the students of the 20th century. Nehama made us understand that Torah is a book with a challenging text which can be interpreted in many different ways – it is also a book of life, a book with an existential message meaningful to our generation.

Nehama made it clear in her writings, in her lessons, and in her lifestyle that Torah study is not only an intellectual challenge and an emotional endeavor, but a committed way of life. A student (and a teacher!) of Torah must serve as an example to society. Her attitude on this matter can be demonstrated by the following incident.

In Yeshivat Hakotel it was decided some years ago that outstanding students might postpone their army service for three years. Shortly after this decision the director of the Yeshiva, Rabbi Benjamin Adler, visited Nehama, and she strongly reproached him for the decision. "But don't the universities, also, have this privilege of postponing army service for exceptionally gifted students?" was his counter-question. "There is a fundamental difference between these two institutions. The university aims to develop the potential intellectual capabilities of its students, but the Yeshiva wants to build a fully integrated Jewish personality who can serve as a model to society, and it is for this reason that students of the Yeshiva should be the first ones to be ready for army service."

9. Torah Study with Nehama Leibowitz Continues

About a year before Nehama passed away I took part in a convention in New York and prayed on Shabbat in one of the big synagogues on the West Side of Manhattan. There I saw a large announcement: "Shabbat with Nehama Leibowitz." I wondered – could it be possible that at the age of over ninety years, after so many decades during which she had never left Israel, Nehama would be coming to New York? I looked more closely at the details of the program, and saw that the "event" was a study evening with three of Nehama's students who were planning to teach Torah using her method. So it really was a Shabbat with Nehama, even if she herself was not present.

"Studying with Nehama" will go on even after she has left us. As people learn Torah with Rashi and Abarbanel, with Malbim and S. R. Hirsch – so they will learn Torah with Nehama Leibowitz, and discuss the words of the Bible on the basis of her writings with personal involvement, enthusiasm, and love.

And the many students of Nehama who continue to study and teach Torah in her spirit, and continue her educational and ethical legacy, can be considered as her children in the sense of the verse.

"And your children are those who are involved in the study of Torah" (Isaiah 54:13).

NOTES

1   We are reminded of the reply of Rav Sherira Gaon to Rav Yaakov ben Harav Nissim of Kairwan, ed. Aaron Heimann (London, 5671/1911), p. 106: "The order of priorities in greatness: Rabbi is greater than Rav, Rabban is greater than Rabbi, but (a person known by his) name is greater than Rabban; the early generations who are very great did not need the titles Rav, Rabbi, or Rabban."

2   J. B. Soloveitchik, *Ish Hahalakah, Galuy V'Nistar* (Jerusalem, 1989), p. 232.

3   *Leaders Guide to the Book of Psalms* (Hadassah Education Dept. USA, 1971), p. 1.

4   "Tanach for Advanced Students" in *Torah Insights* (Eliner Library: Jerusalem, 1995), p. 161.

5   "The Haftarah of the Second Day of Rosh Hashanah," op. cit. n. 4, pp. 4, 92.

6   On the study of the Scriptures in general schools in Israel, see J. Schoneveld, *The Bible in Israeli Education* (Assen, 1976).

7   Despite the reservations of some of her colleagues, Nehama included among the commentators whom she cited scholars like M. D. Cassuto, M. Buber, etc. However, she hardly ever quoted from non-Jewish commentators except for technicalities of translation. In this connection it is worth nothing that both Buber and Cassuto were nurtured on classical exegesis. Buber was close to his grandfather R. Shlomo Buber, an outstanding editor of old Midrashic texts, while Cassuto served as a rabbi.

8   *Al Ha'Teshuvah*, ed. Pinchas Peli (Jerusalem, 5735), p. 296.

9   *Iyunim Hadashim beSefer Vayikra* (Jerusalem, 5743), p. 253f. In this study Nehama cites seven different views in *Hazal* which widen the scope of the Torah injunction and subject it to detailed analysis. She demonstrates that not only deliberately misleading another person, or bringing him into a situation in which he is liable to commit a sin, belong to this commandment. Anyone who has failed to mark the location of a grave so as to guide *Kohanim* has transgressed this prohibition (*Moed Katan, 8a*). From this Nehama in her characteristic way – using care and delicacy in her actualization, but forcefulness in her message arrives at the following important existential conclusion:

The Torah teaches us that even if you remain totally passive (sitting and doing nothing), even if you distance yourself from communal life or activity, even if you remain confined to your four cubits, to your private life, you cannot escape responsibility for communal actions of injustice, violence, and wickedness. The fact that you did not protest and let your voice be heard loudly, that you did not designate graves and other vulnerable places, means that you bear responsibility for the evil which has been perpetrated, and you have transgressed: "You shall not put a stumbling block before a blind man."

10   The last chapter of the Open University program on Rashi (pp. 495–570) is concerned with the historical background to Rashi's creative work, and was written by Prof. Avraham Grossman.

11   Indeed, sometimes, Rashi emphasizes that he is not making use of Aggadic Midrashim (e.g., Genesis 3:8): "There are many Aggadic Midrashim, and our Rabbis have already arranged them in proper order in *Bereshit Rabbah* and other Midrashim. My purpose is only to provide the plain (p'shat) meaning of the text, and Aggadot which explain the text in a manner that enables it to fit into context." But in most cases where Rashi does use the Midrash, he does not mention it.

12   This is how Prof. Moshe Greenberg formulated the importance of Midrash for biblical exegesis in a symposium which was published in *Petahim* 4(40) (Ellul 5737), p. 22.

13   Compare the Index to the gilyonot prepared by Prof. Moshe Sokolov, and published by the Torah Education Dept. of the Jewish Agency, New York, 1993.

14   Cf. *Iyunim Besefer Bereshit* (Jerusalem, 5727), p. 28 and compare Gabriel H. Cohn, *Ekronot Behoraat Hamikra*. Mose Ahrend's Jubilee Volume (Touro College: Jerusalem, 1996), pp. 281–292.

15   Cf. op. cit. n. 14, first reference, pp. 14, 86–87 and *Limmud Parshaei Torah u Derakhim LeHoraatam* (Jerusalem, 5738), p. 67.

16   Cf. op. cit. n. 14, first reference, pp. 14, 137.

17   "How to Read a Chapter of Tanach," op. cit. n. 4, pp. 4, 163–164.

18   Cf. Y. Blidstein, "On the Many Different Meanings of the Torah," *Deot* 44; pp. 270–274 (5737).

19   Cf. E.E. Urbach, "LeMikra Gilyonot le Parshat hashavua," *Maayanot* 4, pp. 55–58 (5714).

APPENDIX D

Torah Insights

Nehama was especially interested in teaching teachers how to give lessons in Torah. Thus her efforts were equally divided between putting out the gilyonot and giving guidance to teachers on how to use them or similar approaches in teaching Tanach. This is one sample with which the Jewish Agency was involved.

– L.A.

Eliner Library, Jewish Agency, 1995

USE OF THE COMMENTARIES TO UNDERSTAND SCRIPTURE
The Twelve Spies

(Numbers; Chapters 13–14)
This article should be read with the original Hebrew open in front of the reader.

The story of the Twelve Spies, related in the book of Numbers and referred to in Deuteronomy, has fascinated Jews throughout the generations, and in particular the classical commentators. Here we present a selection of their remarks on various portions of the text dealing with different aspects of the story. These have been chosen to illustrate suitable ways of deepening and enriching our understanding of Scripture using the approaches of the classical commentators. It is not suggested that pupils should learn or read all of them, but that the teacher should make use of the material in preparing his lesson.

What follows is not intended as a plan for a lesson, but hints and advice for the teacher, from which he can choose what is suitable for a class of children aged approximately 11–14. Our purpose is to illustrate how the study of the words of the commentators can be integrated into the study of the text, both when the class is dealing with the general aspects of the section as a whole and when it gets down to details and starts to discuss a solitary verse or a small group of verses.

The use of commentaries must be variegated considerably. At times the commentary acts as a stimulus to indicate a difficulty in the verse, one which the pupil has not noticed or even sensed at all. (Possibly, if the teacher has not looked at the commentary, he too has not noticed it.) The difficulty is overlooked because the student is not used to reading slowly, making a critical appraisal, and examining the text carefully for anything unusual in the style, any exception in language, or any problem in the realm of ideas and concepts. Sometimes the commentator provides an answer, which should be presented only after the students have attempted to solve the problem themselves – with or without success. Sometimes the teacher may use the commentary to help in a discussion in class, either reading it out to them or conveying the gist in a language more suitable for them, while the students themselves might possibly not read it at all. Sometimes two different explanations, from different commentators, can be placed before the students so as to train them to weigh up the pros and cons of each interpretation, or to show two different aspects of an issue. Of the pieces selected, about half appear to be suitable for the students to read themselves, as will be indicated, while the remainder can be used by the teacher in one of the ways mentioned above.

It is recommended that the first chapter of Deuteronomy should not be invoked for comparison with the story as related here until

Deuteronomy is actually being studied in itself. First let the students learn the story of the Twelve Spies as it is written in Numbers, and absorb it. When they reach Deuteronomy, where Moses recapitulates events with which they are already familiar, the problem will arise on its own: 'What is different? And why?'

*

The students can prepare the two relevant chapters (Numbers 13 and 14) at home. The first two verses of chapter 13 can be read out in class, and then the comments of Rabbi Moses **Nachmanides** (Ramban) should be quoted:

> One may well ask 'What did the spies do?' (viz. What was their sin?). Moses had instructed them to 'see the country, what it is like, the people who live there, whether they are strong or weak, few or many....' and regarding the settlements in which they live 'whether they are in camps or in fortified towns' (verses 18–19); and it was their duty to report on what they had been instructed to ascertain. So what was their fault and sin when they said 'the people are strong and the towns are big and well fortified'? Did he send them to bring back a pack of lies?
>
> Do not reply that their fault lay merely in the remark 'It is a country that devours its inhabitants' (verse 32), because Caleb had already argued against them before they said that to the Israelites.

In other words, what was their sin? Did they not fulfill their errand? The reply should be delayed until the whole story has been studied in detail from beginning to end.

*

The questions Moses asked (verses 18–20) can be written on the blackboard in the following format. (The reader is advised to compare also the original Hebrew, in this and in all the quotations.)

Look at the country:	What is it like?
And the people who live there:	Are they strong, or weak?
	Are they few, or many?

What is the land on which they live:	Is it good, or bad?
What are the settlements in which they live:	Are they in camps, or fortified towns?
What is the land:	Is it fat [fertile], or lean [barren]? Are there trees there, or not?

The students should first make an effort to understand fully the questions Moses asked, to determine how many there are, to sort them out into questions regarding the people and questions regarding the land, and so on. Then, and not before, the teacher may care to read out (rather than encourage them to read for themselves) the comments of Don Isaac **Abarbanel**, which may serve as a summary to their work:

Moses instructed them in general terms to 'see the country… and the people who live there', and then gave details. Notice that Moses asked in all six questions.

The first two concerned the people: 'Are they weak or strong? Are they few or many?' First he asked about the quality, are they well built and strong, or weak and feeble? Then he asked about the quantity, are they few or many?

Next he asked two questions about the settled part of the land. One concerned character of the land on which they settled and of the life there: 'Is it good or bad?' Is the air good? Does it have nice houses, orchards, and sources of water? The second, 'Are the settlements in which they live camps or fortified towns?' In other words, do they simply live in open camps, like nomads who live in tents and camp wherever they find suitable pasture for their livestock? Or do they live in well-fortified towns?

Finally he asked about the part of the land that people did not actually live on but worked. First whether it was fat or lean, second whether there were trees or not. Here, unlike in the previous verse, he did not refer to the land 'on which they live,' since these questions did not refer to the settled part of the land. The first of these two questions, 'is it fat … ?', means 'is it fertile?' The second is to determine whether there are trees there to provide fruit and also wood for fuel, because trees are most essential for life. Note in particular that he asked about trees, because Egypt, which they had just left, is largely devoid of trees. Egypt is known to be plentiful in ground crops but sparse with respect to trees....

*

Ve hithazaktem V'lokachtem Mipri Habretz

(Verse 20) **And have courage, and take the fruit (produce) of the land.**

Nachmanides explains:

When helping themselves to the produce of the land, they should not be afraid of being recognised as spies.

Nachmanides is puzzled as to why the special encouragement ('have courage') is given here concerning taking samples of produce, rather than at the beginning when they were told to go into the country.

It is possible to compare the words of the spies on each of the three occasions that they speak.

Verses 27–29

(They reported to him and said:)
'We went to the land to which you sent us,
it is indeed a country that is an emitter of milk and sweetness,
and this is its fruit;
But the people who live in the country are powerful,
the towns are very large and fortified,
and we saw the giants there;
Amalek lives in the South (Negev),
the Hittites, Jebusites, and Amorites live in the hills and the Canaanites live by the sea and alongside the Jordan.'

Verse 31

(But the men who went with him said:)
'We will not be able to attack [lit. go up against] the people because they are stronger than us!'

193

Verse 32

(And they produced a report for the Israelites on the country which
they had explored, saying:)
'The country which we traversed to explore
is a country that devours its inhabitants,
and all the people that we saw there are men of stature!'

The first: a report as to what they had actually seen, in answer
to Moses's enquiries.
The second: an unsolicited opinion.
The third: a [false] report, a description contrary to fact, a lie.

The students can now be given a little silent work to do: 'Write
down the difference between the three statements of the Ten Spies,'
adding emphatically 'in two or three words, not at length' because
students tend to relate the story, to paraphrase the text into simpler
language, without making any effort to spot the essential differences
between the statements and express these clearly. This silent work
takes up time: it takes the students ten minutes or more to study,
think, and write that which the teacher could explain in three minutes. But the reward of independent effort certainly outweighs the
loss of time.

*

V'gam Zavat Chalav U'dvash Hi

(Verse 27) '**...and indeed it is an emitter of milk and sweetness.**'

Rashi comments:

Any lie that does not begin with a little truth is not upheld (viz.
does not acquire credibility).

Rashi answers the question 'If their intention was to deter the
people from entering the country, why open with words of praise?'
This is an example of explaining a verse within its context. The stu-

dents should note the apparent inconsistency between their initial words in praise of the land and their wicked intention that emerges from their subsequent remarks.

When we compare the three statements, we may recall **Nachmanides's** question that we quoted earlier: 'What was their sin?' Did he send them to bring back a false report?' The first statement appears to be entirely devoid of anything wrong, they appear not to have deviated from their terms of reference. But careful examination indicates that even in the first statement their bad intention was hinted at. Rabbi Isaac **Arama**, author of *Akedat Yitzhak*, explains this well:

> They exceeded their terms of reference as spies and appointed themselves as advisers. This recalls the case of a man who sent his representative to visit a clothing shop and look at a particular garment they had for sale. 'Examine the quality of the material, its length and width, and its appearance, and give me a report, because I want to buy it.' On his return the representative reported 'I have seen it, the material is good, it is long and wide, but it is greenish (or reddish) and it is very expensive, about a thousand gold coins.' He thereby exceeded his terms of reference as a reporter and turned himself into an adviser.

The remainder of **Arama's** comment, included here for the teacher, should not be presented to the students:

> His use of the word 'but' implies 'the quality is suitable for you, but the price is unsuitable for you.' The shopkeeper then has a valid complaint against him for giving an unsolicited opinion, and the one who sent him cannot rely on his report, because he, the one who sent him, knows what is good for himself and what is suitable. The same applies here. Had the spies said simply that they had gone to the country to which they were sent and found the population large and strong, and the towns strongly fortified, they would not have sinned at all. An agent is obliged to do what he is asked to do and to report back truthfully, but when they said 'but the people are strong' they already indicated their intention to make a recommendation regarding the advisability of Israel's proceeding.

As suggested, the students should be given simply the first part, the analogy. They should then be asked to work out the parallel for themselves, and to pinpoint the actual words with which the spies exceeded their terms of reference, namely to provide an objective report without adding personal opinions. This exercise, in distinguishing between reporting the facts and arranging the facts, is more important than understanding the meaning of the text. It also illustrates how one tiny word can cunningly insert a personal opinion into what appears to be an objective report.

Alternatively, the subject may be approached from the opposite end: ask the students if the first statement of the spies is indeed objective or if it includes a personal opinion. Arama's comments can be read out to them afterwards, confirming their answer if they have found the correct one, and giving it if they failed to do so.

*

V'yotziv Dibat HaAretz Asher Taru
Ohtah Al B'nei Yisrael Lemon
HaAretz Asher Avarnu Ba Latur Ohtah
Aretz Ochelet Yoshvaha Hi

(Verse 32) **They produced a report for [lit. to] the Israelites on the country that they had explored, saying 'The country through which we passed is a land that devours its inhabitants....'**

Nachmanides comments:

They produced a report to the Israelites: When they left Moses and Aaron they started to say in their tents that it was a land that devoured its inhabitants. Previously, when they reported to Moses and Aaron, they simply said that it was a land that emits milk and sweetness ('a land of milk and honey'), only that the people there were strong, while Caleb kept insisting 'We can [conquer] it.' The people were in two minds, some trusting their own strength and others trusting in God to provide strength. Thereupon the spies gave the people a direct report, saying that it was a country that devours its inhabitants, until they persuaded all the community to complain: 'They returned and induced all the community to complain against him [Moses], producing a [detrimental] report on the country' (14:36).

What happened was that when these men saw the local inhabitants, who were tall as cedars and strong as oaks, they were terrified of them, and they discouraged their brothers; and when they saw that despite this the Israelites were willing to go ahead, with Joshua and Caleb encouraging them, they produced a false report so as to ensure that the people would not go ahead at any cost.

Nachmanides here explains the technique of incitement, namely creating panic. It is important that the students, on reading the text, should find the basis of Nachmanides's explanation and verify it. In 13:26 we read 'They came to Moses and Aaron and the whole community of the Israelites to the Desert of Paran to Kadesh [Barnea], reported to them and to the whole community, showed them the fruit ... and told him [Moses]....' viz. the report was delivered publicly in front of the whole community. Even when they reported directly to Moses who had sent them, they said 'We went to the country to which you sent us', i.e. you, Moses. But in verse 32 we find 'They produced a report ... to the Israelites.' Here they no longer spoke in the presence of Moses and Aaron, but produced a private report containing their negative attitude, directly to the people in their tents. (See also Nachmanides's comments on 14:3.)

Students, and even adult readers, do not generally notice the subtle distinction between 'they reported back ... and told him...' and 'they produced a report to the Israelites,' but Nachmanides's comments will draw their attention to this. He adds a further comment, on verse 32, which is also worth noting:

Note that one who '*produces* a report' is a liar who gives false facts, whereas one who tells the truth is referred to as one who '*brings* a report' – compare 'Joseph brought a detrimental report about them to their father' (Genesis 37:2). It was for this that the spies were punished with death (in a plague), as explained in 14: 37: 'The men who had produced a detrimental report on the land died in a plague before God.'

197

With Nachmanides's last comments we have found an answer to our initial question 'what was the sin?'

*

Vatehi B'einiham Kehagavim V'chein Hayinu B'eineiham

(Verse 33) **We were like grasshoppers in our own eyes, and were likewise in their eyes.**

Here we have two commentators who offer different answers to the same question.

Rashi comments:

'We heard them saying to one another "There are grasshoppers[1] in the vineyards that look like men!"'

Rabbi Obadiah **Sforno** comments:

'And also in their eyes' – like grasshoppers or even less, for which reason they did not attack us, because they regarded us with contempt as insignificant and felt it beneath them to do us harm.

Both commentators face the problem of how the spies knew what the giants thought of them. All they can really tell is how they felt about themselves. The rest is deduction – according to Rashi by direct inference, and according to Sforno by indirect inference. Rashi states that they deduced it from what they heard with their own ears. (It is worth pointing out to the students the humor of the situation, according to this midrash, where giants look down from a great height on tiny men walking among the vines looking like grasshoppers.) Sforno, however, assumes that they deduced the attitude of

---

1. Our editions of Rashi read "ants" which makes no sense. This is almost certainly a printing error for members of the locust family like "grasshoppers".

the giants from their behavior, from the negative reaction of the local inhabitants to their presence.

*

Before studying chapter 14 in detail, it is worth considering the relative merits of the two forms of chapter division. The traditional Jewish system of paragraphs divides the story into three parts, the first from 13:1 to 14:10, the second from 14:11 to 14:25, and the third from 14:26 to 14:45. The Christian system (used in our printed editions) divides the story into two chapters, 13 and 14, starting the second with the reaction of the people. The question to ask is not 'which is correct?', but 'what is the reasoning behind each?', because in this particular case even the latter is not without its logic.

The Jewish division saw the first section as dealing with the sin (of the spies and of the people) and the second and third as dealing with the punishment. The other sees the first chapter as dealing with the sin of the spies, the remainder as dealing with the sin of the people and the punishment.

Searching for the correct answer is suitable for silent work in class, or possibly, since it is not too obvious and requires considerable mental effort, even more suitable for homework.

*

The sin of the people is described in terms of both their actions and their words, in 14:1–4, and reaches it climax in verse 10. It is worth quoting **Nachmanides**'s comments on 14:3:

> 'Why is God bringing us to this country to fall by the sword, our wives and children to be as spoil?' The people did not mention the [bad] report or say 'the land is bad,' because they wanted to conceal this from Moses. The spies had not said this in their official report to him and to the whole community, and Moses and Aaron would have denounced it as false [being contrary to the official report]. The spies themselves concealed this from Moses, knowing that he had learned about the country while living in the neighbouring lands of Egypt and Midian … so they passed this false report around surreptitiously to the people in their tents.

Here too the teacher can set the students the task of finding out which of the words used by the spies (quoted in chapter 13) are mentioned now by the Israelites in their complaints against Moses and Aaron, and which are omitted. This will further support Nachmanides's earlier remark (on 13:2) that the spies did not dare to mention 'a country that devours its inhabitants' in the presence of Moses and Aaron, but only 'surreptitiously' when they went from tent to tent to incite the people.

The importance of this study lies in the opportunity it affords for practice in making a precise and painstaking comparison of texts and drawing inferences from the differences. If one person quotes another's remarks it is important to ascertain that the quotation is accurate, and if it is not, to ask what the motive was for adding to, subtracting from, or changing the original wording. Once the students have made an effort, successfully or unsuccessfully, to identify any differences, the teacher can read out the views of the commentator who considers these differences; but the main value of the commentary lies in making the *teacher* aware of the need to compare the texts here.

Such comparisons were popular mainly with the later Sephardic commentators Arama, Abarbanel, Alshikh, Ibn Attar, and in the nineteenth century with Malbim and 'Netsiv of Volozhin.' If the two parallel passages extend over a number of chapters, the parallels can be set out and presented to the students in tabular form. (These are illustrated in my Gilyonot for *Bereshit* 5715 and elsewhere.)

*

The principal speakers in the latter part of chapter 13 are the spies: In the first ten verses of chapter 14 the main speakers are 'the whole community' on the one hand, and Caleb and Joshua on the other. The earlier commentators compare and contrast the words of the Ten Spies with those of the other two. (The reader is advised to compare also the original Hebrew.)

THE TEN SPIES	JOSHUA & CALEB
13:32 The country through which we passed to explore	14:7 The country through which we passed to explore

is a land that devours its inhabitants	the land is extremely good
13:27 We went to the land to which you sent us and it is indeed an emitter of milk and sweetness	14:8 If God wants us He will take us to this land and give it to us a land which is an emitter of milk and sweetness

Don Isaac **Abarbanel** explains the words of Caleb and Joshua:

Do not be incited by the reports which these men have produced
and invented concerning the land, because we also went through
the land, explored it and saw all that they saw.

The relative clause 'through which we passed to explore' is
identical in each case (13:32 and 14:7), but as against 'a land that
devours its inhabitants' we have 'the land is extremely good' ... The
commentators ask why the word 'land' is repeated, why not simply
'is extremely good.' The answer is that just as the Ten repeated this
word after the relative clause, so Joshua and Caleb imitated their
words by repeating it. Corresponding to 'and *it* is indeed an emitter
of milk and sweetness,' a sort of forced admission, so the other two
said a land *which* [lit. 'that *it*'] is an emitter of milk and sweetness.

I do not recommend here that the students should read the commentary, nor even that the teacher should read it out to them, but that
the teacher should stress the need for comparison, let the students be
impressed by the similarities and differences, and explain these.

*

Moses's prayer (14:13–19) is fundamentally difficult to understand, on account of its extremely complicated syntax structure. It
might help the students to look at Rashi's comments; it might be
preferable for the teacher to explain the gist of Rashi's interpretation without reading the original. Alternatively, the original text can
be written on the blackboard in the following form. (The reader is
advised to compare also the original Hebrew.)

Moses said to God
'When the Egyptians hear that You have lifted up this people from
among themselves with Your power,
they will say about the inhabitants of that country
    (—they have heard that You are God among this people
    You God Who has appeared face to face [lit. eye to eye]
    Your cloud standing over them, and
    You walk ahead of them in [the form of] a pillar of cloud by
day
    and a pillar of fire by night,
    and when You will have killed this people as one man, then
the nations who have heard your reputation will say:)
"Through the inability of God to take this people to the country
that he promised [lit. 'swore'] to them he has slaughtered them
in the desert!"'

Rashi explains in a continuous comment (which is uncharacteristic of him):

14:13 *When the Egyptians hear;* When they hear that you have
killed them
    that You have taken up: 'that' [and not 'because', which is
the same word in Hebrew, "Ki".] They have seen how with Your
great power You have lifted them [Israel] up from among them
[Egypt], and when they hear that You have killed them, they will
not say that this is because they [Israel] have sinned against You,
but will say that whereas You were able to grapple with them [the
Egyptians], You were unable to grapple with the inhabitants of the
country [Canaan]. This is the meaning of the next section, that
they will say, concerning (not 'to') the inhabitants of that country.
[Note: Rashi wishes to point out that the word "al" which normally
means 'to,' is frequently used as a substitute for "aal" meaning
'about' or 'concerning', and that is the meaning here.] And what
will they say about them? That which is written at the very end,
'Through God's inability,' because they [the nations] will have heard
how You, God, live among them [Israel], appear to them face to
face, all by way of affection, and up to now they have seen no
indication of that affection for them having been terminated.
14:15 *and when You will have killed this people as one man:*
suddenly, as a result of which the nations who have heard Your
reputation etc.

14:16 *through the inability:* because the inhabitants of the country [Canaan] are strong and powerful, and Pharaoh cannot be compared to thirty-one kings. This is what they [Egypt] will say concerning the inhabitants of this country: 'through the inability,' because He was unable to take them there, He slaughtered them.

Rashi therefore understands 'they will say about the inhabitants...' (verse 13) to refer not to the Egyptians in particular, but to all who have heard God's reputation regarding the Exodus etc., and 'then the nations ... will say' (verse 15) as effectively a repetition of this, necessitated by the long interruption in parentheses, which is inserted [by Moses] to show that the dreadful massacre would follow a long period of kindness and love by God towards his people; the other nations would therefore not see the massacre as punishment for misdeeds but as proof of the ineffectiveness of the Israelites' God against the inhabitants of Canaan.

*

It is worth comparing this prayer of Moses with his prayer after the sin of the Golden Calf. There Moses pleads for forgiveness on three grounds: God's mercy, to which he appeals; the need to avoid God's reputation throughout the world being adversely affected; and the promise made to the Patriarchs. Here Moses resorts only to the middle one, avoiding God's reputation being tarnished (*chillul HaShem*) through misunderstanding. The teacher has probably dealt with the meaning and implications of this when teaching the prayer of Moses in the earlier story, that of the Golden Calf. It is worth waiting to see if any of the students raise (in either case) the big problem regarding Moses's prayer. **Abarbanel** has formulated this, his third question, as follows:

How could Moses expect the Supreme Judge to refrain from executing justice through fear of what the Egyptians might say in their ignorance and stupidity? Being complete and self-sufficient He is not afraid of people, so what does He gain or lose if the Egyptians honor and respect Him or otherwise, for this to cause

Him to abstain from executing justice in His world and against His people?

Rabbi Isaac **Arama** (in *Akedat Yitzhak*) expresses this even more sharply:

'Why should the Egyptians say...?' What sort of argument is this? Should justice be sullied on account of fools?

If the students do not ask this question, this indicates that they have not gotten used to the idea of raising problems on their own, but simply try to answer those raised by others. In other words, they just wait for the teacher to point out the problem, and the text itself does not challenge their minds. In such a case, it is necessary to present the problem to them – either in the words of Abarbanel or Arama, or in the teacher's own words – and, without waiting for an answer, to explain the whole concept of *chillul HaShem*, undermining God's reputation.

They have learned earlier that the purpose of all the Ten Plagues was 'so that you should know that I am God,' 'so that you should know that there is none like Me,' etc. The word 'know' in such a context occurs ten times in the story of the Plagues [and the Red Sea Crossing,[2] nine of them in reaction to Pharaoh's remark 'I do not know God' (Exodus 5:2). This proves that God wants his creatures to be enlightened and drawn onto the path of truth. 'If you kill them,' Moses argued, 'the punishment will be misunderstood, and conclusions will be drawn that are the opposite to the correct understanding of "knowing God." Instead of Your name being sanctified in Your world, so that all its inhabitants recognize Your integrity, Your reputation will be tarnished and people will become entrenched in their misconceptions. It is universally recognized that justice must not merely be done, it must also be seen to be done (i.e. understood and appreciated).'

This idea is reiterated in the book of Joshua: 'And what will You

---

2. Exodus 7:5; 7:17; 8:6; 8:18; 9:14; 9:29; 11:7 – in connection with the Plagues; Exodus 14:4 and 14:18 – in connection with the Red Sea; and Exodus 10:2 referring to the Israelites.

do for Your great reputation?' (7:9); Jeremiah: 'Act for the sake of Your reputation!' (14:7); Ezekiel: 'when I act with regard to you for the sake of My reputation' (20:44); and Psalms: 'Why should the nations ask "Where is their God?"' (79:10 and 115:2). It is expressed even more forcefully in Deuteronomy in the song of *Ha'azinu* (32: 26–27). There, nobody is praying for punishment to be deferred, for justice to be abandoned lest God's reputation among the nations be tarnished; there God himself declares that He will not execute full justice against Israel 'lest [their enemies] say "We ourselves have been victorious, God has not done all this."'[3]

Nachmanides also deals with the question as to why Moses does not invoke here the promise regarding the Land made to the Patriarchs, as he did after the sin of the Golden Calf:

> 14:13 *Now let My Lord's power be enhanced:* Moses did not invoke the merit of the Patriarchs or even mention Abraham, Isaac or Jacob in this prayer, because the country was given to the Patriarchs who were very keen to have it, yet the people, who were to inherit it, rebelled against their ancestors and refused to accept the gift. How could Moses say 'Remember your oath to Abraham, Isaac and Israel your servants ... that "I will give all of this country to your offspring as I have promised, and they will own it for ever".' (Exodus 32:13), when that very offspring had declared 'We do not want this gift'?

*

It is also interesting to compare what Moses feared the Egyp-

---

3. **Nachmanides** explains this concept in greater depth in his comment on '*Let me obliterate their memory from mankind!*' (Deuteronomy 32:26).

The motive is not a desire to prove His power to His enemies [viz. the nations], because all the nations are of no significance to Him and considered as nothing; but God created man in order that He should recognize His Creator and thank Him, and he has the choice of doing right or wrong. When they all deliberately sinned and denied God, this people alone remained faithful. Through them, with signs and wonders, He publicized that He is the God of gods and Lord of lords, and thereby made it known throughout all the nations. If He now retracts and destroys their memory, all the nations will forget His signs and deeds, and will no longer talk about them.... so that the Creator's original intention concerning mankind will have been totally annulled, because none of His creatures will remain that recognize their Creator.

tians and other nations might say (leading to God's reputation being tarnished) in the two instances:

After the sin of the Golden Calf: *Lamah Yomru Mitzraim Lemor B'raah Hozeiam Laharog Otam Beharim U'lechalo-tam Meial Penei Haadamah*

> **Why should the Egyptians say 'He has taken them out with a wicked intention, so as to kill them in the hills'?**
>
> (Exodus 32:12).

After the sin of the Spies: *V'Omru Hagoyim Asher Sham'u Et Shimacha Lemor, Mibilti Yecholet HaShem l'Havi Et HaAm Hazeh Al HaAretz*

> **Then the nations who have heard your reputation will say 'Through God's inability to take this people to the country...'**
>
> (Numbers 14:15–16).

The Egyptians, who saw all the great signs and wonders, including the splitting of the Red Sea, could hardly talk about 'God's inability'; but they could claim that while He is strong and powerful He is also cruel and abuses his creatures.

Some claim that there is a reference in the former to the Egyptian god Ra, and translate the former verse as 'He has taken them out with the help of Ra to kill them on the hills.' Rashi comments on Exodus 10:10:

> I have heard a midrash that refers to a certain star called 'Ra.' Pharaoh said to them [Moses and Aaron] 'I can see in my horoscope that a star signifying blood and massacre is rising up against you in the desert.' When Israel sinned by worshipping the Golden Calf and God wanted to kill them, Moses pleaded 'Why should the Egyptians say that he has taken them out under the influence of Ra ... ?' referring to Pharaoh's remark here 'Look out! Ra is against you!'

Professor Umberto **Cassuto** comments likewise on Exodus 10:10:

> Perhaps here too, as has already been suggested, there is a reference to the Egyptian god Ra, the sun god, head of the Egyptian pantheon. 'Take note that the power of *my* god will rise against you!'

After the sin of the Spies, however, Moses argued that the Canaanites, who had not seen God's power and might, would claim 'through the inability ... .'

*

In the section in which the punishment is stated, there are differences between the first section (14:20–25) where Moses is informed of the punishment, and the second section (14:26–35) where, in greater detail, he is told how to pass on the information to Israel. More important than noting the differences in wording is appreciating the character of the punishment, which is intended not merely to cause pain, distress, and suffering, but also to rectify, to educate. The teacher should read to the students, in his own words, the remarks of Maimonides in his *Guide for the Perplexed*, 3:32.

> It is not compatible with human nature for a person who grows up as a slave working with bricks and mortar to simply wash the dirt off his hands and then suddenly fight against giants ... it was God's wise idea to lead them round the desert so that they might learn to become tough. It is well known that wandering in the desert where the body enjoys a minimum of washing and similar luxuries toughens up a person, just as the opposite leads to softness. Furthermore, men will be born who are not accustomed to humiliation and slavery....

*

It should be stressed that those who went up to attack after being told not to do so (verses 40–48) were not performing an act of repentance. One who repents fully and sincerely, recognizes his errors and wishes to make amends, accepts judgment against him and is prepared to face the consequences of his actions, not to run away from them. These people, however, wanted to avoid the punishment and defy authority. **Abarbanel,** at the end of his comment on 14:20, comments:

> Moses rebuked them: 'Why are you doing this, disobeying God's instructions? It will not succeed' (14:41). In other words, 'Even in this action you are rebelling. When I told you to go up and take possession, not to be afraid and not to be discouraged (Deuteronomy 1:21) because God would fight for you, you did not want to go. Now that God says "Turn round and re-enter the desert on the Red Sea Road" you say "Here we are, we are ready to attack"! Do not do this.'

The well-known passage from Bialik's 'Those Who Died In The Desert' refers to something entirely different, and should not be quoted here, since for fourteen-year-olds the comparison and contrast is far too complicated.

Gilyonot for the Study of the Weekly Torah Portion

The World Zionist Organization's Council for Torah Education began putting out Nehama's gilyonot in Hebrew and English after the Keren Kayemet stopped doing so. They, too, used the Internet and e-mail, and were able to ignite interest among students in Israel and abroad who had never met Nehama personally.

– L.A.

> By Nehama Leibowitz – Twenty-ninth Year
> Rabbi Stan Peerless, World Zionist Organization
> Council for Torah Education

Pinchas (5730/1970)
Ch. 27:1–11
Tzelofhad's daughters

I. Rashi – Questions and Analysis

1. Rashi Num. 26:64: And among these there was not a man of those numbered by Moses and Aharon: But the punishment for the sin of the Spies did not extend to the women, because they cherished the

Promised Land. The men said (Num. 14:4), "Let us appoint a chief and let us return to Egypt," the women said, "Give us a possession" (Num. 27:4).

Where does Rashi find a hint in the verse that the women were not affected by the Divine decree?

2. Rashi Num. 27:1: Of the families of Menashe, the son of Josef. Why (state, son of Josef) seeing that it states, "son of Menashe"? To let us know that Josef cherished the land, as it is stated (Gen. 50:25), "and you shall carry up my bones from here" – and his daughters cherished the land, as it is stated, "Give us a possession" (Num. 27:4).

1. What is his problem?
2. *Ha'amek Davar* asks: How is this proof of their cherishing the land? Could they return to Egypt? What then is surprising about their asking for a possession in Eretz Israel?

3. Rashi Num. 27:5: And Moses brought their cause before the Lord: He had forgotten the law. He was thus punished for taking undeserved credit saying (Deut. 1:17), "and the cause that is too hard for you, bring it to me" (*Sanhedrin* 8a).

The author of **Sefer Hazikaron** asks: He did not know the law for the gatherer of wood either (Num. 15:32–36) nor the law for those who were impure (and could not offer the pascal sacrifice – Num. 9:1–8) and he had to ask (God). Why is it not said in those cases that his ignorance of the law was a punishment? Answer his question.

II. Num. 27:5: And Moses brought their cause before the Lord: See Rashi (above).
Tzeda Laderekh: Some comment that since Tzelofhad's daughters revealed in their argument that their father was not among Moses's adversaries he might be influenced, and if he were to judge their case he would be as if **bribed by words.** It was for this reason – and not because he had forgotten the law – that he refrained from judging their case.

This does not seem right!

Can you explain the weakness of this comment, and that we must accept Rashi's explanation that forgetting the law was a punishment?

III. Num. 27:7: The daughters of Tzelofhad speak right...

Rashi's comment: The daughters of Tzelofhad speak right: (The meaning is) as translated by Onkelos: It is proper. This is how this passage is written before Me in Heaven. This shows that their eyes saw what Moses's eyes did not see.

1. **Be'er Yitzhak** amends Rashi's version as follows: I think the correct version is: As translated by Onkelos: It is proper. The Midrash says: This is how this passage is written before Me in Heaven.
   Explain the reason for this amendment.
2. Why does Onkelos not translate *ken* (right) as he does in Gen. 18:5 and Ex. 7:6?
3. Why does Rashi find it necessary to bring a second explanation, s. v. The daughters of Tzelofhad speak right: Their claim is justified; happy the person with whom God agrees.

What does this explanation put right?

IV. Num. 27:3: ... and he was not in the company of those that gathered together against the Lord in the company of Korah.

Baba Batra 118b: And he was not in the company – of the Spies; of those that gathered together against the Lord – those who murmured; in the company of Korah – in its plain sense.

Rashi Num. 27:3: And he was not: Since they said that he died in his own sin, they had to say that not in the sin of those who murmured, nor of the company of Korah who had incited against the Lord, but in his own sin, and he did not cause others to sin with him.

1. **Torah Temimah** asks: Why the Gemara's interpretation and not simply that he was not in the company of Korah? Answer his question.
2. Why did the expounder change the chronological order of the

211

events, which was: a) murmuring, b) Spies, c) the company of Korah?

Guide for Nehama Leibowitz's Gilayon on the Weekly Torah Portion 5730/1970 *Pinchas*

(5730/1970) Ch. 27:1–11
Tzelofhad's daughters

This gilayon does not deal with the practical and conceptual aspects of the inheritance of Tzelofhad's daughters. The teacher who is not acquainted with Israel's inheritance laws would do well not to go into this question for he is liable to pass on partially or entirely wrong information. Furthermore it would be difficult for a teacher to prepare such an involved subject on one leg.

The gilayon deals almost entirely with Rashi and with his ways of interpretation.

Re Question I/2: The teacher ought to show several places where Rashi seeks the purpose of stating the descendancy or the name of the place of residence of a person, or family relationship or his position where this has been known to us for some time. Why does the Torah give us the information, which is unnecessary seeing that we have been told of them previously in several places. See this kind of problem in:

Gen. 18:1, s. v. Mamre
Gen. 25:20   Daughter of Betuel
Ex. 18:5, s. v. To the Desert
Deut. 1:4 s. v. Sihon. who dwelt in Heshbon.

(See also the *Lech Lecha* 5615/1955 gilayon Question II/1,b [the same question]).

If the students find difficulties in finding a solution to Question I/2 b, let them look up Num. ch.32: **Ha'amek Davar's** question is justified; does the fact of seeking the possession of property imply love of Eretz Israel? It is important for the students to realize that Rashi does not quote a Midrash exclusively for educational or propaganda purposes without any **logical** necessity. The same applies also to Question I/3. Unless the teacher asks questions like: Whence does Rashi derive ... ? What induced him to say what he did? Or, if that is so why does he not explain the same way in such-and-such a place? Unless the teacher is particular the students will gain the impression that Rashi's words are arbitrary and inconsistent.

In Question IV, too, this must be emphasized. The unusual style must be pointed out as well as the verbosity, the awkward expression "in the company of those that gathered together against the Lord in the company of Korah" and this way understand the Midrash and Rashi.

It should be added to Question IV/2 that the Midrash as well as Rashi always adhere to the chronological order of events. Whenever this is **not** observed – as in our case – it must be investigated to find in the text a reason for deviating from it.

The teacher may cite the following examples of observing the order:

Ex. 18:1: s. v.	And Yitro heard
Ex. 18:1: s. v.	All that God had done
Ex. 18:8: s. v.	All the travail
Num. 16:4:	He fell on his face
Num. 31:21: s. v.	And Eleazar (the priest) said.

Against this there is the deviation from the chronological order in our case and also in Deut.11:13: s. v. And to serve Him: where he quotes Daniel before David! Likewise in Gen. 37:14: He came to Shekhem.

Something else to be added to Question IV is the comparison between the text in the Midrash and Rashi's version, which we dealt with also in the *Korah* gilayon (see also Deut. 5704/1944) Question V.

We must explain to our students the importance of every word added or omitted by Rashi. I do not think the students are going to find it difficult to find the reason why Rashi omitted to mention the

Spies and only mentioned the murmurings of the people. (The comparison we cited in the 6709/1949 *Lech Lecha* gilayon I/6 is very instructive for this kind of omission.)

In conclusion the teacher should pass on to Question III to see that Onkelos's is not a mechanical literal translation but contains abundant commentary. He is very meticulous not to use always the same translation but rather to fit the translation to each case.

(One may compare his translation of the verb "take" in the following places: Gen.7:2; 11:4–5; 12:5; 14:11–12; 15:9; 16:3 (and Rashi ad loc.); 19:15; 28:11; 29:23; 37:24!)

Answers for the Gilyonot for the Study of the Weekly Torah Portion Prepared By Yitzhak Reiner

Pinchas (5730/1970) Ch.27:1–11
Tzelofhad's daughters

I. 1.   Because it is stated, "Among these there was not a **man** of those numbered by Moses and Aharon, and not "Among these there was none of those numbered by Moses and Aharon" (*Be'er Yitzhak*).

2. a. Why is it stated Menashe son of Josef, which is well known?!

   b. *Ha'amek Davar* answers in v.4: "Give us a possession among the brothers of our father," where "brothers of our father" is redundant. However, since half the tribe of Menashe was already settled in Transjordan, but they wanted an inheritance in Eretz Israel, among the brothers of their father (sons of Gil'ad, son of Makhir, son of Menashe – Num. 32:39–40). The proof is the fact that they wanted a possession in Eretz Israel that had not yet been conquered and not in Transjordan, already conquered, because they cherished Eretz Israel.

3.   The author of *Sefer Hazikaron* answers: In matters of laws of inheritance, of common occurrence and necessary for

214

the orderly conduct of human affairs, it is to be presumed that he knew the law but forgot them. Not so the other laws of rare application. Moses did not have to be expected to remember them until he was consulted.

II.   If he did not want to deal with the matter lest he be accused of accepting word – bribe, he would have told Eleazar to judge their case.

III. 1.   Onkelos and the Midrash differ in their translation of the term *ken*. According to the former it is an adjective = right, proper. The Midrash regards *ken* as a relative adverb – **They speak as it is written before Me.**

 2.   In this case there is something to be compared to, namely, they speak as it is written.

 3.   The words *ken ... dovrot* are superfluous, why does the answer not state simply, "you shall surely give them a possession...." Why is this compliment being paid to the daughters of Tzelofhad?

IV. 1.   Their address is rather long. If they had been referring to only one episode – the one of Korah – they could have stated simply, "he was not in the company of Korah." The convoluted wording indicates that they meant that their father did not take part in any of the rebellions against God. (*Torah Temimah*)

 2.   Because the interpreter follows the **terms** of the text, and *edah* (company) is reminiscent of the Spies – *edah hara'ah* (evil congregation) – hence he must mention them first.

Tips on Methodology
from the Teachings
of Nehama Leibowitz

The same World Council for Torah Education of the WZO also published a number of essays written by Rabbi Stanley Peerless on Nehama's teaching method and her use of commentators. Using her approach, the essays explained each point by using examples from the texts she taught.

Tips on Methodology
from the Teachings of Nehama Leibowitz z"l

I. The Goals of Torah Instruction

Nehama identified three goals of teaching Torah: 1) The accumulation of factual knowledge; 2) the development of independent learning skills; and 3) the development of a love of learning. She stressed that *kiyum hamitzvot* is not a primary goal of Torah instruction. Rather, success in instilling a love of learning will in itself lead to the fulfillment of mitzvot.

II. Active Learning

In order to fulfill these goals, the teacher must involve the student in active learning. Active learning is easy to achieve in the science laboratory, but is much more difficult to create in a Torah lesson. Nehama suggested several "trickim" (as she called them), strategies designed to achieve that goal. The following are a few of her tips on teaching methodology.

III. The Prohibitions

Nehama listed four common practices from which teachers should refrain:

1. Do not lecture.
2. Do not allow students to write while you are speaking.
3. Do not give an introduction to the material that is to be studied.
4. Do not ask students to answer factual questions or to paraphrase.

IV. The Introductory Lesson

The purpose of the introductory lesson is to provide the context, to give an overview of the chapter or section to be studied before examining the details. In place of the teacher providing the students with background information, Nehama suggested that students be given an assignment that would force them to independently read and think about the section being studied. One of her favorite methods was to ask students to divide the section into a specific number of subsections and to give each one a title or definition. This method can be used in both narrative and halachic sections of the Torah.

This method can be used, for example, in studying the Ten Commandments. Prior to beginning the in-depth study, students could be asked to divide the commandments into two categories, and then into three categories. The following are some of the possibilities that the students might generate:

Two categories:
1. positive commandments and negative commandments
2. mitzvot between man and God and mitzvot between man & man

Three categories:
1. mitzvot that are fulfilled with a positive action, mitzvot that are fulfilled by refraining from a negative action, and mitzvot that are fulfilled in thought only
2. mitzvot relating to the holiness of God, mitzvot relating to the holiness of man, and mitzvot relating to the holiness of time

This exercise accomplishes several things:
1. It forces the student to study the entire section and to give thought to the content.
2. It validates the ability of the learner to generate ideas (there is no wrong answer).
3. It raises issues of interest, many of which may be dealt with by the commentators. For example: Is "I am the Lord your God" actually a commandment? Is it possible to command something that is only fulfilled in thought? Are honoring your parents and observing Shabbat considered to be between man and man or between man and God? Is Shabbat a positive or a negative commandment?

V. Asking the Right Questions
Nehama believed that it is not worthwhile to ask any question where the answer is obvious from the context. Rather, questions should be thought provoking, requiring the student to demonstrate an understanding of the material. For example, Nehama advocated comparison of texts as a worthwhile learning exercise. She applied this method to Chumash texts in which information is repeated (i.e. when the Torah describes a plan and then its implementation, when two people describe the same event, etc.) and to the comparative study of commentaries.
For example:
1. Comparison of the Laws of Shabbat – *Shemot* 20:8–11, *Shemot* 31:13–17, and *Devarim* 5:12–15:
a) What differences do you find with regard to the reasons stated for the observance of Shabbat?
b) The *Amidah* on Shabbat morning states: "Moshe rejoiced in the gift of his portion.... He brought down two stone tablets

in his hand on which is inscribed the observance of Shabbat. So it is written in Your Torah: 'B'nei Yisrael shall keep Shabbat, observing Shabbat (*Shemot* 31:6)...'" If the prayer mentions the two tablets, why does it bring the quote from *Parshat Ki Tisah* rather than from the Ten Commandments?

   2. Comparison of commentaries on *Shemot* 20:8 – "Remember the Shabbat day and keep it holy"

Rashi: Take care to always remember the Shabbat day – that if, for example, you come across a nice item of food during the week, put it aside for Shabbat.

Rashbam: Every act of remembering is with respect to the past.... So here, too, "Remember the Shabbat day and keep it holy" refers to the six days of creation, as in the continuation of the verse: "For in six days the Lord made...". Therefore, what is written here is "remember" in order to keep it holy, to refrain from work.

Sforno: Always remember the Shabbat day while you go about your weekday activities, as in "Remember what Amalek did to you." "And keep it holy": This is what you should do so that you may keep it holy: it cautioned us to arrange our affairs on weekdays in such a way that we can turn our minds from them on Shabbat.

Questions:
   a. In what way do Rashi and Rashbam differ in their interpretation of the word "remember"?
   b. Which of them do the following verses support?
      "You did not remember how this will end (Isa. 47:7)"
      "She remembered not how this will end (*Eichah* 1:9)"
   c. Did Sforno follow the approach of Rashi or Rashbam, or did he choose a third approach?

VI. The Teacher as Role Model

Although Nehama did not emphasize the importance of role modeling in her discussions of teaching methodology, she served as a paradigm in this regard. She was a giant among Torah scholars, yet she always demonstrated genuine humility. Nehama's love of Am Yisrael, Eretz Yisrael, and Medinat Yisrael was always evident in her lessons and had a great impact on her students. She was truly a role model for her students to emulate. Her impact on a generation of teachers has had a significant influence on Torah education in our times.

More of Nehama Leibowitz's tips on methodology can be found in *Torah Insights*, published by the Eliner Library (Jerusalem, 1995).

Tips on Methodology from the Teachings of Nehama Leibowitz zt"l
Part II: Rashi's Use of Midrash

Introduction

A significant challenge to the teacher of Chumash is to develop an approach to the teaching of Rashi's commentary. Rashi, the father of the school of *peshuto shel mikra* (the simple meaning of the text), is clearly the focal point of most Chumash curricula. Yet, many find it difficult to understand and adequately transmit the innovation that Rashi introduced to Torah study. One of the primary challenges is to understand Rashi's approach to Midrash. In a cursory reading, Rashi seems to rely heavily on Midrash, and one might question whether he really reflects the approach of peshuto shel mikra. Ibn Ezra, by comparison, seems to utilize a textual analysis that is more faithful to the p'shat (simple meaning). In order to foster a more sophisticated understanding of p'shat as it manifests itself in Rashi's commentary, it is necessary to understand his selective use of Midrash.

Rashi's Use of Midrash – Homiletics or Interpretation?

The super-commentaries on Rashi differ regarding the role of Midrash in Rashi's commentary. Some contend that Rashi refers to Midrashim both to explain a difficulty in the text, but also to teach a lesson. In other words, some of the Midrashim brought by Rashi are necessary to properly understand the text, while others are supplemental embellishments to the text. Other commentators, on the contrary, claim that Rashi only quotes Midrashim when they are necessary to understand difficulties in the text.

Nehama Leibowitz clearly ascribes to the second position. She claims that Rashi is systematic in his use of Midrash. Rashi, however, did not write an explanatory introduction to his commentary, and it thus falls on the reader to understand his approach through an analysis of the commentary. Nehama believes that the key to understanding Rashi's system is to pay attention to those situations in which Rashi rejects the use of existent Midrashim and those instances in which he selects one Midrash over another. The methodological implications are clear. The teacher must guide the student through such an analysis, which will simultaneously engage the student in a meaningful learning process.

Rashi's Criteria for the Use of Midrashim

Nehama posits that for Rashi to utilize a particular Midrash in his commentary, it has to meet two criteria:

1. It must answer a particular difficulty in the text (i.e. a grammatical inconsistence, a redundancy, a divergence from the context, a theological difficulty, a divergence from the chronology, etc.).

2. It must fit into the context of the larger section within which the verse appears.

In this sense, Rashi the *pashtan* differs from the *darshanim* who preceded him. The darshanim explained verses in order to teach a particular lesson, similar to rabbinic sermons today. As such, the drasha can utilize a verse out of context and does not have to be consistent with other drashot. Rashi's innovation is that he explains the verse as part of a larger whole, selecting only Midrashim that when pieced together create a unified picture. Thus, while Rashi's commentary may appear at times to be simplistic, it is, in Nehama's opinion, a sophisticated work of scholarship. The tapestry of grammatical, literary, and Midrashic explanations that Rashi presents is, in his opinion, the simple meaning of the text.

Explicit Evidence – Instances in Which Rashi Rejects Existent Midrashim

When Rashi utilizes the term *peshuto kemashma'o* (the simple meaning is the same as the literal meaning) he is implying that in this instance, the literal meaning is to be favored over a Midrashic explanation. The implication is clear – in other instances the Midrashic explanation, and not the literal translation, is indeed the simple meaning of the text. Thus, Rashi's statement of 'peshuto kemashma'o' is an invitation to analyze the existing Midrashim to understand why Rashi did not see them as suitable for inclusion in his commentary.

Nehama points out several places in which Rashi discusses his rejection of specific Midrashim, such as *Bereshit* 3:8, *Bereshit* 4:8, *Bereshit* 49:22, and *Shemot* 23:2. As an example, let us examine the way in which Nehama would suggest *Bereshit* 4:8 in order to give students a greater appreciation of Rashi's methodology:

> "And Cain said to Hevel his brother, and it came to pass when they were in the field and Cain rose up against Hevel his brother and slew him."
> Rashi: "He started to argue and fight with him in order to fall on him and kill him. There is Midrash on this, but the above is the plain meaning of the verse."

Students should be asked to identify the difficulty in the text that Rashi is addressing. Clearly, some important information is seemingly missing from the text. The Torah refers to a conversation that took place between Cain and Hevel, but then fails to record the content of the conversation. The students should now be presented with the Midrash that Rashi does not utilize and analyze why he rejects it. The following Midrash from *Midrash Rabbah* records three possible conversations that might have taken place between Cain and Hevel:

> 'Then Cain said to Hevel while they were in the field.' What were they arguing about?
> They said: Come and let us divide up the world. One took the land and the other took the movable property. The former said: 'The land that you are standing on belongs to me,' and the latter said: 'The clothes that you are wearing belong to me.' The latter

222

said: 'Take them off!' and the former said: 'Get off!' The result: 'Cain rose up against his brother Hevel and killed him.'

Rabbi Yehoshua of Sakhnin quotes R. Levi: Each took both land and movable property. What did they argue about? One said: 'The Temple will be built on my property', and the other said: 'The Temple will be built on my property'.... As a result, 'Cain rose up against Hevel his brother and killed him.'

Yehudah the son of R. Ami: They were arguing over Eve....

Students should be asked to analyze the differences between the three arguments described in the Midrash. Each Midrash identifies a different source of the conflict between Cain and Hevel. According to the first opinion it is the ownership of property, according to the second it is the desire for religious supremacy, and according to the third it is the desire for a woman. This Midrash posits that competition over wealth, religion, and sex are the primary sources of conflict in the world.

While Rashi may agree with this homiletic message, he cannot consider any of the opinions to be the simple meaning of the text. The students should be asked why these opinions are unacceptable to Rashi. All three of the cases adequately solve the difficulty in the text by providing the missing conversation. None of them, however, are consistent with the larger context. In the Midrashic accounts, both protagonists are equally responsible for the argument. In the Torah account, however, Cain is clearly the antagonist and bears responsibility for precipitating the argument. This is suggested, as well, by the fact that the verse begins with the phrase "And Cain said to Hevel." It is for this reason that Rashi rejects the Midrash. Rashi does not suggest an alternative conversation since the content of the argument is not significant. Cain simply precipitated an argument as a pretext to attack his brother.

Implicit Evidence – Selective Use of Midrash

There are many instances in which Rashi makes selective use of Midrashim without explicitly referring to the process. In some cases, a Midrash refers to several verses in the Torah but is only quoted by Rashi in reference to one or some of the verses. In other cases, Rashi may transfer a Midrash from the verse for which it was originally addressed to another verse. And, of course, many times Rashi refrains from utilizing available Midrashim without referring to them. Through an analysis of these instances, students can gain further insight into Rashi's concept of 'peshuto shel mikra'.

Let us examine a prototypical case. The Midrash often identifies anonymous people in the Torah with well-known personalities. For example, the refugee who brings a report to Avraham is identified as Og the King of Bashan (Bereshit 14:13), the two lads who accompany Avraham and Yitzhak to the Akeidah are identified as Yishmael and Eliezer (Bereshit 22:3), and the wood gatherer who violates Shabbat is identified as Tzelofhad (Bamidbar 15:32). In some cases, Rashi utilizes the Midrashic identification and in some cases he does not. Let us look at one such section and how it might be taught.

> "And there remained two men in the camp, the name of one was Eldad and the name of the other was Medad. And the spirit rested on them ... and they prophesied in the camp. And the young man ran (vayaratz hana'ar) and told Moshe and said: 'Eldad and Medad are 'prophesying' in the camp.' And Yehoshua Bin Nun, the servant of Moshe from his youth, answered and said: 'My master Moshe restrain them.'"
>
> (Bamidbar 11:26–28)

Rashi identifies the lad who reports to Moshe as his son Gershom. This is consistent with one opinion brought by the Midrash. The Sifre identifies the lad as Yehoshua based on the fact that he is referred to as "na'ar" elsewhere (Shemot 33:11). The Tanchuma identifies the lad as Gershom. The students should be asked to analyze why Rashi chose to identify the lad as Gershom rather than Yehoshua, and why he felt the need to identify the lad at all. The first question can be answered by looking at the continuation of the text: "And Yehoshua answered...." Certainly Yehoshua would not answer himself. Thus, the context forces the identification of Gershom as the anonymous lad. The question as to why Rashi needed to identify the lad at all can be answered by comparing this section with a similar situation in which Rashi does not utilize a Midrashic identification. For example, students might be asked to compare the section in *Bamidbar* with chapter 24 in *Bereshit* dealing with the search for a wife for Yitzhak. The Midrash identifies Avraham's servant in the story as Eliezer. Rashi, however, does not identify the servant even though the Midrashic identification fits in quite well with the larger context of the Biblical narrative. The perceptive student will note that when the servant is introduced in verse 24:2, the noun is used without the definite article. In contrast, the lad who reports to Moshe is referred to as "hana'ar," the lad, utilizing the definite article. If the Torah had stated that "a lad ran," Rashi would not have been compelled to identify him. In other words, the verse in *Bamidbar* has a textual difficulty that must be solved. In the verse in *Bereshit*, however, since there is no textual difficulty, Rashi omits the Midrashic identification even though it fits in well with the context.

Conclusion

The methodology demonstrated in the above examples can be replicated numerous times throughout the study of Chumash. Nehama believed that by engaging the students in analyses of this sort, they not only internalize more fully both Rashi's commentary and the content of the Midrashim, but they also gain an appreciation of the sophistication of Rashi's approach to 'peshuto shel mikra.'

Note: Information in this essay was gathered from Nehama's shiurim and her writings. For a more thorough treatment, consult "Rashi's Criteria for Citing Midrashim" in *Torah Insights* (Eliner Press) and Volume II of *Perush Rashi La'Torah* (The Open University of Israel).

A Review of the Pedagogical Approach of Nehama Leibowitz

Nehama's disciples can be found in the most unlikely places. A friend in Toronto, a real estate agent, decided to go back to school and become a teacher of Tanach. He discovered Nehama all on his own and even wrote a critical paper on her method. Needless to say, he is now "sold" on her approach.

– L.A.

Prepared for a Directed Reading Course
With Dr. Alex Pomson
York University Graduate Program in Education
Summer 1999
(October 4, 1999)
Prepared by Jerry Tepperman

A Review of the Pedagogical Approach of Nehama Leibowitz with Particular Attention to the Role of the Student in the Educational Process

Introduction

After the death of Nehama Leibowitz (z"l) in 1997, numerous obituaries were published praising her contribution to Jewish education. These obituaries carried titles such as "The Teacher of the Generation," "The Exemplary Teacher," and "Nehama of the Masses." These flattering articles, in addition to many others, have all expressed their admiration for Nehama Leibowitz. In turn, I have no reservation in echoing the opinion expressed in many of them, namely, that there is no other person in the field of modern Jewish education who has developed such an impressive following of devoted students dedicated to her pedagogical methods and ideals. Now that she is no longer with us, there is a perceived need to better define those methods and ideals in order to preserve them for future generations of teachers. This paper is an effort to examine one aspect of her approach in order to define and delineate it by pulling together her comments from a selection of sources. More specifically, I will try to examine how Nehama Leibowitz (or as she will be referred to henceforth, Nehama) views the role of the student in the education process and ask whether it is possible to identify the central approaches that she uses in order to engage the student in the process of learning.

The story is told[1] that a colleague once asked Nehama Leibowitz to explain what the secret was to her successful teaching methods. Reportedly, and perhaps for lack of time, she answered abruptly, and in a very concise Hebrew as follows, "Just make sure that it [the class] is interesting." One may assume that this answer was offered tongue-in-cheek and was not meant to encapsulate her methods or her approach. However, one must also assume that it contained an element of truth. Exactly how did she go about making sure that the

---

1. Daf Letarbut Yehudit, Misrad Hahinuckh Hatarbut V'hasport, Shoshana Rabin, "Minitsutsot Nehama", 1997.

students remained interested? Was this casual comment truly indicative of her approach to Jewish education or was she merely trying to be amusing? Assuming that this brief response is not a complete answer to the original query about her teaching methods, can we find other clues in her published works that may help us to answer the question properly?

Very little information appears in the written legacy of Nehama that clearly expresses and defines her philosophy of Jewish education or her theory of Jewish education.[2] The bulk of her writings are directed toward the analysis of Torah texts. Her gilyonot are made up of questions without answers guiding the reader through the study and analysis of a variety of specific texts. Her style therein involved presenting a selection of perplexing problems with the explanations of commentaries on the text. The answers to some of these problems required a great deal of expertise and sophistication. Corrections could be obtained by correspondence with her directly. Her studies in the weekly portion of the Torah are perhaps directed to a less sophisticated audience, but they too contain biblical exegesis and not a description of how to teach that material or of what objectives are to be achieved through the study of that material.[3]

This paper will focus on several pedagogical pieces written by Nehama that do contain specific recommendations, suggestions, and references relevant to answering our questions. These are *Limud Parshanei Hatorah Uderakhim Lehoraatam, Sefer Bereshit*[4] (LPHUL),

---

2. Rosenak defines these terms as referring respectively to the goals of Jewish education and to the techniques and methods to be used to achieve those goals. Rosenak also divides theories of education into four categories. They may be centered on any one of the following elements in the educational process: the teacher, the student, the subject matter, and the context. See Rosenak, Michael, *Roads to the Palace: Jewish Texts and Teaching,* Oxford: Berghahn Books, 1995, page 45.

3. A doctoral dissertation by Marla Frankel examines the *Gilyonot* and *Studies* in the five books of the Torah of Nehama Leibowitz in order to compare the approach taken and suggest whether the approach was different when directed at different audiences. See Franel, Marla, "Iyun V'Horaah: Hanharat Shitata Shel Nechama Leibowitz," The Hebrew University, 1998.

4. Leibowitz, Nehama, "Limod Parshanei Hatorah Uderakhim Lehoraatam (LPHUL), Sefer Bereshit," Hamahlaka Lehinukh Uletarbut Toraniim Bagola, Histadrut Hatsionit Haolamit, 1975.

and a collection of essays titled *"Lilmod Ulelamed Tanach"*[5] (LUT). These two pieces of her work, written at different times, contain brief comments and advice intended as instructional tutorials for teachers that demonstrate how Nehama would herself approach the task of teaching the respective texts to a class of students. Here, more than in any other samples of her writings, we may find clues that can be used to answer the questions posed above.

To begin with, we will look at an important quote from Nehama's introduction to LPHUL that has appeared in print several times. After introducing and setting the stage for this detailed analysis of selected passages from *Bereshit*, Nehama anticipates the objection that there is not enough time in the classroom to study these passages and the commentaries in such depth. To this objection she answers that it is preferable to limit the quantity of textual analysis and the commentaries covered, but to teach them in such a way as to endear the material to the students by making them aware of the complex analysis and scholarship contained therein. Then she adds;[6]

> The teacher should always remember: Our main purpose in school is not to impart knowledge, and it is not in our power to produce wise students familiar with all the books of the Torah. However it is our goal to spread love of the Torah, so that the words of the Torah are precious and cherished by the student, so that he/she will see the awesome light which shines forth from our commentators and illuminates the text, and so that the hearts of our students will be warmed by their light.

These brief introductory comments shed light on Nehama's pedagogical goals and her personal philosophy of teaching. It is clear even from this brief quote that the student's love and appreciation for the beauty inherent in the text of the Torah is at the center of this philosophy and what it seeks to achieve. Nehama does not seem to be concerned with general knowledge, or performance of the mitzvoth. Nor is it love for God, or identification with the community of Israel,

---

5. Leibowitz, Nehama, "Lilmod Ulelamed Tanach (LUT)," Jerusalem, Israel, Elinor Publications, 1995.
6. All translations from the Hebrew in this paper are those of the writer.

that concerns Nehama. She makes no mention of them. The possible implication from this brief quote is that in Nehama's view, all of these other worthy objectives will follow if we can impart a sincere love of the text of the Torah to our students. Thus, Nehama emphasizes the point here in her introduction. In her approach to education, the ultimate objective is to instill the students with the *love of Torah*. This objective supersedes all dictates of curriculum, and all considerations and decisions regarding quantity over quality in the classroom.

Moreover, it is clear from this quote, in the context of this introduction, that in Nehama's view it is the judicious use of the commentators on the text of the Torah that provide the practical key to generating that love of Torah. That is why an in-depth understanding of the commentaries is so important.[7] This is in fact the argument Nehama is making in her introduction to this book about the commentaries. This is her justification for writing a book written to highlight the approaches and idiosyncrasies of a selection of those commentaries. Perhaps we might even suggest that this judicious use of the commentaries stands at the center of her methodology for teaching biblical texts.[8]

Methodology and Findings

As mentioned above, the book LPHUL is really a collection of brief analyses and insights into selected texts throughout *Bereshit*. Clearly, Nehama has written this book because she felt it was imperative that

---

7. See Marla Frankel in a recent article investigating how Nehama Leibowitz selects different problems and materials in her publications that are directed toward the general reader than she presents in her gilyonot, which are intended for the more accomplished reader. Frankel, Marla, "The Teacher in the Writings of Nechama Leibowitz," Jerusalem, Israel, The David Yellin Teacher's College, Freund Publishing House Ltd., and Bar Ilan University, 1999.

8. Howard Deitcher, in his article, "Between Angels and Mere Mortals: Nehama Leibowitz's Approach to the Presentation of Biblical Characters," employs the same quote as in order to derive two approaches in Nehama Leibowitz's methodology. One is a normative approach whose goal is the love of Torah and the other a deliberative-inductive approach, which is based on problem solving. He suggests that there is an interaction and synthesis between the two in the general approach espoused by Nehama. Although Deitcher's terminology is quite different we believe that his analysis moves along similar lines to those presented here.

teachers have an appreciation for the types of textual problems and questions that were addressed by the commentaries in order to clarify their understanding of the texts. Each commentator tends to develop distinctive approaches for dealing with certain types of problems and utilizes a depth of and breadth of knowledge that is not always appreciated by those uninitiated in higher levels of biblical scholarship and exegesis. Nehama seeks to begin to clarify these issues for the teachers who would read her book.

Sprinkled randomly among these short analyses are also random comments and instructions aimed at teachers who might want to use the book as an aid in preparing their lesson plans while teaching classes in the book of *Bereshit*. From Nehama's introduction, it is also clear that she expected the book to act as a reference guide such that teachers would not necessarily read the entire volume. Thus, where she felt a comment was important she would repeat it, even if there were other similar comments in other sections of the book. In developing the thesis expressed above, I undertook to carefully review these side comments and classify them into categories. As I will endeavor to demonstrate, this review yields some interesting patterns, which will be the main subject of this paper. It is our contention that these patterns provide a road map to Nehama's methodology. From these patterns, we learn what techniques and strategies were significant to Nehama, and while there are no dramatic surprises, they do provide a concrete basis from which to draw some conclusions.

The first step necessary in order to categorize the types of advice offered by Nehama required a careful reading of each section of her book and a concise summary of each section. This summary included a description of the difficulty in the text and a brief indication of the contents of the answers offered by Nehama or her view of the relevant commentaries on that difficulty. Each section summary was then listed in a tabular format and next to each there was an indication of the appropriate page in LPHUL and the biblical reference for the relevant passage. Also in the same row, I paraphrased any pieces of advice for teachers that were suggested by Nehama for that section. These included explanations for why something was done, or how to select material for presentation, or side comments about the lesson. A sample page of this summary is included here for your review.

231

After the initial step was completed, all of the comments and pieces of advice were listed and divided into categories. A letter code followed by a number was placed in the third column of the table next to the corresponding comment or advice. The letter codes indicate the type of advice as listed in the chart on p. 234. The number next to the letter code indicates whether this is the first time that this type of advice appears or the second time and so forth. On the first round of categorization there were a large number of comments that naturally seemed to belong together in a few larger categories. Other categories were smaller and some were actually quite similar to each other with only minor differences separating one from the other. Then a second review of all the comments and categories was conducted and in this second round of categorization the definitions of certain categories were broadened so that in effect some of these smaller categories were combined together to form the classifications you will find listed below.

Note that these classifications are also listed in two groups, and within each group the classifications are sequenced according to the frequency[9] of their appearance. The first four are didactic in nature and among the largest classifications. In other words, most of the advice offered by Nehama in this group focuses on issues that are instructional in nature. The remainder are comments about the interpretive style of the commentaries cited in each relevant section and are listed next in the lower half table. The last category of miscellaneous comments are generally interpretive in nature (three of them could also be considered didactic), but none fall easily under the umbrella of one of the other classifications.

---

9.   A detailed summary of LPHUL and a classification of the various comments and advice can be made available as an appendix to this paper.

Comments On Selected Classifications

A. How much of the available relevant material on a given passage should be included in the classroom and which portions should be given priority

In order to clarify these classifications for the reader, we will now cite examples of most as they appear in LPHUL and briefly discuss each one. Note that almost 25 percent of these comments fall into the first category and address the need for teachers to be selective when choosing the commentaries and teaching materials so that they are appropriate for the particular classroom environment. All of Nehama's comments in this regard are consistent with the general goal suggested above, which is to instill the love of Torah in the student. This selectivity is important to Nehama for a variety of reasons. In some instances, her advice is to skip certain material because it would be too challenging or frustrating for most students, or because it would not be enjoyable for the students, or because a comprehensive treatment of the topic would take too much time from other more productive texts. The selection of materials is one of the few elements of the teaching environment that is almost entirely under the teacher's control. Nehama's emphasis on this area indicates that this factor is in her view one of the basic building blocks of a successful lesson. For example, in *Bereshit* 15:14, God notifies Avraham that his descendants will be slaves in Egypt and that they will be rescued from Egypt and the Egyptians will be punished. Nehama quotes several commentaries[10] who ask why the Egyptians should be punished when they had no choice in the matter. The descendants of Avraham became slaves because God decreed it, not because of the Egyptians who implemented it. The issue at stake in this passage is whether the Egyptians exercised free will and if they did not, whether they are to be held accountable. Among those commentaries cited are Rambam and Ramban, but Nehama advises that the explanation of Rambam is too sophisticated for most students and would require too much time

---

10. LPHUL, page 44.

Type of Advice	Code	Frequency
Didactic Classifications		
How much of the available relevant material on a given passage should be included in the classroom and which portions should be given priority.	S	22
Suggestions for individual student exercises, student analysis, and class preparation particularly where the students are asked to compare the commentaries and contrast their merits and deficiencies, and even voice their preferences.	B	18
Suggestions for the inclusion of outside sources relevant to the student that do not relate directly to the text but that contribute to the theme, moral, or lesson embedded in the text.	O	12
Visual techniques for assisting students with grasping complex issues or facilitating successful seat work.	V	12
Interpretive Classifications		
Demonstrations of the importance of careful attention to details of expression and textual variations in the biblical text and in the commentaries.	A	13
Situations that demonstrate how what seem like midrashic commentaries can be considered the plain sense of the text.	P	5
Situations where disagreements regarding technical grammatical or syntactical interpretations result in conceptual thematic differences.	X	4
Situations where the commentaries take an objective approah to the behavior of biblical heroes. They do not hesitate to criticize when necessary or attempt to take sides when it is unnecessary.	W	3
Miscellaneous suggestions that do not fall into any of the above categories.	M	8
Total		96

and discussion. She suggests that it should be skipped even though it is quite important, and in fact a part of the commentary of the Ramban refers to the views of the Rambam. Nehama recommends just the latter two answers offered by the Ramban for presentation in the classroom.

Similarly, in *Bereshit* 4:10 Nehama introduces a technical grammatical issue[11] that receives attention from the Ibn Ezra. In order to illustrate the details of the problem she also presents a couple of other instances where the same isssue is crucial for an understanding of the text. In Nehama's view, it is important for the teacher to realize that such grammatical fine points are instrumental in understanding a whole series of problematic texts. Given unlimited quantities of time it might even be interesting for the students. However, Nehama strongly recommends that this Ibn Ezra not be introduced into the classroom setting. She insists that there is too much material in the specific chapter at hand that has moral and ethical significance to expend precious class time on grammatical issues that will do little to enhance their enjoyment of the text.

In contrast to those two instances where Nehama suggests that sometimes technically relevant material is not appropriate in the classroom, on at least one other occasion Nehama gives the opposite sort of advice. She recommends that the teacher take the time to make sure that other examples of a certain moral issue should be included and emphasized in the class presentation. For example, in *Bereshit* 24:10, while speaking of the trip of Eliezer to Haran to find a wife for Yitzhak[12], the text says that Eliezer took ten camels from the camels that belong to his master. Rashi comments on the extraneous wording "From the camels that belong to his master." Rashi suggests that this indicates that the camels of Avraham were always muzzled in public so that they would not graze in private property. The extra wording teaches us the extent to which Avraham and his household went in order to avoid accidental theft. Nehama points out other similar instances such as the story of Lot's disagreement with Avraham, the story of Yitzhak sending Eisav out to hunt, and

---

11. LPHUL, page 6.
12. LPHUL, page 93.

the story of Moshe grazing his flocks of Yitro in the desert. In each of these instances Rashi explains extraneous wording by associating it with lessons in the avoidance of dishonesty[13] and strongly suggests that the teacher present them to the class as well.

What is the principle guiding Nehama in deciding what should and should not be included? On one occasion Nehama suggests leaving out comparable sources from other biblical texts and then in the other she suggests going far afield in order to demonstrate that the same explanation is used to solve problems in a variety of texts. Our contention is that Nehama asks herself if the material will contribute to the "love of Torah" in the students. Her position is that grammatical issues, while very worthwhile and important in the appropriate circumstances, would tend to be dry and boring in the classroom. Spending time on a sophisticated philosophical issue that is beyond the grasp of many of the students will only also serve to demoralize the students. On the other hand, a moral ethical issue, such as theft versus honesty, is a topic that the students can relate to and lends itself to classroom presentation and discussion. Petty theft is an unfortunate reality that many students live with and take measures to counteract on a daily basis. For Nehama this practical ethical issue is important enough to emphasize with multiple examples and comparable situations.[14]

B. Suggestions for individual student exercises, student analysis, and class preparation

The type of advice that appears next in order of frequency in LPHUL includes suggestions for appropriate individual student exercises, student analysis, classroom preparation, and homework assignments. These comments often suggest that the students compare two related texts and examine them for slight variations in wording and terminology. The students may be asked to suggest explanations in writing

---

13. LPHUL, *Bereshit* 27:3, *Vetsuda li tsayid,* "And hunt game for me" (but not on private property). *Shemot* 3:1, *Ahar Hamidbar,* "out in the desert" (but not on private property). *Bereshit* 13:7, *Vayehee Reev,* "And there was a fight" (concerning whether to graze the sheep on private property). See LPHUL, p. 95.
14. Perhaps this is also exactly the type of situation where Nehama would be tempted to relate one of her anecdotes about the price to be paid for dishonesty.

for these variations in writing and/or to consider how they contribute to the themes[15] introduced in the text. On occasion, these exercises are to take place prior to a class discussion that analyzes the commentaries on that text. This provides the opportunity for the students to see their own insights repeated in the commentaries. What better reinforcement for the students' diligent work and careful investigations than for them to have the same insight as a respected biblical scholar? On other occasions, this sort of individual analysis may take place after the commentaries have been studied. Here the students may be asked to review the text and find references that support one commentary or the other. The text itself often dictates which of these approaches is most appropriate. Some situations lend themselves to student analysis before class discussion because the material differences to be uncovered are relatively obvious and not grammar related or technically complicated. Others are best assigned after the class discussion to reinforce the commentaries studied in class.

In places, Nehama insists that it is not really relevant whether the answers are correct or not. The essential element in the exercise is the involvement of the students in the process of analysis and exegesis.[16] Almost always, the answers are to be prepared in writing so that the entire class must participate in the activity and not sit by while the brightest in the class answer for them. The students may be asked to write down the difference between several commentaries on a given passage. Always, Nehama is careful to stipulate that the answers must consist of concise abstractions that provide insight into the essential difference between the commentaries and must not consist of mere repetitions of the interpretations themselves.

---

15. LPHUL, See *Bereshit* 15:18, page 48, where Nehama suggests that the students compare the texts of four separate instances where God promises the land of Canaan to the descendants of Avraham. Also see *Bereshit* 37:26, page 176, where Nehama recommends that the students chart the changes in the way Yosef is referred to in the chapter and relate the changes to the contents of the story line.

16. LPHUL, See *Bereshit* 37:2, page 157, where various interpretations of the term *Naar* are provided by the commentaries and each has its merits and detractions. Nehama suggests the students should be encouraged to voice an opinion as to their preferred interpretation. See also *Bereshit* 44:22, page 198, where she states that the discussion itself is more important than the final conclusion.

In other situations, one commentator, such as Rashi,[17] may present several interpretations to a specific passage. Here Nehama is careful to point out that Rashi never suggests multiple answers to a problem unless each of the answers has some deficiency that makes it unable to stand on its own. The students may be asked to explain what the deficiencies or advantages are within each answer presented. Alternatively, the students may be asked to concisely conceptualize the differences among the answers. Another variation along the same theme may require a comparison of Rashi's treatment of a similar problem in different locations.[18] Here the students may be asked to compare the various commentaries and then write down what is similar in all the locations or perhaps what is different.

In another essay published by Nehama that seeks to provide direction to the teacher in the classroom setting, she speaks at relative length about the advantages of such an inductive activity centered approach. In a similar manner to the examples listed above, she recommends putting the students to work with issues and problems that will make them think. Then she adds yet another nuance[19] directed at stimulating additional classroom discussion. Nehama begins by deprecating the Socratic approach to classroom instruction and points out that even the Midrash, a relatively ancient source, outlines forty-eight different methods through which the Torah can be studied. Then she continues:

> Passive behavior during the class will weaken his [the student's] muscles, deflate his spirits, which will remain dormant, and cause him to fall asleep.... Moreover, if the teacher insists on presenting the material to the students on a silver platter, without any effort or work on their part, they will not absorb the material and if they do absorb it they will immediately forget it, the students will be bored, and the learning will not capture their hearts.

---

17. LPHUL; *Bereshit* 25:28, page 107.
18. LPHUL; *Bereshit* 18:20, 21, page 58. Here Rashi deals with the issue of anthropomorphic language in the Torah. Nehama cites and compares several other locations where Rashi comments on the same problem.
19. Leibowitz, Nehama, LUT: "Lehorot Hatanakh Bekitot Gevohot" (On Teaching Tanach in Senior Classes), Jersualem, Israel, Elinor Publications, 1995, pages 14–17.

In the same vein, Nehama has quoted Rav Yosef Ibn Kaspi,[20] who once said "And I will give them *for free* the treasure which I have accumulated through blood and perspiration." Nehama insists that this is not the way to accomplish our educational objectives. How then does Nehama suggest that we capture the hearts of the students? She recommends selecting texts that lend themselves to several interpretations, each of which contains its own merits and deficiencies. Then in a manner similar to that described above, she suggests orchestrating a classroom discussion that would in effect debate the merits of each of the interpretations. Give students the opportunity to examine, weigh, and prove or disprove the various opinions. Allow the students to form factions, divide into groups, develop the ideas, and argue the points. Then, after presenting her first example, Nehama continues:

> The main thing is that no one is nodding off or sleeping in the class. Instead there are shining eyes and raised hands, with each student adding a point of his own and trying to prove his point with clear and decisive arguments, and the atmosphere is light and lively. For the most part there are no moments in the classroom more beautiful than these.

This technique is designed to actively engage the students in the scholarly discussion of the text as a participant and not merely an observer. It is reminiscent of the position presented by David Hartman,[21] where he argues for an educational system that engages the student in a discussion of the Mishna and Talmud, which is relevant to their lives. The students must feel that their opinions and analyses will allow them to understand the intricate discussion of the rabbis and that they have the ability to contribute to that discussion. Nehama tries to accomplish similar goals with her approach to the

---

20. Leibowitz, Nehama, "LUT: Horaat Haftorat Yom Bet Shel Rosh Hashana", Jerusalem, Israel, Elinor Publications, 1995, page 68.
21. Hartman, David, *A Heart Has Many Rooms: Celebrating the Many Voices Within Judaism,* Woodstock, Vermont, Jewish Lights Publishing, 1999. Rabbi Hartman argues that it is only possible to engage the students in this sort of relevant discussion if they feel part of a community in which the discussion is significant.

biblical texts. One of the greatest gifts that this form of instruction bequeaths to the students is the training in how to conceptualize the discrepancies between the various interpretations, plus the ability to verbalize those discrepancies in an abstract fashion and to evaluate and form an opinion about which interpretation is the most suitable. These skills are bound to empower the student not only in his work on the biblical texts but in any endeavor that he or she may choose to pursue.

C. Attention to details of expression and textual variations in the biblical text and in the commentaries

Thus far, we have seen that Nehama places a heavy emphasis on choosing the appropriate material for presentation in the classroom setting. We have also seen that once the material is selected it must in her view be presented in such a way as to animate and empower the student to take responsibility for his or her own learning. Between these two categories of advice we have already included almost forty percent of the comments made by Nehama in LPHUL. Clearly these are two issues that she considers worthy of emphasis.

Next on the chart by frequency of occurrence are situations where Nehama finds an opportunity to convey to the students interpretive skills such as the necessity for reading the biblical text and even the commentaries with precision and accuracy. Nehama also directs the teacher to train the students to pay attention to variations in expression between similar texts and expressions. Often it is the commentators who are able to open the eyes of the students to the significance of these seemingly minor variations. The first example[22] we have chosen demonstrates how the commentaries take note of the appearance of a single extraneous word in the text, the word *Bidorotov*. In this biblical passage, the narrator tells us that Noah was a just man, and he was pure *in his generation*. Nehama contrasts the two ways in which the commentaries, in the footsteps of the Midrash, interpret this phrase. Is it derogatory or complimentary? Some say Noah was pure *even* in his generation, while others say Noah was pure, *but only* in his generation. The fact that this one

---

22. LPHUL, page 17, *Bereshit 6:9*.

word can be construed either way and potentially change the meaning of the text so dramatically points to the significance of each and every word. Nehama also suggests that a dramatic reading of the line with contrasting inflections will serve to emphasize the difference to the students, in a manner to which it will be easy for them to relate. Similarly, at the beginning of the next chapter[23] we find a phrase again describing Noah as just, but not as pure. The commentaries base a new lesson on this change. They suggest that when the narrator is speaking to the reader about Noah he is able to give a full and accurate description and mention that he is both *just* and *pure*, but in speaking directly to Noah, God restricts his comments and only mentions that he is *just*. Perhaps this is done so as not to embarrass him.

Nehama insists[24] that it is important to emphasize to the students that scholars of secular literature also analyze minor variations in the wording of modern poetry with exacting detail. Therefore, it should not be surprising that in order to fully appreciate biblical texts we must also employ a similar meticulous attention to detail and literary style. In other places, Nehama points to situations where we can even learn lessons from changes in the order in a listing of names,[25] or subtle changes in the references to certain personalities and the adjectives used to describe them.[26] Nehama highlights the habit of many commentaries of defining unusual terms in the text at the first occurrence.[27] In other places she even demonstrates the way in which commentaries themselves, such as Rashi, are meticulously precise in the use of wording.[28] When Rashi employs different terminology to discuss similar situations, it is worthwhile asking why.

The net effect of Nehama's emphasis on a precise reading of the text is ultimately consistent with what we have defined as her basic goal and objective. What better way to instill a love of Torah than to train the student to treat each and every word with reverence and

---

23. LPHUL, page 23, *Bereshit 7:1*.
24. LPHUL, page 90, *Bereshit 24:7*.
25. LPHUL, page 99, *Bereshit 24:50*.
26. LPHUL, page 176, *Bereshit 37:27*.
27. LPHUL, page 126, *Bereshit 29:17*.
28. LPHUL, page 154, *Bereshit 37:1*.

respect? What better way to instill admiration for the scholarship of the commentators of the text than to demonstrate their mastery of the subtle nuances that escape most of us and certainly fly directly over the head of the casual reader? Having demonstrated the level of sophistication and challenge involved in engaging in a serious discussion of the text, the student is more inclined to try to enter into this discussion himself. Thus, this emphasis on precise reading reinforces and supports the exercises and tasks that we have discussed earlier and that play such a central role in Nehama's approach to education. By choosing the material appropriately, by encouraging the students to tackle challenging problems tailored to their skill level, and by emphasizing the complexity and precision inherent in the text, the teacher is able to capture the imagination of the students and perhaps even inspire them.

D. Suggestions for the inclusion of outside sources

However, inspiration is an elusive goal. The biblical text is full of stories and lessons and morals, but if the students are unable to relate to the stories and personalities in them, then it is doubtful whether they will be able to treat it as more than just an interesting intellectual pursuit. Love of Torah will not be achieved merely on the basis of intellectual challenge alone. Torah must also speak to the lives of the students and provide some insight into their own everyday problems. To that end, Nehama often introduces unusual external sources not directly related to the text, in order to bridge the gap between an interesting biblical lesson or story and a message that is meaningful to the student. Thus, it is no surprise that the next category of comment presented in LPHUL includes situations where a variety of outside sources can be employed to make the text more relevant to the student. For example,[29] on the passage that describes Yaakov leaving Be'er Sheva for Haran in order to escape the wrath of Eisav and find a bride, the commentaries question the necessity for both phrases, one mentioning *leaving* and the other mentioning *going*. If Yaakov was going to Haran it is clear he was leaving Be'er Sheva. Rashi explains that the text is conveying the extent of the community's feelings of loss in the

---

29. LPHUL, page 117, *Bereshit* 28:10.

city of Be'er Sheva. Nehama suggests the following brief anecdote that highlights that people still use this type of expression in their everyday speech. This apparently normal dialogue conveys the identical concept that Rashi is presenting in his explanation of the text.

> A classmate from school emotionally tells his friends, "Can you imagine! You know John Doe, the guy who was at the top of his class, and our teacher's favorite student, and the most popular kid in the school? Well, *he left our school* and transferred over to school X." (The meaning of the phrase *He left our school* is that his leaving will have an impact.)

In Nehama's approach, no outside source is a priori off limits[30] if it can contribute to the insightful understanding of a particular text and help the students find relevance in the lessons contained therein. She has often been known to quote from what some might consider non-traditional sources such as Buber, Cassuto, even non-Jewish biblical exegetes. Nor does Nehama ignore more ancient traditional texts if they can shed light on a particular text. Often Midrashim[31] expand beautifully and timelessly on an idea and convert the task of interpreting the text from an intellectual exercise into a meaningful life-enhancing experience. For example,[32] Rashi points out that the text uses different descriptive terminology for the attributes of Avraham and Noah and suggests that this is indicative of the fact that Avraham operated at a higher spiritual level than Noah. Noah required support but Avraham did not. In order to reinforce this concept, Nehama quotes a Midrash that beautifully compares the actions of Noah and Avraham and Moshe in standing up to defend their fellow men. Similarly, Nehama refers to an essay by Buber on the same topic and suggests that it might be a good source for relevant outside reading as well. The criteria for including these sources ultimately depend on

---

30. Marla Frankel demonstrates that Nehama is motivated by the need to engage the students. Outside sources are introduced when they contribute to that end, and they are chosen to complement the circumstances and the needs of the students. See Frankel, Marla, *Iyun V'Horaah: Hanharat Shitata Shel Nechama Leibowitz,* The Hebrew University of Jerusalem, 1998, pages 61–62.
31. LPHUL, page 5, *Bereshit* 4:9.
32. LPHUL, page 19, *Bereshit* 6:9.

the intrinsic merits of the ideas that are presented and on whether they add to the students' understanding of the text and make the text more meaningful for them.

In one other case, Nehama quotes from a book of English grammar[33] in order to help the student relate to a difficult philosophical issue. Here, the text has God himself asking Kayin, "Where is your brother Hevel?" Rashi anticipates the problem dealt with by several commentaries. If God knows everything and he knew exactly what had happened to Hevel, then why did he ask? God should have confronted Kayin directly and asked him how he could have stooped to murdering his brother. Rashi explains that God was initiating a conversation with Kayin in a congenial, friendly way to see whether he might admit what he had done and repent. Nehama quotes the following anecdote in order to clarify what Rashi is proposing.

> An older man, the owner of a large car, stands next to his car on the side of the highway because his car has a flat tire. A good-hearted young man drives by, stops his car, and walks back with the intention of trying to help him. He asks, "Got a flat tire?" If the older gentleman wanted to interpret the words literally he might have regarded the question as silly. He might have responded, "Of course I do, you dumb ox. Can't you see that the tire is flat?" Instead, the older gentleman responds, "Yes, I guess I do. How wonderful of you to stop. I don't know how I would have been able to change the tire on my own." The older gentleman realized that the young man was merely stating the obvious in order to engage a total stranger in conversation.

Presumably, Kayin did not speak to God regularly either. Thus in the wording of this text, we experience God's tolerance and sensitivity as he gently engages Kayin in conversation in order not to appear confrontational and in order to patiently give Kayin the opportunity to admit his sin and repent.

In yet another instance Nehama employs a technique typical of modern biblical scholarship. She quotes from archaeological evidence

---

33. LPHUL, page 5, *Bereshit* 4:9. Here Nehama refers to a book by S.I. Hayakawa: *Language in Thought and Action*

regarding the code of Hammurabi[34] in order to clarify what may have been the legal rights of Sarah in her relationship with her maid Hagar, who became Avraham's second wife. This contributes to a better understanding of the text. In addition, we suggest that another purpose of utilizing this source is to transform the text in the eyes of the students into a real-life situation about people with very real feelings and emotions, who are fully aware of the legal ramifications of their actions.

E. Visual techniques

Yet another of the didactic classifications of advice listed above prescribes various visual exercises that the students can be asked to perform. Although Nehama does not explicitly discuss the possibility that students will have different learning styles, she does seem to anticipate this need by introducing these visually oriented problems and techniques. Often certain commentaries will notice slight variations in language that would go unnoticed by someone only casually familiar with the text, but can be clearly illustrated by employing a visual prop. In addition, there are a myriad of examples in the Bible of stories that are repeated or retold under slightly different circumstances.[35] A technique frequently used by Nehama asks the student to study the two texts while they are written side by side. Similar phrases are placed opposite each other for ease of comparison. This serves to highlight the differences and permits even those unfamiliar with the text to pick out the areas of concern for further study. This technique may be used before the fact in order to shift the responsibility over to the students to discover the difficulties and suggest possible solutions. Or it can be used after the commentaries have been studied in order to clarify their interpretations and opinions. One elegant example of this technique[36] compares the language and sentence structure in two separate biblical texts. One is at the beginning of the first test of Avraham when he is asked to abandon his homeland, and the other is

---

34. LPHUL, page 50, *Bereshit* 16:2.
35. Obvious examples include the multiple retelling of the meeting between Eliezer and Rivka, the repetition of the dreams of Pharaoh for Joseph, and Yehudah's plea for mercy before Joseph when Binyamin is threatened with slavery.
36. LPHUL, page 67, *Bereshit* 22:2.

at the beginning of the last test of Avraham, the Akeida, the sacrifice of Yitzhak. Both texts use the word *Lech Lecha* and similar sentence structure. Nehama suggests that the two passages should be written on the blackboard side by side so that the similarities stand out clearly. She then comments that the choice of such obvious parallel language connects the two incidents. One test asked Avraham to leave behind his past and the other test asks Avraham to cut off his hopes for the future of his family. This connection serves to emphasize the difficulty of the latter test and the extent of Avraham's faith.

A second visual technique introduced by Nehama examines parallel structures within a given passage to great effect. These parallel structures are characteristic of biblical poetry and sometimes appear in the middle of a section of what most would consider prose.[37] In this instance, the best way to describe the technique is with a detailed example. As Yaakov and Eisav mature the text tells us about each of their personalities and the relationship that they enjoyed with their parents. *Vayehee Eisav ish yodaya tsayid, ish sadeh, veYaakov ish tam yoshev ohalim.* Rashi translates this as, "And Eisav was a crafty person, a man of the fields, and Yaakov was an honest person who sat in the tents." As Nehama puts it, most students will immediately ask how Rashi knows to translate the word *tsayid* as "crafty," when its usual meaning is derived from the word "to hunt." Why not translate it as "Eisav was a man of the hunt, a man of the field"? In order to clarify Rashi's reasoning Nehama presents the following table:

Description	Occupation or Character trait?	Where he worked
And Eisav was	A man of the Hunt or Crafty?	A man of the field
And Yaakov was	Honest	Who Sat in tents

The answer is made obvious by the parallel structure of the sentence highlighted by this table. Each man is described by two phrases, the second of which in each case clearly refers to his occupation.

---

37. For an extensive discussion of biblical parallelism, see Kugel, James, *The Idea of Biblical Poetry: Parallelism and Its History.* New Haven and London, Yale University Press, 1981.

Note that the first descriptive phrase associated with Yaakov clearly refers to a character trait; thus Rashi deduces that the first descriptive phrase associated with Eisav must also refer to a character trait. By using this technique, the students can be encouraged to successfully uncover a completely rational reason for Rashi's interpretation, an interpretation that the students can identify with and understand. This new insight may even encourage the students to develop greater respect for Rashi and for the text itself.

Finally, one last type of visual exercise. Nehama was fond of asking students to copy over a passage and punctuate it appropriately in order to demonstrate their understanding of a given passage. Often different interpretations would require quite different punctuation marks. This exercise would allow the student to demonstrate understanding of the various interpretations and of the discrepancies among interpretations. For instance,[38] as Yehudah pleads for the welfare of Binyamin he says, "And we told my master that the boy cannot leave his father, and if he leaves his father he will die." Several commentaries ask, who is the one who will die if the boy leaves his father, the boy or the father? The text is not clear on the matter. In order to illustrate the opinions of differing commentaries the students might be asked to punctuate the sentence according to each opinion. In this instance, the two ways to punctuate the sentence in order to highlight the difference are as follows:

and if he leaves his father – he will die, and your servants...
and if he leaves his father he will die, – and your servants...

In summary then, these five categories that we have outlined make up over eighty percent of the comments and suggestions that Nehama makes in LPHUL. It has been our contention all along that it is no coincidence that a quarter of her comments are centered around the appropriate choice of the subject material for the class. It is indicative of the centrality of this sort of advice to Nehama's approach. Neither is it a coincidence that almost as many suggestions center

---

38. LPHUL, page 198, *Bereshit* 44:22.

around how to devise interesting and challenging activities that instruct the students in how to read and analyze the text, or that demonstrate to the student the need to read the text carefully and precisely. It is also significant that the bulk of the remaining suggestions and comments relate to other methods through which these activities can be made more meaningful and more understandable to the students. It is clear that these categories of suggestions are at the core of Nehama's methodology and her approach to classroom education.

A Further Illustration and Conclusion

In order to illustrate the centrality of these types of advice further, we will digress and look at one other essay written by Nehama[39] in order to see if we can detect the same methodologies and types of suggestions. Indeed, we will find that the areas of emphasis and the general direction of the advice offered by Nehama here in this essay are remarkably consistent with the categories of advice we have reviewed and derived from LPHUL. This essay is a guide to teaching a chapter from *Yirmiyahu* that also serves as the Haftara for the second day of Rosh Hashana. More than anything else written by Nehama, this particular paper artfully outlines in a step-by-step fashion how she would approach teaching a chapter in Tanach and thus exemplifies her methods and approach to teaching in the classroom.

It is significant that Nehama begins by recommending to the teacher three steps to follow while preparing to teach this typical chapter.

- Study the chapter itself intensively without any thought to the best way to teach the chapter or present the material to the student.
- Decide on the specific goals for this particular class situation and then select which parts of all the material that has been studied will be appropriate for this situation, given the time constraints and the characteristics of the students.
- Design a variety of exercises for the students that will animate

---

39. Leibowitz, Nehama, "LUT: Horaat Haftorat Yom Bet Shel Rosh Hashana," Jerusalem, Israel, Elinor Publications, 1995, page 59.

the students and open their eyes to see and their hearts to understand.

These three steps correspond exactly to the material we have reviewed above in LPHUL. The body of the text in LPHUL is designed to instruct the reader in the analysis and understanding of the Parshanim and their approach to the text. The examples Nehama cites are designed to demonstrate the characteristics of the Parshanim and the depth of scholarship necessary to appreciate those characteristics. This corresponds to the first of the three steps listed above, where the teacher is to take the time to accumulate a broad range and depth of knowledge both with regard to the text and with regard to the commentaries on the text. Next, recall that approximately a quarter of the comments offered by Nehama throughout the text of LPHUL are directed toward the selection of material appropriate to the classroom. These correspond to the second step recommended by Nehama in this article, where the teacher is to select from all that he or she has learned based on the needs and characteristics of the students. Finally, the bulk of the remaining comments in LPHUL recommend a variety of activities and exercises that we have discussed above in some detail. Those identical types and classifications of activities appear in the detailed examples presented by Nehama in this essay and correspond to the third step defined by Nehama. The activities described there are virtually identical to those in LPHUL. These range from the comparison of different views on the interpretation of specific texts, to reading exercises, visual exercises, and the introduction of interesting outside sources. These activities are again the essence of Nehama's methodology and approach to education.

Later in the body of her essay, Nehama goes on to beautifully elaborate how each of these exercises and activities can be sequenced and integrated into the classroom presentation. Finally, at the end of the essay, she once again reviews the last two steps of the three she began with, and recommends choosing judiciously from the ideas presented on this particular chapter so as not to overwhelm the students with too much information. Nehama repeats that too much information will frustrate the students to the point where they absorb very little. Then as if compelled to emphasize yet again the third step, the need to teach by assigning a well-orchestrated variety of exercises and activities, Nehama summarizes a list of numerous suggestions as follows:[40]

> But please pay attention to the multitude of different tasks upon which – in their variety and number – the ultimate success of the lesson will depend. And the following is a list of a portion of them: reading aloud and individual quiet reading, reading the entire chapter and reading individual passages; detailed analysis of one passage and a general overview of a group of passages; interpretive classroom debate concerning a single passage, and in-depth discussion of a problem relevant to the entire chapter and to places in the text outside of this chapter; comparison of passages within this chapter and comparison of passages in our chapter with those of other prophesies and other prophets; comparisons which contemplate similarities between passages and comparisons which contemplate the differences; writing on the blackboard for visual clarity and quiet individual writing in a notebook in order to solve problems or to analyze the structure of the chapter; readings of knowledgeable outside authors in order to provide depth of understanding, and readings of selected Midrashim in order to open up the heart. Many others exist which have not been listed here. Not every lesson will require all these activities, and each one is good at the appropriate time in its place and for the right student. We have listed here many of them in order to show you the multitude of possibilities which exist, and you should choose those that are appropriate for your particular needs.

Why does Nehama go to such lengths to provide a long list of the types of activities available? Perhaps she was anticipating a potential challenge to her views. One might ask whether students might not become complacent when faced with a continuous chain of exercises. It could be argued that the continuous repetition of these exercises would transform them into mundane activities that are less than inspiring. In response to this potential concern, Nehama emphasizes the variety of activities available and strongly recommends that teachers make use of as many of them as possible.

---

40. Leibowitz, Nehama, "LUT: Horaat Hoftorat Yom Bet Shel Rosh Hashana," Jerusalem, Israel, Elinor Publications, 1995, pages 92, 93.

And so we must finally turn again to our original premise and our original question. What is the secret of Nehama's success in motivating students and enabling them to learn? Nehama's facetious answer was to tell us to make sure the class is interesting. It must not be boring. The more difficult answer is how one goes about imparting information and values and yet maintain their interest. We have suggested that her approach in the classroom is centered around the student with the goal of producing students with an innate "love for the Torah." It is clear from the types of activities that Nehama emphasizes over and over again that in her opinion the most effective way to achieve that goal is through the skilled presentation of the text, and the commentaries who are already engaging in a discussion of the text. In other words, Nehama's methodology is centered on the subject matter. By selecting texts and activities appropriate for the classroom situation and by presenting the material in such a way as to entice the students to work diligently on the material, we can instill that love of Torah. By also designing a variety of tasks and activities that are intellectually challenging and that incorporate themes and topics to which the students can relate, we will ensure that the love of Torah is firmly rooted and implanted. The ramifications will be felt in the many positive secondary implications of this love of Torah, namely, ethical behavior, intellectually able students with respect for themselves, respect for traditional scholarship and the scholars themselves, love of the Jewish people and the land of Israel, and the list could go on.

Finally, it is important to reemphasize that all of Nehama's approach seems to be based on one underlying assumption. As we have seen above, this assumption is reemphasized at length at the end of her essay on teaching a chapter in Tanach.[41] She might say that this assumption is born out by many years of experience and supported by an assortment of educational thinkers. This assumption suggests that by avoiding lecturing to the students, and instead insisting that the majority of class time be filled with a variety of intellectually challenging activities, the students will value the results of their work and relate to it in a superior fashion. Nehama insists that when the students successfully engage their minds in the exercise

---

41. See the bottom of page 274.

251

of biblical exegesis at an appropriate level, they will be filled with a healthy respect for their own abilities and mental capacity. In addition to producing self-respect within the students themselves, these exercises will then produce a respect for the text, particularly when the exercises are made relevant to their daily lives. Each choice of wording or subtle variation in the mode of expression will be assumed to be significant to the theme and message the text is trying to convey. Finally, these exercises will also produce a healthy respect for the scholarship of the exegetes who commented on the text and guide us in discovering its secrets. It is they who ask pertinent questions that would not otherwise be perceived by the casual reader, and it is they who provide answers, disagree, and maintain a scholarly level of discussion regarding the text, a discussion that the students are now invited to join. Nehama would argue that these activities are intertwined with situations which contribute to and are in turn reinforced by the love of Torah, Nehama's ultimate objective.

Nehama Leibowitz has had a profound effect on Jewish education because of the unique combination of skills she possessed. Her unparalleled breadth and depth of knowledge combined with her skills as a teacher allowed her to demonstrate how to present the written Torah to students in such a way as to challenge them and capture their imagination. Most of us cannot hope to duplicate all those skills, but we can emulate her methods and hope to copy her successes. As the anecdote quoted at the beginning of this paper suggests, at the very least we can hope to capture and maintain the attention of our students and try to stimulate their interest in the process.

Psalms
for Hadassah Publications

Just as Nehama was willing to teach anywhere and any class, so, too, she accepted requests for articles from all kinds of organizations. The American Hadassah organization has a publishing department and the director decided to put out an English commentary on certain Psalms. When she turned to Nehama to ask her to write the pamphlet, Nehama readily agreed despite her busy schedule. Who knows how many women all over America learned Psalms through this modest publication.

– L.A.

PSALM 23

Psalm 23 is perhaps the most familiar psalm, both to Jew and to Christian. It has been the subject of numerous articles and books in many languages. It is sung in some congregations on the eve of the Sabbath. It is one of the songs for the Third Sabbath meal. In the home, it is sung at the Sabbath meal and at the departure of the Sabbath when it is particularly meaningful. Before the Sabbath – an island of rest and holiness in the sea of secular life and in the rush and speed of the weekdays – is over, before man returns to his work, to his worries, he fills his heart with the faith expressed in this hymn, and feels himself a lamb, sheltered by its shepherd.

Read the whole psalm through. Note its structure. It falls naturally into two parts: verses 1–3 and 4–6.

Note that the trust of the believer in his God is expressed here in two elaborate images: the image of the lamb led by the shepherd (v. 1) and the image of the guest sitting at the table of the host (v. 5). A basic tenet of our religion is the incorporeality of God, who has neither bodily form, nor substance[1]. Although we are well aware of this, yet in mentioning the Lord, or in speaking to Him, imagery is employed. And even though no image can be assigned to the Lord, we illustrate His relationship with us, with His people and with mankind by the use of imagery.

The relation of the Lord to His creatures is pictured in the Bible and in post-Biblical poetry in various likenesses: the lover and his beloved, Song of Songs 6:3; the father and his children, Jeremiah 31:9; the vineyard and its guardian, Isaiah 5; the flock and its shepherd; the servants and their master, Leviticus 25:55; the nation and its king, I Samuel 12:13. And each figure reveals a different aspect of the relation between the Creator and His creatures. In Psalm 23, the relationship between God and His people is depicted as that of the shepherd and the lamb.

Verse 1 in the Hebrew consists of four words only: *Adonai Ro-ee lo echsor.* None of the many translations appears able to render this monumental brevity properly.[2]

> *The Eternal shepherds me,*
> *I lack for nothing*[3]
>
> *The Lord is my shepherd*
> *There is nothing I shall want*
>
> *The Lord is my shepherd*
> *Therefore can I lack nothing*[4]

The last translation illustrates how one word can change the

---

1. See hymn *Yigdal.*
2. See explanation of the Hebrew structure.
3. James Moffat.
4. Revised translation of the Anglican Church.

meaning of the verse and the cadence. The original text does not say: "The Lord is my shepherd, *therefore* I shall not want." The difference between such a translation and "The Lord is my shepherd; I shall not want," is the difference between a logical statement and a poetic one. The first line, which constitutes a stanza by itself, contains positive and negative statements. Its first two words speak of the Lord and its last two words speak of man. Both declarations, in their brevity, in the stark absence of any modifiers, are a symbol of unshaken trust in the Lord.[5]

Immediately after verse 1, two parallel lines follow (in the Hebrew they consist of three and four words respectively) that describe what the shepherd does for the lamb in his care, his concern for its food and drink. But the connotations of "green pastures" and "still waters" are not merely physical. They evoke visions of sweetness, calm, and tranquility. (Other translations for *may m'nuchot* are "tranquil waters" and more accurately, "waters of quietness.") The good shepherd does not lead his flock to a place of rushing, turbulent waters which sweep everything before them, but to a place of slow-moving, restful waters.[6]

Some modern translators (Dahood) have misinterpreted verse 3, appending its first line to verse 2:

*Near tranquil waters will he guide me, **to** refresh my being.*

This is not what the Hebrew says. It is not reflective. Its sentences are short and declarative, each stating what the shepherd does. In each sentence, the subject is the Lord, the object is *me, my soul*. In this context, the Hebrew word *nafshi* does not mean soul as we understand it today. The use of the word soul here would be a

---

5. Ludwig Strauss, *Studies in Literature* (Hebrew), Jerusalem, 1960
6. In a book that interprets our chapter against the natural background of Eretz Yisrael, Frederick Owen writes: "The shepherd moves on with his sheep: into thicker, richer grass. He brings them to the hollow of some valley where there is a well or a quiet stream, bordered by strips of tender grasses. Or he will find some secluded glen hidden away, where grow luxurious grasses, cloves and thousands of fragrant wild flowers." (*The Shepherd Psalm of Palestine,* Eerdman Publ. Co., Grand Rapids, 1958.)

digression from the description of the lamb grazing at calm waters. *Nafshi* in this context means *my whole being* (Dahood's translation is correct).

Rabbi David Kimchi said:

> Like the good shepherd who will not tire the sheep, nor drive them but lead them slowly. "He guides me in straight paths" like the good shepherd who will not lead his sheep in the mountains, and will not shift them from mountain to mountain and will not burden them to pass from mountain to hill – only will lead them in the plain. So will He guide me in righteous paths, and all that, for His Name's sake, not because I merit it.

The closing phrase of verse 3 "for His Name's sake," signifies that all of God's favors, all the good that He bestows on man, are not merited by man, nor are they a reward for man's righteousness. This idea is repeated many times in the psalms, and in our prayers. For the first time, the poet moves from the description of the shepherd and lamb, to hint at the object of the symbol. But at once, in verse 4, he returns again to the image.

The poet does not seek to delude us with visions of life as an idyll suffused with light and sunshine. He knows that besides light and calm, there is also darkness and fear. The lamb passes through the shadows in the valley, the crevices in the rocks. It has strayed from the flock, lost its way, found itself in a narrow, deep and dark valley, or caught in a crevice between the rocks, a helpless prey to predatory beasts.[7]

Note the change that takes place in this verse. In verses 1–3

---

7. Scholars disagree on the meaning of the Hebrew word *tsalmavet,* translated as "the shadow of death." The traditional view of the word is that it is a compound of *tsayl,* shadow, and *mavet,* death. Hence "shadow of death." Many scholars however regard the form *tsalmavet* as having arisen through folk-etymology from a form ts-l-m-v-t=darkness. D. Winton Thomas claims that the word *mavet* in many instances in the Bible means a very high degree, a superlative force. We may compare it with our English phrase "he is bored to death" where we mean extremely bored. It may be that *mavet* in the word *tsalmavet* is another example of *mavet* meaning superlative force. Thus *tsalmavet* would mean a very deep shadow or thick darkness. See Psalm 107:14, "He brought them out of darkness and gloom."

the shepherd is spoken of in the third person: He is my shepherd; He makes me lie down; He restores; He will comfort me. Now for the first time the narrative is not about the shepherd; the words are directed to the shepherd in the second person: "I will fear no evil, for *Thou* art with me." What is the meaning of this change? In poetry such things are never devoid of meaning, neither are they included merely to diversify the text. This is how the poet Ludwig Strauss explains this phenomenon:

> When we speak about an object, it is still in the field of objectivity, but when we address ourselves to the object, it assumes a personal image, stands before us face to face, becomes present. The poets have made use of this distinction not only once; in order to move away from us or bring closer the subject...Just in the hour of trial in the "shadow of death" will the proximity (closeness) of God be felt, like as if He withdrew before, beyond sure knowledge; and suddenly He is present, appears before our eyes; suddenly – out of the darkness.

Following this central verse, verse 5 presents the "image" of the guest sitting at the table of the host, at a table which is set with all the very best.

The expression "thou has anointed my head with oil" appears strange to us. It can be understood only against the background of the customs of the period. The Soncino commentary defines the table, the oil, the full cup, as symbols of plenty, of God's generosity which he has showered upon man, of which the enemies cannot divest him.

Thus far the poet has offered no petition, expressed no demand, no plea. He has stated and described his position. Only in the last verse, following five verses that manifest joy, happiness, security, and confidence, is the hope for the future expressed. Perhaps this verse, too, is only a declaration of fact.

Radak (Rabbi Kimchi) comments: "'I thank you for all the good you granted me till now, still I ask from you, that your goodness and grace may follow me all my days.' This is a petition (request). But there are some who translate: 'Yes! Kindness and goodness pursue me all through my life.' And this is a statement of fact, and describing his condition."

It should be noted that it does not say here "Goodness and kindness follow me," but *pursue me*. The Hebrew verb *yar'dfuni*, pursue me, is commonly used in reference to enemies; yet here the pursuers are none other than the Lord's good messengers: kindness and goodness. (Compare with Exodus 14:9; 159; Psalms 7:6; 31:16.)

Rabbi Ibn Ezra offers a different comment: "I have such urge to do the kind and good – good to myself and kindness to others, to instruct them in the service of the Lord; till it becomes for me a rule – even if I were to abandon for a minute that good, it would pursue me."

According to Ibn Ezra then, the goodness and kindness are not to be taken as the Lord's, but as the poet-singer's. Which appears to you the more in keeping with the context of the psalm?

Dwelling in the house of the Lord (v. 6) cannot be taken literally. It does not express a desire for a contemplative life in the Temple. (No one sat or lived there.) The "House of the Lord" is a symbolic expression for closeness to God.

There is yet another question to be answered: who is speaking (in this poem) in the person of "I"? Who is the object of the parable: the lamb, the guest? Read the Soncino commentary.

Ludwig Strauss comments:[8]

> The two images (of the lamb and the guest) appearing together in this work reflect the historic fate of the people, whose beginning was a people of wandering shepherds. And in the end it became a nation settled around the sanctuary. Thus the life of the individual was described against the background of experience of the entire nation. The "I" of the individual was extended to the "I" of his nation. Moreover, when the poet went about, to compose the two images, he built his poem on the agelong basis, typical of the way man views his own life and that of humankind: long wandering along twisted paths; the end being set beforehand – happiness and security.

Now reread the entire poem. Which commentary seems more appropriate?

---

8. Ludwig Strauss, 1. c.

Questions for Study and Discussion:

1. Note where the name of the Lord is mentioned in the poem. In what way does this positioning aid in the proper understanding of the composition?

2. The image of the Lord as shepherd appears in a number of other places in the Bible. See Isaiah 40:9–11; Ezekiel 34. In what way does the image and its meaning in the latter passages differ from that of our poem?

3. Some commentators believe that this psalm consists of three images: the lamb and the shepherd, the wanderer and the guide, the guest and host. Divide the chapter in line with this conception. What is the basis for such an understanding? What is your opinion of this conception?

4. Do you think that a knowledge of Eretz Yisrael and its nature is helpful to an understanding of the psalm, or do you think that anyone, in any country or climate, is able to understand it equally well?

5. A Christian author advises his readers to recite this poem, but to change it somewhat: "Use the words of the psalm (for your prayers) substituting 'Thou' for 'The Lord' and 'He' and changing the other words accordingly." (John Scammon, *Living with the Psalms*, 1967, p. 18.) What do you think of this suggestion?

6. The National Geographic of 1926 carried an article on the life of shepherds in Israel with a photograph for *each* verse of Psalm 23. Refer to it if possible. Do the photographs contribute to an understanding of our chapter?

Active Learning in the Teaching of History

Nehama's range of interests were wide and varied. She taught courses on pedagogy and specifically how to teach subjects such as history. This essay translated and published by the Torah Education Network teaches how to make the study of history come alive and be interesting for students in different age groups. As usual, Nehama used examples of different ages in history to illustrate her point.

– L.A.

> *by Prof. N. Leibowitz.*
> *Translated from the Hebrew by Moshe Sokolow*
> *Published by the Torah Education Network 1989*

INTRODUCTION

Although the article for which the following serves as an introduction is certainly dated, and is predicated upon an education scene which is rather different from the prevailing reality in our schools in the United States in the latter part of the 20th century, it is remarkable that so much of what Prof. Leibowitz wrote some 50 years ago remains relevant to today's Jewish history classroom.

In particular I would point to her advocacy of what might be termed the "inductive method," in which the teacher begins with the careful study of a specific primary source (or group of sources) and proceeds toward appropriate historical generalizations, a method which the five sample lessons ilustrate well. My experience has shown this type of approach to be an extremely effective one in the high school classroom, not only from the standpoint of increasing student motivation but also from the standpoint of promoting understanding of the subject matter and furthering students' "skills development" in the study of history. In addition, such an approach fits nicely into the educational program of Torah high schools in an overall sense, in that it stresses that which is universally proclaimed to be a central element in a Torah education: the development of sensitivity to the meanings and nuances present in a text.

I would also cite and heartily endorse Prof. Leibowitz's suggestion that fictional works, inasmuch as they are frequently able to evoke social, cultural, and political milieu in a way that more "objective" source materials do not, be utilized as a resource by the Jewish history teacher. To mention one example which might be added to hers, for a number of years I have used a chapter from I.J. Singers's novel *The Family Carnofsky* to help students get a sense of German Jews' reactions to Hitler's rise to power in the early 1930s. The use of such works, incidentally, presents an opportunity for some integration within the curriculum, if the Hebrew literature courses and the Jewish history courses can be coordinated so as to be dealing with the same periods at the same time.

As to the concern for "literalism," with which Prof. Leibowitz begins, I would regard this as something which remains a problem to a degree. My most unscientific perception is, however, that it is not a major issue in the teaching of Jewish history in our day schools and high schools today, for the simple reason that the danger of overdoing it with abstractions and jargon is greatest when the teacher has been trained at the university or graduate level in history. Unfortunately only a small minority of today's teachers of Jewish history are in this category. I would add, though, that notwithstanding Prof. Leibowitz's comments, which I accept, I do think it both useful and worthwhile to introduce high school students judiciously to technical terminology and historical generalizations, provided that these are properly explained and illustrated, since this is the language of the discipline of history, of which Jewish history is a sub-category.

My final comments return to the matter of methods. It is my view that Prof. Leibowitz's strong condemnation of the frontal lecture method is too extreme. The lecture method has its place, so long as, like any other method, it is not overused. Lectures that are structured so as to engage the mind of the student succeed; an example might be a lecture structured around three or four provocative questions to which the teacher suggests and evaluates possible answers. It should be added that, thankfully, Prof. Leibowitz's survey of conventional teaching methods in Jewish history is out-of-date; I have never encountered, for example, a teacher who employs the "textbook lesson". Today's skilled teachers, moreover, use additional methods which are extremely useful in overcoming the problem of student passivity. In particular I would mention the use of role-playing, either by individual students or by groups of students; this is an enormously effective way to get students involved in what they are studying. Also worthy of mention is the discussion method, in which students discuss an issue, not just the meaning of a text; this can be a particularly valuable tool for promoting critical thinking skills, since students are asked to present their own views, while considering and evaluating the merits of the views of their classmates (and their teacher!).

In conclusion, let me emphasize that the use of someone else's methods, strategies, and approaches always requires individualized adaptation to one's own strengths in terms of knowledge and teaching style. Teachers reading this article are urged to adapt its suggestions and to apply them in a way which will work successfully for them in their own classrooms.

Jon Bloomberg

PREFACE

There are two major dangers that always lie in wait for the teaching of history and it requires great caution and special shrewdness to avoid them:

A. The absence of contemplation, the empty exaggeration, the abstraction and generalization of expression; in a word – literalism.

B. The absence of activity on the part of the student; in a word – passivity.

A. Literalism

Of all the school subjects, it appears to me that none is taught in such opposition to the age-old demand for analysis and antiliteralism as history, and not only in our midst but throughout the world. Even before Pastalucci schools were fighting for analysis, for illustration, and from its inceptions the new Hebrew school (as opposed to the Cheder) took pride in analysis and fought against the empty conceptualization devoid of tangible illustration. Only in the study of history does empty exaggeraton rule the day. If, in the study of Bible, the modern teacher makes fun of the "Melamed" who explained *eilon ve-'alah* as "a type of tree," and *tziyim ve-'iyim* as "an animal," and does not rest comfortably until he explains them to his students and exhibits them at least in picture form or drawn on the board (even though sometimes the recognition of the noun neither adds to nor detracts from the understanding of that prophecy or psalm, and, quite to the contrary, it is liable to deflect the students' interest from the main object, which is the idea), in the teaching of history the teacher feels free of the need to illustrate and he allows his lectures, the textbook, and the students to use such generalized expressions and empty and vague words that no student can imagine anything when he says them other than the way the letters look when they are spelled.

With us, as with other nations, history teachers and textbooks – even in elementary schools are permitted to use such expressions as "the economic collapse that followed the change of government," "the high cultural status," "the influence and mutual fructification of the two cultures, the Jewish and the Arab" (7th grade); "the Hellenism that led our youngsters astray" (6th grade); and many like them. An American pedagogue[1] who deals with the subject of history reports that the reason – supplied by the textbook – for the Puritans' emigration to America is "because they couldn't behave as they wished in their own country," and faithfully guarantees that in many classes the teacher will accept this answer from his students with complete satisfaction and without requiring any supplement.

While it is clear that the study of history does not allow illustration, contemplation, and exhibition of subject matter to the students to the same degree as they are feasible in natural science or civics, does that mean we must conclude that they are entirely impossible and abandon our search for means of bringing the subject to life, illustrating it and exhibiting it before the student to observe and contemplate it with his mind's eye?

B. Passivity

It would appear that no school subject paralyzes the student's independent activity as does the subject we are discussing. The student's entire activity consists, most of the time, of repeating the words of the teacher or the text. It makes no difference whether he is in the 6th grade in elementary school or in an upper high school grade; in both cases the student sits and remains silent. In other subjects – even outside of natural science – the opportunities for independent work and activity are obvious.[2] The Tanach student can wrestle with a difficult verse (rough comparison with other subjects, by analysis of commentaries, rational deliberation, and his own knowledge of grammar) and pave the way towards his own interpretation; in learning a foreign language he can approach comprehension by means of a dictionary and a grammar book; and in mathematics he solves equations and problems by utilizing rules and forms that he has learned.

In all other subjects we can see the student activating his spiritual abilities and training them, while in studying history we see him sentenced to be the recipient, the one being influenced, the silent one. All work is done by the teacher, only the reception and memorization – the unproductive and uninteresting part of the job – are done by the student.

Must the situation be this way?

The three conventional ways to study our discipline – both in our and other types of schools – have impeded the demand for observation, contemplation, internalization, the creation of a (learning) experience for the student, on one hand, and the strengthening and training of his skills, on the other.

1. The first approach – which held sway in the past, even the near past (some would whisper: it still exists!), primarily in European countries – is the presentation of new subject matter by the teacher's frontal lecture. I shall not waste words on its negative aspects since it has been well criticized in didactic literature. Many have pointed out its drawbacks, every language of explanation has been used to point out – through bitter experience – that this approach is not useful either for formal goals, since it does not teach the student to work or think, nor for material goals, since the material presented in lectures is not absorbed and, in general, leaves no impression in the student's heart, not even while the class is going on![3] Even if, once in a while, the material is swallowed up, it is spit out as soon as the lesson is over. In spite of all the above, while the frontal lecture has been chased out of all didactics it still cannot be budged from the teaching of history.

2. The second approach to obtaining new material is reading the textbook during class and giving explanations after the teacher's every pause. The "textbook lesson" rules the day in America, and it has some followers in Israel, too.

Yet, there is a rule in didactics that learning occurs primarily from the individual, specific case and not from generalizations (this is well known to propagandists who in order to impress even an audience of adults by describing the troubles and suffering of a group, prefer to describe the predicament of an individual or a single family in that group in order to play on their emotions), while textbooks are all written in opposition to this requirement in the form of abstract reviews and summations that are lacking all the contemplative points that could possibly leave a lasting impression on (the student's) mind.

As we approach the lower grades and the need for observation and tangible illustration grows greater, the textbook gets even more brief and, in its desire to limit itself to the important and fundamental, it becomes increasingly general, noncommittal, and bland. If we were to say – as the older methodicians advised – that the teacher should provide, from time to time, the tangible, individual material and place flesh and skin on the skeleton of the textbook, then there is no difference between this approach and the frontal lecture and all the criticism we noted above applies here, too.

In addition, the method of annotated reading does not suit textbooks at all, rather source books, such as Tanach, Mishnah, and literature, because those books were not written for schoolchildren and they require explanations, or because they have to be read very closely and between the lines. Textbooks, on the other hand, are written from the outset for schoolchildren in a simple, comfortable style that demands no penetrating analysis.

3. The third approach, which was followed in most German schools before the war, is the developmental approach. The teacher does not lecture on all the material, rather he relates some of the parts and asks the students questions about causes and results, the sequence of events and their relationships. This way the teacher "extracts" the new material from the students.

This approach, while it appears to activate the student and converts him from silent to speaking, is really an illusion. The teacher isn't "extracting" from the student but depositing the desirable answers into his mouth, by means of his questions. The student does not have to think and his answers are not born of his spiritual endeavors but they are simply what his teacher wants to hear – like a mechanical echo of the teacher himself. (Students who are accustomed to learning by this method develop a kind of sixth sense by which they guess the answers the teacher wants and they can answer without any thought.)

Besides this, it is worse than the other two approaches on account of the lack of truth in it, and on account of the false impression it conveys that historical occurrences do not have to be studied from documents or traditions (oral or literary), rather they can be arrived at by rational deliberation, and logical analogies (like mathematics, for instance). In doing so, this approach falls wide of the mark set by its own discipline.

"The emotional and intellectual participation of the learner in the experiences of (past) generations,"[4] without which there is surely no value in studying one's national history, cannot be achieved by means of any of these three approaches. Not emotional participation, since how can the student feel the experience, how can his passion be kindled, if instead of showing him fathers, mothers, and children; a particular tailor, butcher or tanner; living conditions improving or impoverishing; persecutions, emigrations, studying Torah and dying for her; instead of flesh and blood human beings like himself and his father – he is fed "situations," "social strata" (high and low), "regimes" (social and economic) that are either "strengthened" or "collapsing," and with all this, lines and lines of names, names, names....

Nor is there room here for intellectual participation since the student has no opportunity to think, to understand, to comprehend, to distinguish between things or compare them one to another, because everything is generously provided him ready-made and all he has to do is listen, repeat, and remember.

In the following five examples of lessons for both elementary and secondary schools, I would like to demonstrate different approaches to the study of Jewish History by which means it is possible, I think, to avoid the mistakes described above and to meet the requirements of which I spoke. These approaches – the use of a single source, a group of sources, belle lettres, a source ad belles lettres – are not novelties and in didactic literature.[5] One can find instructive examples from general history or from an author's national history. Rather, the conditions in those authors' countries are different from our own; they have historical chrestomathies, booklets of sources for every era and of every type, and numerous reference works that make the work of those teachers much easier.

I should like to show by means of these examples that even if we lack all these we can use these approaches, in any event, even before we acquire all the means at the disposal of the teachers abroad. All these lessons were given once or several times in class during the past years and are, therefore, the fruits of experience and not of imagination.

The sample lessons are:

a. the activities of the Anshei Knesset HaGedolah (Men of the Great Assembly) (6th grade)

b. life of the Jewish villager in 18th century Poland (8th grade)

c. the kidnapped children (8th grade)

d. the essence of Hassidism (Upper high school)
e. the Jewish question at the Congress of Vienna (Upper high school)

a. The activities of the Men of the Great Assembly

I have deliberately chosen material without wars, or other tangible activities such as building cities or discovering countries, and without names (those same names which often are of so much help, particularly in our area, in creating for teacher and student a false sense of knowledge where none really exists), but abstract material, since my intention is to demonstrate how abstract material, too, can be made tangible.

Let me stipulate that the purpose of the lesson is to impart to the students a concept of the activities of the Men of the Great Assembly, and to demonstrate that they desired "to educate the people through worship and deed, to realize the ideals of Torah in their national life in such a manner that Judaism would no longer be monopolized by a few but would become the possession of the general public in a form which each and every person will find suitable."[6]

When students are learning new material, it is good to first pose a question to them and then present the new material as an answer to that question. Otherwise we teachers appear, all too often, as someone trying mightily to solve a great problem for a friend while the friend doesn't feel it is problematic at all. It is even better if the teacher doesn't actually pose the question but directs the class in such a way that the question arises by itself. Although, in truth, it is the teacher who is stimulating the questioning, the students will still feel as though it were their own and that will arouse their interest.

For this purpose it is good, perhaps, to begin this lesson … by reading *Nechemiah* 12:15–16 (which begins): "In those days I saw people in Judea threshing wheat on Shabbat," etc.[7] (I presume that these verses are not new and that they were studied in previous lessons.) Immediately thereafter the teacher should read aloud the following passage from I Maccabees 2: 32–41:

"They (the Greeks) arose, suddenly, to fall upon them on Shabbat saying to them: how long will you refuse to obey the King?…And the men in their midst did not raise their hands to hurl a stone or to silence them … and they fell upon them on Shabbat and killed all those in the cave."

The teacher should indicate the number of years that had elapsed between the two incidents and since numbers don't signify much to children in this grade, he should concretize the number by counting the number of generations or the like.

After the preliminary reading – and certainly after a second reading – the question should arise in the class regarding the striking change in the nation's attitude towards Shabbat. Immediately the class will take a critical attitude: How can we speak of "the nation" when we don't know whether everyone behaved this way? (Students at this early age – and not only at this age – are quick to offer superficial generalizations and the battle against this must begin even in the lower grades. If you draw the class' attention to this error, it will try itself to correct these kinds of mistakes. Here we are helped by a psychological factor: the joy in catching someone – even oneself – in a much repeated error; the joy of making progress.)

The question regarding instruments of this change leads us to the question of the people's leaders and educators between these two eras and to the means they employed to exert their influence. At this point it is possible to review, briefly, the means and activities utilized by Ezra and Nechemiah. Now we come to the main part of the lesson, to the presentation of new material: What were the means used by the leaders who followed Ezra and Nechemiah? Here there is a need to supply the student with facts; it is not the place for deliberation or for questions and answers.

Each student should be given a sheet with the following four texts:

A. Ten Enactments were introduced by Ezra: [The Torah] is read on Shabbat; [the Torah] is read on Monday and Thursday; we enact courts of law on Monday and Thursday…. (*Bava Kama* 72A)

B. Men of the Great Assembly enacted for Israel blessings and prayers, *kiddushim* (sanctification over wine) and *havdalot* (separation of Shabbat ceremony).

C. The Prophets in Jerusalem ordained 24 "stands" (*ma'amadot*) corresponding to 24 watches of the *Kohanim* and *Levi'im* (*Tosefot Ta'anit* 4:2). These are the "stands": As it says (in the Torah): "Command the B'nei Yisrael and tell them, My offerings, my food [to be consumed] by fire, for a pleasant scent, you should observe to offer at the appointed time." (Numbers 28:2) How was a person's offering made in his absence? The Prophets ordained 24 watches. At each watch there was a shift of Kohanim, of Levi'im and of Yisraelim. When the time came for each "stand" to serve, Kohanim and Levi'im would go up to Jerusalem and Yisraelim in that shift would stay in their cities and read the verses relating to Creation in Genesis (*Mishne Ta'anit* 4:2).

D. How are the First Fruit offering brought? All the [inhabitants of] the smaller towns in a "stand" gather in the main city [of that area], and sleep in the streets, and don't enter houses. For the early risers, an appointed person would proclaim: "Arise, let us ascend Zion, to the House of HaShem, Our God." (*Mishne Bikkurim* 3:2).

(Rabbi Ovadia Bartenura explains: 24 "stands" were in Israel, corresponding to 24 "watches" of the Kohanim. The Yisraeli members of the "stand" were sent by all Israel [as their representatives] to stand next to the Kohanim and Levi'im of that same shift, each one in his predetermined week. They were called, "the men of the 'stand'" (*Anshei Ma'amad*).)

Those that lived close [to Jerusalem] would bring figs and grapes and those from afar would bring dried fruit and raisins. A bull would lead [the procession going up to Jerusalem] adorned with gilded horns and a wreath of olive leaves on his head. A flutist would play before them until they arrived in the vicinity of Jerusalem. When they got close, messengers were sent from Jerusalem to decorate the first fruits. The leaders would come out to greet the guests. According to the honor [or size] of the pilgrimage was the honor [or size] of the receiving committee. And the artisans of Jerusalem would stand before the guests and ask about their welfare: "Our brothers from....., welcome in Peace." (Ibid 3:3)

Before we begin our analysis, let us examine these texts one by one. A and B need no linguistic explanation beyond the word "kiddushim" since the students do not know that it refers to the "*kiddush*" of Shabbat eve. D should be known to the students from previous grades since it is printed in 4–5th grade readers and is studied in the context of *Bikkurim*. C requires explanation.[8]

Now the class should be asked whether it can detect an overall line or direction among all these four sources, or among some of them. This direction will emerge – bit by bit – from the classroom discussion. Permission to speak should first be given to the more superficial students, those who see the external and obvious. Let them make their contribution first, followed by the better students, and, finally, the penetrating ones who spot what the others have missed. Finally, the review and summation can be conducted, again, by the moderator or weak students. The superficial students spot the connection between C and D – an external connection since both mention the Beit Hamikdash and the service connected with it which is performed outside the Beit Hamikdash but in conjunction with it. The fourth text emphasizes celebration, publicity, mass participation – the participation of the Israelites in the service of God; even if they are forbidden to offer sacrifices, they are given another way of participating.

From this observation the students – or the teacher – can make the connection to text: The Men of the Great Assembly were not satisfied with the situation (described in C and D, i.e. of "vicarious" participation), so they instituted individual prayer; not only in the Temple, not only in public, but even at home, alone with the family, and including women and children. The value of Kiddush and Havdalah for establishing a pattern of religious life within the family is well known to every child in whose home they are observed. In any event, it will be easy for the teacher to arouse the feeling of their importance.

Here the students, too, can easily see – even without the teacher's help – that the Men of the Great Assembly intended to beautify and sanctify the Shabbat; not to be content with the prohibition of work which, by itself, is negative and spiritually unfulfilling. Afterwards attention should be paid to the institution of Berachot and

Tefillot. What is the value of a fixed text for national unity? What is its individual educational value? When we move along to text A we will encounter the value of public Torah reading and of including the whole community in its understanding, and we will recognize that the Men of the Great Assembly were continuing the policy which Ezra began.

One can, of course, follow the opposite course, beginning with Ezra's institution of Torah reading in A and continuing with the institution of prayers in B, and so on. Choose whichever way promises to open the class up and just make sure they don't digress.

In Conclusion

The Men of the Great Assembly tried to bring all the people (not just certain elements) nearer to a life of Torah and to have a knowledge and love of Torah penetrate each and every home, and they are the ones who fashioned the practices that are most characteristic of the religious Jewish experience down to our own day.

The use of sources in this lesson is not intended to instruct the students in historical analysis, to bring them into the historian's workshop, or to show them how an edifice is constructed of small and scattered stones; none of these purposes suit an elementary school. The sources were cited before the class only to insure that the final conclusion, the goal of the entire lesson, will not be abstract and empty of all meaning – just "words" – but full of insights and capable of awakening in the students desirable associations.

Even though the text, in this lesson, serves as an illustration, it will nevertheless lose all its values – methodologically – if it is brought down only as an illustration (as textbooks habitually cite sources), that is to say after the main abstract point has been made by the teacher or by the textbook. In such a case the student only has to listen and absorb the new material which is being served to him in an already crystallized form (by the teacher or the book) and studying the source does not require more than affirming what he has already heard.

This work is not individualized work and deprives the student of any opportunity for activity or thought. The source – if we utilize it – must be given to the student before he knows what he is expected to discover in it, and it really must serve as a source from which the student will draw his knowledge by means of intensive study.

NOTES

1   Henry Johnson: *Teaching of History in Elementary and Secondary Schools* (NY, 1920)

2   That method of teaching history, which truly wishes to introduce "activity" and "contemplation" (borrowing the terms from natural science, transferring them without change, and applying them to our subject), but which concerns itself with pictures and diagrams of furniture, buildings, and clothing of different periods, or their manufacture by the students out of clay, cardboard, etc. – is clearly not a method for teaching history (which is a discipline of the humanities) but for teaching the history of objects and their manufacture. Even if this has, from time to time, a value for the understanding of history – there is certainly no being satisfied with this alone, nor making it the focus (of a lesson).

The entire method only came about on account of an erroneous understanding of the application of the term "contemplation" to the discipline of history and of the restriction of the term "activity" to manual crafts that have almost no place in this discipline.

Details about this method and its application in schools may be found in: Ulr. Peters: *Methodik des Geschichtsunterrichts an Hoheren Lehranstalten* (Frank. a.M., 1928). 14–15.

3   Even if we assume that the teacher is an exceptionally gifted lecturer who can excite the students and motivate them, in any event the strong effect he may be able to create at the start of the school year will surely wear off after a few weeks on account of the repetition of these periods of excitement on fixed days and at fixed times each week. By the second month of the school year the students' interest and excitement will dissipate and their place will be taken by a gentle sweet sleep just like every other class that depends upon frontal lecturing.

4   B. Dinabourg (= Ben Zion Dinur) "The Last 100 Years in our Schools," supplement to *Davar* #2209; 24 Av 5692.

5   Keating: *Studies in Teaching of History in Secondary Schools* (London, 1927), which cites many examples of the use of sources, and written exercises based on sources, for the middle high-school grades. Cf., in particular, E. Willmanns: *Die Quelle in Geschichtsunterict* (Berlin, 1932), for the high school.

The teacher of Jewish history will find particular interest in the lesson about the battles of the Hasmoneans – based upon 1 Maccabees cpt. 1 – brought in the *Lehrerbuch zum Grundriss der Gesch. fur Oberstufe* (Der Neue Geschichtsunterrichti, Band I; Teubner, 1929.)

A good, detailed example of the use of ancient literature can be found in an interesting book by Kaweran: *Alter u. Neuer Geschichtsunterricht* (1925).

The first and last books on this list – and all others mentioned in this article – can be found in the national library in Jerusalem.

6   Talmudi: "The Talmud," *HaShiloach* 7, 496.

Clearly all analyses of the relationship of the Men of the Great Assembly to the Soferim and the latter Prophets – or whether the Men of the Great Assembly and the Soferim are identical – have no place in elementary school. It is also possible to posit a different goal for this lesson but that is not my concern now. My intention is only to show the ways which can be taken to insure that the teacher's goal (whatever it is) won't remain unachieved but will be made into a reality.

7   There is no need to describe at length that it is possible, necessary, and even easy to teach the era of Ezra and Nechemiah in elementary school through selected chapters. I deliberately did not want to bring a model lesson from this period because it is methodologically simple and straightforward. The chapters concerning the building of the walls and the opposition of the Samaritans, etc., have all the necessary ingredients for a vibrant lesson, close to the child's heart.

8   One must always pay attention that the text which the teacher wishes to use for a history lesson should be easily understood linguistically and thematically so that the lion's share of the time can be devoted to using it for the main purpose of the lesson – learning history. If the text requires many linguistic or thematic clarifications before the class can get to the heart of the matter then it has lost in time whatever it might have gained (in content).

Exchange of Letters with Professor Hugo Bergman

This interesting exchange of letters between two very brilliant and committed Jewish scholars says a great deal about both. It also shows how Nehama was able, in most instances, to win over any antagonist with her extreme modesty and personal characteristics.

– L.A.

The following is a translation of segments from an exchange of letters between Prof. Nehama Leibowitz and Prof. Hugo Bergman. The letters appeared in full in the original Hebrew in Meimad Magazine, 1998.

Chanukah 1957

To a very dear Nehama Leibowitz,

I feel compelled to tell you how deeply dismayed I was by your explanation of the episode which describes the meeting between Esau and Jacob. I was shocked to read that "what happened to our ancestors at the hand of Esau, will continue to happen to us at the hands of Esau's descendants."

I was even more shocked to hear the manner in which you juxtaposed, on the radio broadcast, the commentary of Hirsch to that of Benno Jacob. You ended your broadcast with the latter, as if concluding your broadcast with an exclamation point! Don't you understand that you are sowing in the hearts of your students and listeners the seeds of hatred towards others?

Even if one can understand, from an historical perspective, the narrow-minded viewpoint of the commentators, can we then allow ourselves to perpetuate this horrible, anti-humanist tradition now that we have our own State? Is this how we are going to transform the beginning of redemption (*Tchilat hageulah*) into the era of full redemption?

Sincerely yours,
S.H. Bergman

Chanukah 5718

Dear Professor Bergman,

I was startled to read your letter. If you had criticized what I said and wrote for not being sufficiently persuasive, or for making assertions which were weakly supported, I certainly would have accepted your criticism immediately. I know full well that I am a "very cracked shofar" as far as being able to transmit Torah, the words of the living G-d, is concerned. But it never would have occurred to me that my words could be misconstrued as sowing seeds of hatred in people's hearts towards others who are created in G-d's image (and for me this is certainly no empty cliche). On the one hand I thought that I had emphasized two views of our sages. One that said Esau kissed (*nashko*) Jacob sincerely, and the second that he did not kiss him, but intended to bite him (*nashkho*). On the other hand, I do not think that if we remind ourselves that our position has been and is still today that of a sheep among seventy wolves (and I do not know what the creation of the State has done to change this), we are thereby sowing seeds of hatred. As a teacher and educator, I do not intend to erase from the memory of our students everything that has happened to us and that included the pogroms of "TATNU" (1648), the Expulsion from Spain (1492), the pogroms of TAT v TAT (1171), and certainly the Holocaust in this century … Nevertheless I do not think that reminding ourselves of these events sows seeds of hatred among the majority of the human race. (I feel similarly obligated to point out the shortcomings and faults, narrow-mindedness, shallowness and copying of the faults of the world by our countrymen.) Nevertheless, it would never occur to me that doing so would impinge upon my educating for loyalty, along with love of the people of Israel for their land and country, the beginning of our redemption. Thus even you will agree with me that we dare not educate people to respect all humans and to hope for a world of brotherhood in the end of days by hiding the travesties done to us. You certainly would agree with me that we should educate towards love and fear of G-d, without minimizing the faults and weaknesses of Jews throughout the ages, including those who were G-d fearing or even used their religiosity as a veneer to hide their sins.

Therefore I did not understand why we're forbidden to analyze Esau's position vis-a-vis Jacob throughout the generations. This would not necessarily lead to hatred and a desire for revenge, but rather to hope for the end of days when we would truly be able to say (as in the aleynu prayer) "that all the world's peoples will recognize and know that every knee should bend to You...."

Another thing I did not understand was why it seemed to you that I juxtaposed Benno Jacob to Hirsch? It was the comments of Rabbi Naftali Tzvi Yehudah Berlin, the Netziv, head of the Volozhin Yeshiva, whom I juxtaposed to Hirsch. The Netziv's words are suffused with love of humanity. I wanted to show that although Hirsch, the product of a German humanistic education, came to the concept of brotherhood by closing his eyes and being incapable of or refusing to see what was going on around him (during the period when he observes Esau casting aside his sword, Jewish children in Russia were being kidnapped and sent to serve in the Czarist army or tortured into apostasy.) At this time the talmudic "Sage of Volozhin" wrote words that were truly humanistic – words which drew upon Jewish sources exclusively – but without erasing the memory of what had happened to our people in the past.

You make a point in your letter which pained me more than anything else. You wrote about what you termed the "narrow-minded viewpoint of the commentators." You have corrected me in the past when I referred to non-Jewish commentators whose hatred of Israel surpassed their wisdom. You made me aware that one must be careful about making such generalizations. Do I know ALL such commentators? Furthermore how can you say about righteous souls such as Ramban/Nachmanides, who plumbed the depths of the mystical tradition and saw every human being as G-dly ... how can you say about them that they were narrow-minded? Narrow-mindedness can be found in greater abundance among leaders of political parties, including those close to my viewpoint. But not among our greatest teachers whose intentions were to convey to us an understanding of G-d.

In any case, a lecture on the radio should not be evaluated on the basis of the intentions of the speaker but rather by what is actually understood by the listener. Thus, if what I said sounded like incitement to hatred then I admit this is not good, and I must be more careful. Perhaps there should be a different emphasis, or additional aspects should be stressed. I am extremely grateful to you for pointing out to me what you heard and how you understood my words. I am sending you a printed copy of the lecture that I read this time, and perhaps you will see for yourself that there was no call for hatred there. It could be that I should have omitted the comment by Benno Jacob whose words – now I see – are not more than interesting remarks, and perhaps they are only of minor interest. I did not see it that way when I was writing...

Again thank you for your help and suggestions. I wish that I could truly teach Torah as it should be taught in this generation. But for this much Divine help is needed.

With great respect and appreciation,
Nehama

Bergman's rejoiner:
6th Candle of Hanukah, 5718

Most dear Nehama Leibowitz,
First I must thank you for your reply and for the spirit in which you received my comments. I am sorry that I caused you to write me (and such a long letter at that!) during the 25th hour of your very full day: but perhaps the matter is so important that it justifies the effort.

The differences between us may be only differences in taste, but in these matters "the tone sets the music" and I dare to influence and affect your "tone." I cannot, to my regret, see our people only as "a dove on the wings of an eagle." Would that I could feel the way you do! From the day that I saw the joy that the populace of the country received the news about the murder by the *Hagana* of DeHaan, may his memory be blessed, something broke inside me. Since then I feel all the dangers that accompany an attitude of self-justification in which we are educating ourselves. This gives rise to the notion that we are better than others, whereas we are "made from crooked wood" as are all other humans. The difference is that "they" are arbitrarily bad, so-to-speak innocently so, rather than being bad and accompanied by sentimental, superficial self-justification. I don't have to list for you [the terrible things we did in] Kibia, Kfar Kassem, the scaring off of residents of Ramle and Lod, the "prisoners" of Yizhar, and our indifference to the fate of the Arab refugees, etc, etc. When I sense this type of sentimentality in your words, this pains me twice as much because I hold your work in such high esteem....

If I termed the approach of our commentators narrow-minded, then that was my intention. The Torah itself does not support, in my understanding, any interpretation that diminishes the image of Esau and the verse "and Esau ran towards him" is so wonderful, so messianic (sic), so full of the feeling [of brotherhood expressed in Schiller's words in Beethoven's 9th symphony] "millions marching hand-in-hand." Anyone who detracts from this meaning is making a grave mistake in my opinion, in misinterpreting the spirit of the Torah in this episode. We need not be surprised that our commentators due to historic experience and bitter trials and tribulations, could no longer describe Esau as a figure who could be a partner in the verse "and they embraced one another." But even when I view them as coming to their understanding from a certain milieu, I still cannot exonerate them from my reproach that they were narrow-minded, and that their narrowness prevented them from understanding the text in its simplest and most wonderful meaning....

Again I thank you.

S.H. Bergman

APPENDIX K

Articles Recognizing
Nehama's Contribution

Already in 1951 Nehama's unique contribution to Torah scholarship was recognized. Professor A.E. Simon wrote an outstanding analysis of her method and success, and may be the first to target in on her special regard for Rashi, her constant rejoiner being, "What's bothering Rashi." Professor Cyril Domb is quite proud of the fact that he, too, was one of the first to describe her expertise and influence in an article that appeared in the *Jewish Chronicle* shortly after she received the Israel Prize in 1956. Dr. Rachel Salmon, one of her devoted disciples, wrote her personal impressions and appreciation of Nehama's qualities in *Kol Emunah*. Finally, Dr. Moshe Sokolow wrote a moving eulogy on his beloved teacher after she passed away, in which he describes the person and her love for Torah.

(Appeared in HaTzofeh 26.10.51)

Torah Commentary[1]

By Professor A.E. Simon

When the late Franz Rosenzweig opened the new Jewish Seminary in Frankfurt in Mein in 1920 he made a pragmatic speech on "the New Learning." This approach to learning was designed to bring

---

1.   Torah Comm. by Prof. A.E Simon, appeared in *HaTzofeh* 26.10.51.

the students back from the periphery of Judaism to the hub, to the Torah.

The direction of Nehama Leibowitz's "New Learning" is just the opposite because she focuses not on the uninitiated, the babes who were lost among the nations, but the young Israelis who never left their father's "table" but who need, nonetheless, new approaches to learning. Here too the hub is Torah, and the many paths which lead to and from it. (This approach) never loses its focus to foreign influences but rather constantly returns the students to their roots. One can compare her method to a tree that grows not only vertically, but spreads its branches widely horizontally as it grows annually in its scope. So (too) is the Torah with its ever-spreading commentaries, very much in line with the famous saying: "It is a living tree to those who grasp onto it."

How did the author accomplish her goal? She began her project alone, and only later, with the support of the American Women of Mizrachi, she received minimal but important organizational and financial assistance (to put out the weekly gilyonot worksheets). However the contents remain her sole responsibility. The worksheets cover the complete world of Torah exegesis, including midrashim from both Talmuds; continuing with the works of the Gaonim, especially Rabbi Saadia Gaon; the classic commentators of the Middle Ages, particularly the Rambam and on to the more modern works of the Malbim, HaNetziv, Hirsch, Buber, and Rosenzweig's important translation into German, and finally Prof. Cassuto. Lacking are Bible criticism and non-Jewish commentaries (translator's note: this was in 1951; later Nehama used many of the latter sources). This feminine scholar (*Talmidat Chachama*) remains internally oriented.

Nehama Leibowitz is an outstanding teacher, and this trait is obvious in her written lessons. In the first years she related to her readers, her correspondents, her students as if they were sitting in her classroom before her. She was right from a pedagogical point of view, because once a pupil accepts her approach, it becomes habitual. Gradually she introduced a new system, marking progressively more difficult questions with stars. With the passing years she added another innovation, often referring the student to previous gilyonot to learn certain basic principles, to help the student progress and gain expertise in the wealth of meaningful details. Just as the author maintained a synoptic approach to the Torah so too she expected her students to demonstrate mastery of the overall view, which is after all the Rabbis' and the commentators' way.

The worksheets are not standardized. There is a certain style, but not a constant form. Usually each gilayon consists of four divisions: general questions (on the Portion of the Week); attention to grammatical and linguistic details; understanding Rashi; and midrashim. Of course if the Parsha demands a different division or if there is no division at all, there is more scope for flexibility.

There is less flexibility in the educational principles which Nehama maintains. The author demands and also inculcates wide scholastic knowledge, understanding in depth, ability to analyze text and explain differences in exegesis. She will never make a point without a purpose; she will inevitably ask questions that make the pupil think independently.

If, according to a German linguist, philology is "the art of reading carefully" then Nehama Leibowitz is an expert philologist. But the linguistics (in the Torah) are not a goal in themselves for her, but rather the means to an educational end. She doesn't particularly like direct moral preaching, but she has considerable indirect influence (by the choice of her subject matter). She teaches us again and again to marvel at the text and the commentaries, and this awe is not only the basis for any philosophy, according to the Greeks, but is the foundation of the new learning approach.

And indeed there is need to renew traditional learning. In the long Middle Ages the Torah remained the treasure of the privileged few, the religious scholars who alone were able to approach it through the key of the Holy Tongue. But, today, when this key is again available to the entire population, it is little used to decipher this marvelous treasure, the Torah, and there is danger that we will lose out.

To counteract this danger we have the gilyonot – which encourages anyone interested to delve into the expressions found in the sources more effectively in our effort to renew the language of our fathers. But (a word of caution): we must be careful not to "overeat" and to swallow the words of the Torah per se which over the years were often forgotten. Just as the ignorance of ages warps the Torah so too deceptive interpretations can be harmful. The author fights such tendencies with her worksheets, much as Buber and Rosenzweig fought them with their translation.

Her greatest admiration Nehama Leibowitz reserves for *the* commentator, Rashi. There are two main approaches to exegesis. The Rambam categorizes the Torah material into concepts without relating to context. Rashi, on the other hand, pays careful attention to the context and what can be learned from the text itself. Nehama Leibowitz has chosen the second method. She rejuvenates the way our forefathers learned. "What is bothering Rashi?" she asks and reveals the hidden difficulty which his brief comments bring to light. Thereby she turns back the calendar to a time when Torah learning flourished and 'the words of the Bible rejoiced as on the day they were given on Mt. Sinai.'

Ten Years Since the Gilyonot Appeared

On Wednesday, the second day of Chol HaMoed Succoth, a party was held at the Youth Aliya Seminar for Religious Madrichim in Beit V'gan, Jerusalem, to celebrate a unique event. Some of the many students who study Dr. Nehama Leibowitz's worksheets weekly, gathered to commemorate their tenth anniversary. Among those present were Minister Yosef Burg, university professors, the religious 'intelligentsia' of Jerusalem, Youth Aliya group leaders, teachers in Mizrachi schools, settlers from all types of religious settlements, and especially those who had studied at her Seminars and who were the initiators of the party.

The director of the Seminary, Rabbi A.S. Rozenthal, spoke enthusiastically about her activities. Prof. Ernst Simon talked about the weekly gilyonot and their educational value, and a representative – of the students, Aaron Langerman, announced that they had inscribed Dr. Leibowitz in the Jewish National Fund's Golden Book. During a short intermission the guests were invited for a little reunion between friends and former teachers in the Seminary's succah. The main event of the evening was the honored guest's speech about "Torah Exegesis in Our Day."

At the end of the event, the words of one student were read out, including the following section: "I wasn't born as an observant and kosher daughter of Israel. I came a long way from complete assimilation to faith in a living G-d, His Torah, and acceptance of the Yoke of Mitzvot. Of course many factors had an influence on me, but almost at the beginning of my journey, I happened to discover the worksheets. A new world opened up to me, and without your guidance it would never have opened up to me in such a moving way. You taught me how to delve into the holy writs, and the love and commitment which your unique approach reflects, have immeasurably contributed to my development in the direction I've come to choose."

New Approach to Biblical Study[2]

Dr. Nehama Leibowitz's Discussion Sheets
By Professor Cyril Domb

The recent announcement of the award of an Israeli prize for education to Dr. Nehama Leibowitz is a timely recognition of the influence of this remarkable woman on the study of Tanach. Dr. Leibowitz (or "Nehama" as she is known to her friends and disciples) personifies a vitalising approach to our traditional texts and sources. For the academic scholar these may provide material for historical or archaeological research; but for the Jew their primary purpose must always be one of moral inspiration and guidance. This is in accord with the rabbinic dictum (*Meg.* 14a), "Many prophets arose in Israel double the number of (the Israelites) who came out of Egypt; only prophecy which contained a lesson for future generations was committed to writing." Every part of the Bible – including the section devoted to pure narrative – embodies moral teachings which maintain their validity throughout the whole of human history.

Brilliant Pedagogue

In addition to being closely familiar with all sections of traditional literature Dr. Leibowitz is a brilliant pedagogue, and has succeeded

---

2. New Approach to Biblical Study, by Professor C. Domb, appeared in *The Jewish Chronicle*, May 25, 1956.

in passing on her technique to hundreds of young teachers all over Israel. As a lecturer her services are in continuous demand, and she gives her time and energy unsparingly and without discrimination to kibbutz, ma'abara, teachers' seminary, or Army Educational Institute. But the originality of her approach is most clearly seen in the "*Gilyonot l'Iyun b'Parshat Hashavua*" or discussion sheets on the portion of the week. These gilyonot first appeared in 1942, and have come out regularly every week subsequently, and are now in their fifteenth year. Rarely is there any repetition, every recurrence of a particular Sidra bringing new material for consideration; even Sidrot which seem to give little scope for detailed analysis produce their quota of questions and discussion topics. Answers or comments are welcomed and dealt with by correspondence, and as a result Dr. Leibowitz has spread her teaching beyond the borders of Israel to the whole of the Jewish world.

Dr. Leibowitz's method is described in detail in her article in *Maayanot I*, a recent publication of the Jewish Agency's Torah Education Department devoted to the teaching of traditional subjects. In the introductory remarks she refers to the passage in the sixth *Perek*, which says that Torah can be acquired in forty-eight different ways; only one of them is "listening by ear," yet we are apt to put all our faith in this one method. It is most important to find an alternative approach in which the student is not merely passive, but aroused into thinking for himself and taking an active part in the proceedings. Dr. Leibowitz selects the method of "discussion with pupils."

When Commentators Differ

In applying the method to Tanach one should look for points in which the classical commentators differ in their interpretation. This provides a ready source of material for discussion. What is the actual difference between the explanations? What reasons impelled any one commentator to reject the point of view of the other? Which point of view does each individual student prefer? The resulting discussion, and the particular view of each student, add greatly to the interest of the teacher, and throw considerable light on the psychological makeup of individual pupils. But the essential feature is that a high level of interest is maintained in the class, and everybody is keen to demonstrate that his point of view is the correct one.

In the gilyonot Dr. Leibowitz has prepared the ground for the application of her technique by selecting discussion points, quoting the relevant portions of the commentaries, and concentrating the difficulties in a series of questions. The questions are graded into three categories of difficulty, and the "two-star" questions are quite capable of providing the experts with a good deal to think about. One cannot fail to be impressed by the brilliance with which Dr. Leibowitz will quote a comment or Biblical passage from a completely unexpected source; only after a good deal of thought does one realise that the quotation has particular relevance to the problem under discussion.

Incidentally, the gilyonot provide a solution to another formidable problem. At every period in Jewish history distiguished scholars have devoted their attention to the study of traditional sources; as a result we are the fortunate possessors of a vast literature of commentaries which is a treasure house of ideas and suggestions. But the student with limited time at his disposal hardly knows where to begin his reading, and would normally not expect to proceed beyond one or two of the most famous standard commentators. By her process of filtering Dr. Leibowitz concentrates attention on a number of topics of importance, and enables a student in a reasonably short time to learn something of the contribution of many additional Jewish thinkers. The sources from which Dr. Leibowitz draws are wide and varied, starting with the Talmud and early Midrashim, passing through the standard commentaries of the Middle Ages, Rashi, Maimonides, Ibn Ezra, Nachmanides, Sforno, Kimchi, and Abarbanel, to the more recent commentaries of Malbim, Hirsch, the Natziv of Volozhin, Hoffmann, Benno Jacob, and Cassuto (including many others not listed here).

The time has surely arrived now for Dr. Leibowitz to present her results in a more permanent form than that of duplicated sheets. A privileged few have in their possession all the gilyonot from the beginning. (It is possible even now to acquire a complete set by direct application to Dr. Leibowitz in Jerusalem.) However, if the gilyonot were available in book form they would undoubtedly reach a far wider audience; a few hints for the solution of the more difficult questions would also be most welcome. Dr. Leibowitz has not undertaken this task so far, since it would require a detailed editorship, and would involve taking time off from her other important activities. But she could justifiably be persuaded that time devoted to this purpose would greatly increase the influence of her ideas and teachings.

It is worth considering the application of this technique to education in the Anglo-Jewish community. A detailed knowledge of the Hebrew language is not a *sine qua non* of the method, and an introduction to traditional Jewish thought throughout the ages would provide a useful addition to routine studies of the Hebrew language and texts. It might even stimulate some of our youngsters to a more profound appreciation of their cultural heritage.

Nehama Leibowitz
Scholar & Teacher[3]
by Rachel Salmon

Rachel Salmon, a longtime student of Nehama Leibowitz reminisces about her first encounter with this master teacher and analyzes her literary methodology.

Twenty-odd years ago, shortly after my arrival in Israel, Nehama Leibowitz became my first Bible teacher. Today I can fathom some of the difference that has made, although the initial encounter was not especially propitious. Although a graduate student in English literature I was nevertheless, in respect to what Nehama was teaching, the most retarded member of the class. Having heard from those who had already studied with her what was in store for us, I was full of pleasant anticipations, in spite of the fact that this was my first experience with classical Jewish studies. My anticipations proved short-lived. Nehama entered the classroom briskly – in the neat, dark, simple clothing she always wears, which makes a clear statement about her values – and got straight down to business. Each student was told to read a few verses aloud, and when my turn came – I don't think I pronounced one word correctly – I was told to leave the room. I soon

---

3. Nehama Leibowitz, Scholar & Teacher, by R. Salmon, appeared in *Kol Emunah Magazine*, Spring 1985.

had a companion. Nehama informed us that we could not rejoin the class until we had read the entire Torah, verse after verse, aloud to each other, and that we were not to attend any other lessons either until we completed the task. Permission was granted – if Nehama said so, it must be done. When we finally finished, I returned to the class with trepidation. To my surprise, Nehama was warmly welcoming, encouraged me when I was near despair about ever being able to learn properly, and – in these long years – has never asked me to read aloud again!!

No literature teacher I had ever known had a sharper eye than Nehama for detail and for deviation in a text. Little by little I discovered why. No one could have as deep a commitment to any text as she had to the Bible, a commitment of the sort which justifies infinite attention.

She was also in constant conversation with the best rabbinical minds of the centuries. She brought them into the classroom, spoke to us in their voices, and manifested, in her own devotion to the study of Torah, what the mitzvah of *Limud Torah* had been for them, and might be for us.

The first thing that a student receives from Nehama is an attitude – the conviction that Torah study is serious fun. There is nothing pedantic about her work in the classroom. After what must have been interminable hours of writing comments upon the weekly Sidra exercises which students sent her from all over the world, and the labor of preparing new exercises and lessons, she never appeared tired or overworked upon entering the classroom. She looked at her students attentively, she remembered things about them over long periods of time, she had something personal to say here and there. I must confess that in an attempt to revise the impression of my backwardness, I would sometimes place some volume of philosophy or theology strategically upon my desk. She would indeed take note, discuss it with me for a few minutes, and then tell me how I might better spend my time and efforts at the moment. No area of study was forbidden or worthless for her, but she had a clear sense of what was most important in each situation.

Nehama has always conveyed a striking impression of wholeness. There is no subject in which she does not reveal genuine interest, but everything which she touches undergoes a passionate integration into the central and pivotal endeavor of Limud Torah. Through casual conversations I have heard between her and others, I have gathered some awareness of the extent and depth of her knowledge and interests. For Nehama, no truth can undermine any other, and everything is potentially relevant to her own work. She has never approved a retreat from the exigencies and responsibilities of daily life for the purpose of intensifying one's spirituality. Her Religious-Zionism, which she exemplifies in all she does, is a statement of the degree to which Jewish living must take place in the everyday common world of land and nation. Actually, her idealism and devotion makes that common world look rather uncommon.

Once I asked Nehama's advice about the possibility of changing professions in order to concentrate my efforts on Jewish studies. Nehama was not encouraging – in fact, she disapproved. In her opinion, it is of utmost importance that religious women teach "secular" studies in the university. I should, she insisted, both do my job, and find time to study. Her admonition is in perfect keeping with her demands upon herself and with her basic belief in the possibility of synthesising all rational activity. For this reason she could never understand the attraction of mysticism in our generation, and is greatly troubled by the denials it seems to imply.

From time to time over the years Nehama and I have discussed literary criticism and questions of interpretive strategies. I would like to examine some of her aims and procedures.

She is very well-read in the theory and practice of Anglo-American New Criticism, and finds the methods of the New Critics congenial to her own practice. I am quite certain that she did not learn her skills or close reading from them – the Rabbis of the classical and medieval periods were masters enough – but they perhaps helped her in making applications to the contemporary educational situation. Like them, she treats whatever text she is considering as a complete unit, and tries to glean its meaning from the text itself, by paying minute attention to all its details. Like them, she foregoes assertions about the intention of the writer – to do otherwise in respect to the sacred text would be pure hubris. She directs her students to discover for themselves the difficulties inherent in the language, so that they will understand, first of all, the issues that the Rabbis addressed. At this point, she goes further than the New Critics, who concentrate upon producing their own reading of the text.

Nehama is teaching not only the reading of the Biblical text through close analysis, but is teaching the reading of readings as well. On the one hand, she brings the text itself to life in the eyes of the imagination. No one who has followed her step-by-step analysis of Eleazer's testing of Rivka can forget Nehama's recreation of the scene with its attention to the physical details of Israeli weather and landscape which we experience in our daily lives. These are surely closer to the conditions which prevailed in Aram-Naharaim than is the imagery which many of us bring from our own backgrounds and which informs some of the traditional commentaries.

On the other hand, she has the traditional commentators confront each other. Even when the Rabbis have not addressed each other, her careful delineation of their points of view and modes of approach enables the student to grasp how they would have reacted to each other's interpretations. Beyond this, the active presence of the Sages is felt in Nehama's classroom; she brings them alive through her own lively intimacy with their words. This is, by no means, merely an intellectual exercise. Reading, as Nehama carries it out, is very much living – the interpretation chosen has quite a bit to say about the way one chooses to live. Furthermore the act of considering, weighing, and choosing is itself an essential act of living.

This brings us to the moral-pedagogical aspect of Nehama's work. She does not recognize intellectual activity as separate from the conduct of life. To study Torah for its own sake means, for her, to realize its teachings in our lives. There is no academic disinterestedness here. I well remember her caricature of the *nouveau* intellectuals who fear that the traditional modes of teaching might lead their children to confuse what is in the Written Torah with what is in the Oral. Simple and wholehearted people who identify with the Avot and try to pattern their lives according to the examples they find in tradition, might forget, for instance, that Avraham's smashing of his father's idols does not appear in the Bible itself. However, for Nehama, they are far nearer the truth than those who try to partition the text off into formally correct units which can no longer touch us.

Her insistence upon the reader's involvement in the text indeed finds much support not only in traditional commentary, but also in sophisticated contemporary literary theory. Nehama herself is wary of the approaches to textuality developed after, and to some extent against, New Criticism because she fears that they will relativize the text and weaken its moral imperative. This is not the place to enter into an evaluation of different theories of interpretation; what is of importance here is the grounds of Nehama's claims: her allegiance to the view that reading should have a pragmatic effect on conduct – that the study of Torah should lead to practice.

I shall conclude with a few words about Nehama's influence on the women she has taught. First of all, she has provided a model for them, as a woman who achieved the highest levels of scholarship at a time when it was most uncommon for women to do so. Then, she went on to teach in almost every possible educational setting including some in which women were not readily accepted. It may even be said that she has proven that a woman, whose expertise equals that of men in the field may have something unique to contribute because of her particular woman's perspective.

In this sense, she has provided inspiration for many women. Nehama has also and always been very human – interested in the way that women are managing their lives, forthcoming with personal encouragement. She has, for me, a unique kind of warmth and womanly concern.

Nehama has also provided an ideal – that of a Talmidat Hachama – for us to attempt to achieve. Many are the women seriously studying Torah throughout the country, who look upon Nehama as their mentor. Surely some of the growing thirst of women for Jewish learning can be attributed to her endeavors. She has also trained many of the Bible teachers in both the religious and non-religious school systems. When we discover that our children are fortunate enough to have a teacher trained in her methods, we know that her love of Limud Torah will be passed on to the next generation.

I remember that Nehama once made us memorize the Rashi on the opening of *Parshat Noah*, which asserts that the essential descendants of a good man are his deeds and teachings. Nehama has many children and grandchildren, indeed. May it be that we shall enjoy her teaching and presence for many years to come.

Nehama Leibowitz:
She Taught Torah Out of Love[4]
by Moshe Sokolow

Nehama Leibowitz, who died in Jerusalem on Shabbat, 5 Nissan (April 12), at the age of 92, was a phenomenon in the world of Torah study and education. A Riga-born graduate of the University of Berlin who immigrated to Isarel in 1931, Nehama (that is the unassuming way in which she even answered her telephone) became the instructor of three generations of teachers and acquired an extensive and profound influence on Torah pedagogy worldwide – no mean feat for anyone, let alone for a woman in what has traditionally been a male preserve. Prof. Uriel Simon once marveled at the perspicacity of the elder Leibowitzes, who, as if knowing that their elder son was going to be the great rebuker of the Jewish people, named him Yeshayahu (Isaiah), and then, almost as if to offer a measure of "consolation," named their daughter "Nehama."

From 1942 through 1971 Nehama issued her renowned gilyonot (pamphlets) on the weekly Torah portions, an undertaking for which she was awarded the prestigious Israel Prize in 1957. Nehama would pose questions about the Torah text and selected commentaries, and students from all parts of the world and walks of life would respond. No correspondence course ever had so many diligent participants over so long a period of time; no other teacher could have sustained such interest for so long. Nearly twenty years after the gilyonot ceased to be formally circulated, her "students" were still sending in their replies to her questions, and Nehama, red pen in hand, would read, assess and return them.

For Torah students in Israel and the Diaspora, Nehama was "*Morateinu*" – our teacher, par excellence. To this daunting task she

---

4. "Nehama Leibowitz: She Taught Torah Out of Love", by Moshe Sokolow, appeared in *The Jerusalem Report*, May 15, 1997

brought a vast erudition in Jewish and secular classics – which she honed through regular forays into the stacks of the National Library at the Hebrew University – and a talent for pedagogy, which she refined through repeated expeditions into every corner of the country to which she was invited. (Her stories about conversations with taxi drivers were legion.) A study of her gilyonot (later collected in the popular "Iyunim" on the weekly portion – translated into English as *Studies in the Weekly Sidrah*) reveals citation from the Mishnah; the Babylonian and Jerusalem Talmuds; midrash; Maimonides and the exegetes of France, Spain, Provence and Italy; Mendelssoh, Luzzato, Hirsch, Cassuto, Buber and Kook; and also Shakespeare, Gandhi, Steinbeck and Bialik.

Erudition has existed before and since, but the panoply of pedagogical devices which she invented or refined was uniquely, and characteristically, hers. If Torah teachers worldwide have trained their students to ask, rhetorically, *"Mah kasheh leRashi?"* (What troubles Rashi?), it is due to Nehama's fastidious attention to that exegete's methodology. If a tried-and-true tactic of Torah teaching (Nehama playfully called them "trick-im") is to have students divide a Torah chapter into its component parts, or to compare versions of the same verse or event, it is because she pioneered these "tricks" as stimulants to what, today, we call "active learning."

Nehama was without affectation and without artifice. She lived in a simple apartment ("modest" would be an exaggeration), furnished mostly with books, slept in an alcove, and prepared her meals in what only real-estate agents would dare call a "kitchenette." Her energies, and such resources as she had, up to the very end of her life, were devoted to her studies and to her students, and they remain her legacy. The quintessence of her pedagogic philosophy can be summed up in her own words: "The most important thing is that the students should study Torah from all angles; search it out and choose or reject interpretations. All providing that they engage in Torah out of love."

Glossary

Aggadah: legend

Aharonim: Halachic codifiers and authorities who lived approximately between the 15th and 18th centuries

Ahavat haEmet: a love for Truth

Akedah: sacrifice

Akedat Yitzhak: the Binding of Isaac, also the name of a famous commentator and his book

Aliyah: immigration to Israel

Am Yisrael: the nation of Israel

Amcha: ordinary, simple people

Amei Ha'aretz: lay people of the Jewish nation

Amidah: the central part of the prayers recited three times a day, consisting of 18 blessings plus an introductional section and a summary

Amoraim: first generation of commentators of the Talmudic era who lived and taught from the culmination of the Mishnah until the completion of the Talmud (roughly between the 3rd to 5th centuries)

Apikorsik: heretic

Avodat Kodesh: holy work

Avot: forefathers; specifically Abraham, Isaac and Jacob

B'nei Torah: sons of the Torah, refers to people who engage in Torah study, or guide their lives by Torah

B'nei Yisrael: the Jewish people
Ba'al Koreh: person who reads aloud from the Torah scroll during prayers according to special notes
Bamidbar: Numbers, the fourth Book of Moses
Beit haMikdash: the Jewish Temple
Beit Midrash: study hall of Jewish learning
Berachot: lit. blessings, also a Tractate of the Talmud
Bereshit: Genesis, the first Book of Moses
Bikkurim: lit. offerings, also a Tractate of the Talmud
Bizayon LaTorah: an insult to the Torah
Blat: pages (of Talmud)
Bnei Akiva: a religious Zionist youth organization
Bohts: mud
Bracha: blessing
Brogus: Yiddish, angry
Chanukah: the Festival of Lights
Chessed: kindness
Chevra: social group
Chevrutah: study partner in learning Jewish texts / study circle
Chidonei Tanach: Bible quizzes
Chidushim: original ideas especially in exegesis of the Bible
Chillul HaShem: desecration of God's name
Chochmat Chaim: common sense
Chol Hamoed Succoth: the intermediary days of the Festival of Tabernacles
Chug: activity or group, which meets for a common purpose
Chumash: the Five Books of Moses
Chutz la'Aretz: Diaspora
Daber Ivrit: 'speak Hebrew'
Daf Mekorot: page of sources of Jewish texts, used to assist in Jewish learning
Dafka: specifically
Dapim: pages
Darshanim: those who take an in-depth approach to the meaning of the text and on the other hand, those who give homiletic sermons
Dati: religious person

Daven/Davening: pray/praying
Derech: approach
Devarim: Deuteronomy, the Fifth Book of Moses
Drash: explanation of the Torah, given with a moral lesson in mind
Drasha/Drashot: sermon/sermons
Emunah: faith
Eretz Yisrael: the land of Israel
Erev Shabbat: the eve of Sabbath, Friday night
Erlicher yid: honest Jew
Galizianer: person originating from Galicia
Galut: exile, the Diaspora
Ganav: thief
Gannenet: kindergarten teacher
Gedolim: 'giants' of Jewish learning, revered scholars
Gemillut Chassadim: acts of loving kindness
Gemara: the Talmud
Genuss: deep satisfaction
Gilayon/Gilyonot: worksheet/worksheets
Goyeh: non-Jew
Hachnasat Kalah: assisting a new bride; a fund for that purpose
Hachshara: training camp, agricultural training camp
Haftara/Haftarot: weekly reading of a section of the Prophets, recited after the Torah reading during Sabbath services
Hagana: Jewish underground movement that fought for the establishment of the State of Israel
Halacha: Jewish law
Halachic: according to Jewish law
Haredi: ultra-orthodox Jew
HaShem: God
Hashomer haTza'ir: socialist Zionist youth organization
Havdalah: prayers recited at the conclusion of the Sabbath
Hazal: abbreviation for "Our Sages, may their memory be blessed."
Hechsher: kosher certification
Hesed v'Emet: kindness and truth
Heter: exemption according to a halachic authority
Histapkut b'Meat: simplicity, frugality
Kaddish: prayer for the deceased

Kal v'Chomer: 'how much more so', expression from the Talmud; one of the basic ways Torah is interpreted – "If this is true, then obviously this must also be so."

Kavanah: meaningful concentration while reciting prayers

Kedushah: holiness

Kedushat Ha'Aretz: the holiness of the land of Israel

Kef: fun

Kerem Navot: Navot's Vineyard

Kibbutz HaDati: the religious Kibbutz movement

Kiddush/Kiddushim: sanctification over the wine, blessings made over wine; also marriage ceremony

Kita aleph: 'first grade', refers to the levels of the study of the language of Hebrew for new immigrants to Israel

Kiyum Hamitzvot: fulfillment of the mitzvot (commandments)

Kohanim: Priests who worked in the Temple and their descendents

Kollel: center of Jewish learning

Kotel: the Wailing Wall

Kriya: a ritual performed by mourners, tearing a small piece of the clothes they are wearing as a sign of mourning

Leining: reciting the weekly portion of the Torah from the Torah scroll

Levi'im: the tribe of Israelites that worked in the Temple and their descendents

Limud Torah: Torah learning

Maabarah: transit camp

Maaser: tithe

Machanaim: Russian new immigrant center in Jerusalem for learning Judaica

Machon l'madrichi chutz la'aretz: institute for leadership of Jewish communities in the Diaspora, under the auspices of the Jewish Agency

Madrich/Madricha: group leader (male) / group leader (female)

Mama loshen: Yiddish, mother tongue

Mehitzah: dividing partition between men and women in synagogue or places of Jewish learning

Mekarev et haGer: to bring the convert closer, to assist the convert

Melamdim: teachers

Melamed: teacher

Menahel: manager, director, principal

Mercaz Klita: Absorption Center for immigrants to Israel

Meshuggener: crazy person

Mesorah: tradition

Metapelet: caregiver

Mezonot: foods that include cakes, biscuits, crackers and other grain-based foods

Midrash/Midrashim: a parable or story that explains a teaching from the Tanach

Midrasha: women's study institution

Midrashic: of a midrash, according to a midrash

Mikrah: the Holy Text

Mikraot Gedolot: the five Books of Moses, incorporating the major classical commentators

Mincha: afternoon prayers

Mishloah Manot: parcels of foods given as gifts on the holiday of Purim

Mishnah: the Oral Law, upon which the Talmud is based

Mishpat: judgement

Misrad Hamedeiyek: an office service in Jerusalem, literally the "accurate office"

Mitzvah/mitzvot: commandment(s)

Mitzvot bein adam l'chavero: social mitzvot, regarding relations between people

Morateinu: our teacher

Motzei Shabbat: the conclusion of Shabbat, Saturday night

Musar: ethics

Musar smoose: a discussion on ethics; sermon on moral behavior, often given in yeshivot

Nach: the combined books of Nevi'im and Ketuvim, from the Tanach (Hebrew Bible)

Nissim v'Niflaot: miracles and wonders

Olim Chadashim: new immigrants to Israel

P'shat: simple explanation, grounded in the text

Parshanim: commentators

Parshanut: commentary

Parshat Hashavuah: weekly Torah portion recited at synagogue on Sabbath day

Pashtan: one who takes a simple approach to the meaning of the text

Peirush/peirushim: explanation(s)

Perek: chapter

Pesach: Passover holiday

Peshuto Kemashma'o: the simple meaning is the same as the literal meaning

Peshuto Shel Mikra: the simple meaning of the text

Pirke Avot: Ethics of the Fathers, Jewish text

Poskim: halachic authorities

Pruta/prutot: penny(ies)/dime(s)

Purim: festive holiday celebrating the Jews of Persia's victory over Haman

Rabbanim: Rabbis

Rebbe: Rabbi, beloved figurehead and role model

Rishonim: Torah and Talmudic authorities roughly from the middle of the 11th century to the 15th century

Rosh Chodesh: new month in the Jewish calendar

Rosh Hashanah: Jewish New Year

Rosh Kollel: dean

Rosh Yeshiva/Rashei Yeshivot: Head of the Yeshiva/Heads of the Yeshivot

Saboraim: sages who codified or "finished off" the Talmud between the 4th century (in Eretz Yisrael) and the 5th century (in Babylon) and until the middle of the 7th century

Seder: the proceedings for the evening of first night Passover, when the story of the Exodus from Egypt is recited

Sefer Torah: Torah scroll

Segulah: virtue; omen of good luck

Shabbat: Sabbath

Shabbat Shalom: greeting, 'have a nice Sabbath'

Shabbaton: an organized Sabbath spent with friends and colleagues, usually incorporating learning, speeches and a festive atmosphere

Shalom: hello, goodbye, peace

Shechinah: Divine Presence
Shemot: the second Book of Moses
Shiur/Shiurim: lesson/lessons
Shevet: tribe / or age group in the Bnei Akiva youth movement
Shitah: method
Shivah: week of mourning following the death of a parent, spouse, sibling or child
Shofar: ram's horn, used as a trumpet on the Jewish New Year as a symbolic call to the Jewish people to repent
Shul: synagogue
Siddur: prayer book
Sidra/Sidrot: weekly Torah portion/s (Parsha)
Simcha/S'machot: celebration/s, e.g. wedding, bar mitzvah
Simchat Torah: annual festival celebrating completion of the cycle of reading the Torah
Spactel: a tirade
Succoth: Tabernacles
Sugiah: issue, problem
Tallit/Tallitot: prayer shawl/s
Talmidat Chachama: a woman who is very learned and knowledgeable in the Hebrew Bible and Jewish texts
Talmidei Chachamim: people who are very learned and knowledgeable in the Hebrew Bible and Jewish texts
Talpiot Maabarah: transit camp located in the Talpiot region of Jerusalem
Tamim: naive
Tanach/Tanachim: the Hebrew Bible, incorporating Torah (Five Books of Moses), Nevi'im (Prophets) and Ketuvim (Writings)
Tanna'im: the sages from the period of Hillel to the compilation of the Mishnah (1st and 2nd centuries)
Tchilat Hageulah: the beginnings of the redemption
Tefillah/Tefillot: prayer/prayers
Tefillin: phylacteries
Tehillim: Psalms
Teshuva: repentence
Teuneh tipuach: disadvantaged youth
Tiyul: hike

Tnua Anivah: Scarf worn by members of the Zionist youth
movements as part of their uniform

Torah: the five Books of Moses

Torah L'Am: Popular Torah

Torat Chaim: the Torah of life

Tsedakah: charity

Tzaddekes: righteous woman (Yiddish)

Tzaddikah: righteous woman (Hebrew)

Tzibur: community

Tzizzit: fringed garment worn by Jewish males

Umlala: distressed; poor kid

Verhorren: when the patriarch of the family tests the children's
knowledge of Parshat Hashavuah

Yahrzeit: anniversary of the death of a loved one

Yasher Koach: expression of praise, 'well done'

Yerushalmi/Yerushalmim: person/people who reside/s in
Jerusalem

Yeshiva/yeshivot: institution/s of Torah learning for males

Yetzer: inclination, instinct

Yetzer Harah: evil inclination

Yirmiyahu: Book of Jeremiah

Yishuv: settlement, also used to refer to Jewish settlement in
Palestine before the establishment of the State of Israel

Yishuv Tov: greeting, 'good luck in your new home'

Yisraelim: Israelites

Yom Kippur: Day of Atonement

About the Author

L eah Abramowitz studied with the late Professor Nehama Leibowitz on different occasions for the last forty-five years. She is, by profession, a medical social worker and works at Shaare Zedek Medical Center. In addition, she is a freelance journalist and has written articles for the past twenty-eight years for the *Jerusalem Post* and various magazines in the U.S. and South Africa. She is the coordinator of Melabev, an organization for the care of cognitively impaired elderly people and their families, and the coordinator of the Geriatric Institute for training professional and paraprofessional workers in the helping fields on subjects related to gerontology. Mrs. Abramowitz is married to Abe, and is blessed with many children and grandchildren. She is privileged to live in the reconstructed Jewish Quarter in Jerusalem.